ESSENTIAL SKILLS FOR
EARLY CAREER
RESEARCHERS

Sara Miller McCune founded SAGE Publishing in 1965 to support the dissemination of usable knowledge and educate a global community. SAGE publishes more than 1000 journals and over 800 new books each year, spanning a wide range of subject areas. Our growing selection of library products includes archives, data, case studies and video. SAGE remains majority owned by our founder and after her lifetime will become owned by a charitable trust that secures the company's continued independence.

Los Angeles | London | New Delhi | Singapore | Washington DC | Melbourne

ESSENTIAL SKILLS FOR
EARLY CAREER
RESEARCHERS

JOSEPH ROCHE

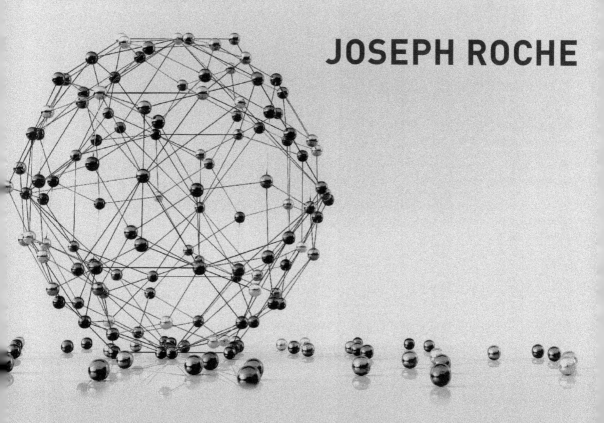

Los Angeles | London | New Delhi
Singapore | Washington DC | Melbourne

Los Angeles | London | New Delhi
Singapore | Washington DC | Melbourne

SAGE Publications Ltd
1 Oliver's Yard
55 City Road
London EC1Y 1SP

SAGE Publications Inc.
2455 Teller Road
Thousand Oaks, California 91320

SAGE Publications India Pvt Ltd
B 1/I 1 Mohan Cooperative Industrial Area
Mathura Road
New Delhi 110 044

SAGE Publications Asia-Pacific Pte Ltd
3 Church Street
#10-04 Samsung Hub
Singapore 049483

Editor: James Clark
Assistant editor: Diana Alves
Production editor: Prachi Arora
Copyeditor: Christine Bitten
Proofreader: Elaine Leek
Indexer: Martin Hargreaves
Marketing manager: Catherine Slinn
Cover design: Naomi Robinson
Typeset by: C&M Digitals (P) Ltd, Chennai, India
Printed in the UK

Library of Congress Control Number: 2021942453

British Library Cataloguing in Publication data

A catalogue record for this book is available from
the British Library

ISBN 978-1-5264-9023-0
ISBN 978-1-5264-9022-3 (pbk)
eISBN 978-1-5297-8918-8

At SAGE we take sustainability seriously. Most of our products are printed in the UK using responsibly sourced papers
and boards. When we print overseas we ensure sustainable papers are used as measured by the PREPS grading
system. We undertake an annual audit to monitor our Sustainability.

Contents

About the Author

Joseph Roche is a researcher and lecturer at Trinity College Dublin. He has worked at NASA and coordinates international research projects exploring the role of research in society. His research interests include public engagement, informal learning, higher education, citizen science, and science communication. He leads the Science & Society research group at Trinity College Dublin.

Acknowledgements

I have benefitted from the insight and wisdom of mentors, friends, family, colleagues, and students countless times as a researcher. I would not have survived in research without such help. There are too many people I need to thank, so here is an incomplete list of those to whom I am incredibly grateful:

Rebecca Amet, Louise Archer, Prachi Arora, Sarah-Louise Ball, Andrea Bandelli, Joanne Banks, Orla Bannon, Gillian Barber, Philip Bell, Alan Bennett, Shane Bergin, Bronwyn Bevan, Marie Boran, Mary Bourke, Sarah Bowman, Matthew Boyd, Ann Marie Brady, Mairead Brady, Christine Bitten, Autumn Brown, Ian Brunswick, Maureen Burgess, Niamh Burke, Jake Byrne, Aimee Byrne, Ellen Byrne, Jason Byrne, Peter Byrne, Vinny Cahill, Anja Cakara, Eoin Carley, Kevin Carney, Nigel Carroll, Jane Chadwick, Ruth Chadwick, Stephen Clarkin, Jade Concannon, Ken Concannon, Paul Conlon, Ruth Connolly, Conor Courtney, Michael Creek, Cian Crowley, Ronan Cullen, Lenna Cumberbatch, Jennifer Daly, Sarah Davies, Nicola Davis, Emily Dawson, Thomas Deane, Tessa Delehanty, Ann Devitt, Marie Devitt, Jen DeWitt, Ángel Dominguez, Niamh Dornan, Úna Dowling, Bevin Doyle, Linda Doyle, Edward Duca, Lara Dungan, Kali Dunne, Sarah Durcan, Keara Eades, Melissa Eitzel, Gea Eman, Katrina Enros, Brian Espey, Amy Fahy, Jessamyn Fairfield, Carmen Fenollosa, Mauro Ferreira, Suzana Filipecki Martins, Laura Finnegan, Geraldine Fitzgerald, Sarah Flanagan, Paula Flynn, Alessandra Fornetti, Giovanni Frazzetto, Na Fu, Arlene Gallagher, Peter Gallagher, Robbie Gallagher, Conor Galvin, Beatriz Gietner, Michael John Gorman, Sinéad Greener, Adam Greener, Muiríosa Guinan, Graham Harper, Raquel Harper, Miriam Harte, Emi Hashem, Nóirín Hayes, Sarah Hayes, Tom Hayes, Sylvia Healy, Theresa Heffernan, Matthew Hickman, Paul Higgins, Caitlín Higgins Ní Chinnéide, Ronan Hodson, Stephen Hughes, Mairéad Hurley, Stefan Hutzler, John Hyland, Raluca Iagher, Claudia Iasillo, Rachael Inglis, Aaron Jensen, Eric Jensen, Keith Johnston, James Jemmer Kavanagh, Áine Kelly, John Kelly, Valerie Kelly, Marita Kerin, Laure Kloetzer, Larisza Krista, Mark Langtry, Didier Laval, Lorraine Leeson, Ruza Leko, Rob Lennox, Giovanna Lima, Kat Logan, David Long, Julia Lorke, Andrew Loxley, James Lunney, Lina Maigyte, Shane Maloney, Ilda Mannino, Ian Martin, Luisa Massarani, Amanda Mathieson, Marzia Mazzonetto, Louise McAteer, Fergus McAuliffe, Liz McBain, Kevin McCarthy, Vincent McCarthy, Joe McCauley, Aoife McCloskey, Jonathan McCrea,

Róisín McGannon, Niamh McGoldrick, Ignatius McGovern, Joanne McGrath, Conor McGuckin, Cormac McGuinness, Linda McHugh, David McKeown, Fiona McKibben, Fiona McLoone, Aoife McLysaght, Ailbhe McMackin, Diane McSweeney, Sam Mejias, Ambika Menon, Kevin Mitchell, Mark Moore, Caroline Morgan, Diana Morosan, Damian Murchan, Colette Murphy, Daniel Murphy, Kathryn Murphy, Patrick Murphy, Susan Murphy, Aisling Murray, Sophie Murray, Anna Mwakitalu, Emer Emily Neenan, Orna Nicholl, Melanie Ní Dhuinn, Aoibhinn Ní Shúilleabháin, Shaun O'Boyle, Gordon O'Brien, Robert O'Byrne, Kevin O'Connor, Mary-Ann O'Donovan, Freddie Oetker, Ciara O'Farrell, Cliona O'Farrelly, Aidan O'Flannagain, Lea O'Flannagain, Eamon O'Gorman, Jane Ohlmeyer, Suchita Ohri, Arko Olesk, Deirdre O'Malley, Rory O'Malley, Alan O'Meara, Noel Ó Murchadha, Neal Ó Riain, Carmel O'Sullivan, Brendan Owens, Lola Pearse, Kylie Peppler, Elaine Pereira Farrell, David Perez-Suarez, Lina Persechini, Erika Piazzoli, Joffrey Planchard, David Prendergast, Mark Prendergast, Nancy Price, Claire Raftery, Sarah Reilly, Abby Rhinehart, Naomi Robinson, Colette Roche, Finbar Roche, Patrick Roche, Mark Rosin, Pedro Russo, Daniel Ryan, Maija Salokangas, Lynn Scarff, Mishael Sedas, Aidan Seery, Michelle Share, Michael Shevlin, Igor Shvets, Catherine Slinn, Chris Smith, Ronan Smith, Aisling Smyth, Ciarán Smyth, Fiona M Smyth, Fiona T Smyth, Phil Smyth, Lena Söderström, Lissa Soep, Frida Sommer, Natasha Spassiani, Jessica Stanley, Colm Stephens, Mary Tallant, Brendan Tangney, Naomi Thompson, Brian Trench, Aengus Tukel, Brendan Tuohy, Shaun Ussher, Alice Vajda, Lupita Valdez Castilla, Joana Vasconcelos, Maria Vicente, Louise Whelan, Lucy Whitaker, Samantha Williams, Silvia Winter, Jen Wong, Michael Wride, Karen Young, Fabiana Zollo, Maria Zolotonosa, and Pietro Zucca.

I especially want to thank James Clark for believing in this book from the very start, Diana Alves for her patience and reassurance, and Laura Bell for her unwavering support, guidance, and encouragement every step of the way.

Online Resources

This book is supported by a range of downloadable and adaptable resources and templates available at: www.JosephRoche.ie/EssentialSkills

One
Introduction

In this chapter, we will cover:

- taking ownership of academic skills
- what to expect in the coming chapters
- how early career researchers can benefit from this book and its companion website.

A very particular set of skills

Academic skills are the foundation of a career in research. They are the skills that let us translate the knowledge we have gained over many years of study into tangible benefits for society. All of us who work in academic environments must develop our skills so that we can contribute to our respective fields of research – but where do we acquire such skills? They are often thought of as a form of tacit knowledge that can only be learned through experience, but for those of us who are too impatient to wait to find out if we will be presented with such opportunities, we can take ownership of our careers in research by identifying the skills we need and proactively developing them ourselves. In this book, we will pinpoint the most important skills for researchers and the most efficient ways to acquire them. Whether you have already embarked on a career in research, or you are an undergraduate or postgraduate student considering becoming an academic researcher, the sooner you start developing your academic skills, the sooner you can fulfil your potential, thrive in your work, and become the best researcher you can be.

Who this book is for

This book is for anyone who has an interest in academic skills, though it is especially relevant to early career researchers. The early career stage is defined differently in different contexts, but generally encompasses the 6–10 years in which a postgraduate researcher engages in doctoral and postdoctoral work. The overarching theme of this period is of a gradual transition towards independent research, but there is no typical experience – it can range from doctoral or postdoctoral study to academic appointments as a junior professor or faculty member.

This is also when each researcher develops their academic skills, and acquiring those skills can be a significant source of stress for early career researchers (Barry et al., 2018). Academic skills are what allow us to work in competitive research environments. They are key skills that every researcher needs – sometimes referred to as generic skills, attributes, or core competencies – and yet they are not described or taught in a consistent way (Clanchy and Ballard, 1995; Virtanen and Tynjälä, 2019). Vital skills such as academic writing are often developed from tacit knowledge; rather than being explicitly taught they are more likely to be acquired through experience, insight, and intuition (Elton, 2010).

There have been widespread calls for skills training in both undergraduate and postgraduate education (Craswell, 2007; Sinche et al., 2017; Hopkins and Reid, 2018) and institutions of higher education are under increasing pressure to ensure their students and staff develop transferable skills – skills that can be used outside of the academic environment (Kemp and Seagraves, 1995; Drummond et al., 1998; Fallows and Steven, 2013). Early career researchers are usually overburdened with content-specific knowledge – information about their research areas – to the detriment of skills like writing, project management, and the abilities needed to address personal motivation and wellbeing (Pretorius et al., 2019; Ålund et al., 2020). By the time they reach full-time permanent positions as professors in universities, most researchers have developed their skills by observing others, emulating, and with some trial and error, hopefully improving over time (Buller, 2010).

All of this can be frustrating for early career researchers, waiting expectantly for their supervisors or employers to teach them academic skills. We are told repeatedly how important these skills are, and yet the anticipated teaching never seems to materialise. Eventually it starts to feel like the academic skills we need are secrets that must be summoned to us from another plane of existence through complex rituals involving incantations, candles, and standing in elaborate chalk circles. There is, however, nothing stopping us from seeking out and developing these skills ourselves. Over the course of this book, you will encounter all the essential skills needed to succeed in academic research and the ways you can learn and hone them. The path of the early career researcher is as challenging as it is rewarding, and with the right tools you can succeed in all your academic pursuits. Whether you want to be a more effective researcher, become a prolific academic writer, publish more of your work, put together successful funding proposals, improve your teaching, be a better supervisor, compellingly engage audiences, stay on top of administration, tackle professional learning, or land job offers, all while staying cognisant of your health and wellbeing – academic skills are at the heart of what is possible.

How to use this book

The chapters in this book can be read as standalone instalments. If there is a particular area that you are especially worried about in the list below, proceed directly to that chapter. You can also read the book in the standard linear fashion. The chapters are ordered to mirror the researcher's journey: the early sections – on research skills, writing, and publishing – cover the basics. The ensuing exploration of topics such as teaching, professional development, and career progression may be of greatest benefit to researchers considering employment as lecturers, junior professors, or similar academic positions.

Each chapter will focus on a different area or set of academic skills:

- *Research*: In Chapter 2, we will review the fundamental skills that we all need if we wish to contribute to a field of research.
- *Writing:* Chapter 3 provides us with the opportunity to strengthen the backbone of our research efforts by looking at the ways we can become more reliable and productive in our academic writing.
- *Publishing:* Writing skills are invaluable, but without the expertise to get our writing published, no one will ever see it. Chapter 4 covers the most efficient strategies for navigating the peer-review and publishing processes.
- *Funding:* One of the key steps to becoming an independent researcher is winning research grants. Chapter 5 takes us through the ploys and manoeuvres that are needed to persevere in the most punishing arena of an already competitive ecosystem.
- *Teaching:* Chapter 6 takes us through teaching in higher education and how to be the kind of inspirational educator we always wished we had.
- *Supervision:* Although some see supervision as simply another form of teaching, it is fully deserving of the limelight provided by Chapter 7 due to the impact that supervisory relationships can have on researchers' careers.
- *Communication and engagement:* Being able to connect with public audiences is a skill that few naturally possess, but in Chapter 8 we see how nurturing appropriate presentation styles across different media can allow us to reach far beyond the ivory battlements of academic sanctuary.
- *Administration:* Administrative skills are the skills that all the other skills used to bully in the playground. Despite being the least glamorous skill set, being able to carry out our administrative tasks as efficiently and painlessly as described in Chapter 9 is vital to ensuring the prosperity of the rest of our work.
- *Professional development:* The wonderful thing about academic skills is that they are ever-evolving. Chapter 10 highlights how we need to find our community and make professional learning a cornerstone of our academic responsibilities.
- *Career progression:* Chapter 11 brings all our skills together to make sure we secure the jobs and the promotions we deserve.
- *Health and wellbeing:* If our health and wellbeing are not always our top priorities then we run the risk of the rest of the skills in this book becoming irrelevant. Chapter 12 concludes our adventures in academic skills by calling our attention to the safeguards we need for a life in research.

Each chapter includes lessons learned from the published literature as well as the perspectives of early career and mid-career researchers whose views are sprinkled throughout the chapters in the form of verbatim quotations. These perspectives were collected over several years through surveys, interviews, and focus groups. The combination of published knowledge and real-world insights provides a detailed picture of what academic skills mean for early career researchers.

There is a list of topics at the beginning of each chapter to outline what will be covered. At the end of each chapter there is a summary so that if you ever need to refresh your memory on the lessons from a particular chapter you can find a quick reminder. The end of each chapter also has recommendations for further reading – books that delve deeper into the topics covered – as well as a bibliography of all the references cited in that chapter.

There are also additional resources mentioned throughout the book that can be found on this website: www.JosephRoche.ie/EssentialSkills. This website is an online companion to the book, and has more than 30 resources and sample templates that can be downloaded and edited for your own use. A wide range of templates are included for research proposals, paper outlines, publication plans, lecture slides, emails, meeting agendas, Gantt charts, academic posters, module descriptors, teaching philosophy statements, resumes, and cover letters. If you have any feedback on the book or the website, I would love to hear from you. Similarly, if there is a particular resource or template that is not mentioned in the book or on the companion website that you feel would benefit your academic skill set then please let me know and I can try to update the online templates accordingly.

The life of an academic researcher is incredibly rewarding. It may not have the same recognition as being a movie star or a professional athlete, but it is a well-respected role, essential to society. No other job gives you the same level of freedom to explore concepts, discover new knowledge, and take an active role in creating positive change in the world. I hope this book will give you the confidence to face the challenges of academic life and fulfil your potential as a researcher.

References

Ålund, M., Emery, N., Jarrett, B. J., MacLeod, K. J., McCreery, H. F., Mamoozadeh, N., ... & Gering, E. (2020). Academic ecosystems must evolve to support a sustainable post-doc workforce. *Nature Ecology & Evolution, 4*(6), 777–781.

Barry, K. M., Woods, M., Warnecke, E., Stirling, C., & Martin, A. (2018). Psychological health of doctoral candidates, study-related challenges and perceived performance. *Higher Education Research & Development, 37*(3), 468–483.

Buller, J. L. (2010). *The Essential College Professor: A Practical Guide to an Academic Career.* San Francisco, CA: John Wiley & Sons.

Clanchy, J. & Ballard, B. (1995). Generic skills in the context of higher education. *Higher Education Research and Development, 14*(2), 155–166.

Craswell, G. (2007). Deconstructing the skills training debate in doctoral education. *Higher Education Research & Development, 26*(4), 377–391.

Drummond, I., Nixon, I., & Wiltshire, J. (1998). Personal transferable skills in higher education: the problems of implementing good practice. *Quality Assurance in Education, 6*(1), 19–27.

Elton, L. (2010). Academic writing and tacit knowledge. *Teaching in Higher Education, 15*(2), 151–160.

Fallows, S. & Steven, C. (2013). *Integrating Key Skills in Higher Education: Employability, Transferable Skills and Learning for Life*. London, UK: Routledge.

Hopkins, D. & Reid, T. (2018). *The Academic Skills Handbook: Your Guide to Success in Writing, Thinking and Communicating at University*. London, UK: SAGE.

Kemp, I. J. & Seagraves, L. (1995). Transferable skills – can higher education deliver? *Studies in Higher Education, 20*(3), 315–328.

Pretorius, L., Macaulay, L., & de Caux, B. C. (Eds.) (2019). *Wellbeing in Doctoral Education: Insights and Guidance from the Student Experience*. Cham, Switzerland: Springer Nature.

Sinche, M., Layton, R. L., Brandt, P. D., O'Connell, A. B., Hall, J. D., Freeman, A. M., ... & Brennwald, P. J. (2017). An evidence-based evaluation of transferable skills and job satisfaction for science PhDs. *PloS One, 12*(9), 1–16.

Virtanen, A. & Tynjälä, P. (2019). Factors explaining the learning of generic skills: a study of university students' experiences. *Teaching in Higher Education, 24*(7), 880–894.

Two
Research

In this chapter, we will cover:

- navigating research philosophies
- research questions
- learning research methods
- undertaking systematic reviews of the published literature
- self-monitoring progress.

Basic skills every academic researcher needs

Everyone plays the role of researcher in their daily lives. We search for information and use the knowledge we discover to help us make informed decisions. The depth of our search, the reliability of the sources we use, and the robustness of our interpretation of what we have learned determine the quality of our research. As academic researchers, what defines our work is that it is *systematic*. We conduct our research following a fixed system, in a methodical way, so that anyone can easily follow our technique and – if they wish – duplicate it to see if they come to the same conclusions.

Basic research skills are numerous enough to warrant whole books dedicated to their description (see the further reading list at the end of this chapter). We will focus on some of the most fundamental and necessary skills, such as situating ourselves in the broader field of research, defining research questions, selecting appropriate research methods, investigating the published literature, and monitoring progress. These research skills are not only the basis of how we conduct our academic work, but are some of the most transferable skills we will have at our disposal regardless of the career paths we choose to take (Allison et al., 1996).

Research philosophies

Philosophy is an expansive discipline, but the reason we need to consider the philosophy of our approach to research is because it demonstrates our interpretation of the world around us. When someone asks us about our research philosophy, our answer sums up our belief system, situates us in our chosen field of research, and governs how we carry out our work. Early career researchers can occasionally get lost in the wilderness when searching for a philosophy to underpin their research. Navigating the paradigms, ontologies, epistemologies, and theoretical frameworks – terms that many of us do not encounter on a daily basis – coupled with a dizzying number of philosophical systems and principles ending in 'ism' (from absolutism to Zoroastrianism) can make this part of our tour of academic skills particularly daunting.

Before getting lost in the philosophy forest, keep in mind that you are not obliged to know your research philosophy. There is probably even a philosophical argument that it *cannot* be known – one of the great things about philosophy is that you can dispute anything. There are plenty of world-leading researchers who would struggle to describe their philosophy or identify which ontologies or epistemologies underpin their work. But when it comes to their methods of research – the more practical *how-to* aspects of their job – they will confidently describe every facet of what they do and how they do it. You can do the same if you wish, and concentrate solely on your research methods, but knowing why you use those methods and how they fit into a wider philosophical view of the world will make you feel more sure of your place in the field.

Choosing your philosophy – the pilgrimage through academic jargon you need to make in order to connect your broad worldview to your specific research methods – can take several iterations. Firstly, you need to choose an *ontology*. An ontology can describe the nature of existence and reality, but for the sake of our research philosophies (and possibly our sanity) it can also simply be thought of as setting boundaries on what can be known. Next, you need an *epistemology* to define your position on knowledge itself. If your ontology describes what can be known, your epistemology describes how it can be known. Now you might need a *theoretical framework* which provides your distinct approach to gathering knowledge, and a *methodology*, which is the specific set of rules and procedures you are going to follow when conducting your research. Finally, you select your *research methods* – the actual tools you will use in your research.

These different components of your research philosophy are sometimes referred to collectively as your *research paradigm*. It may seem more relevant to philosophers than scientists, who can appear to be at different ends of the theoretical and empirical research spectrum, but these two points are inextricably linked. Natural philosophy predates the term *science*, and even Isaac Newton, a key figure in the emergence of modern science, thought of himself as a philosopher of nature (Gale, 1984). If you want a simple way to figure out your research philosophy for yourself, you can use the research philosophy wayfinder available on this book's companion website to steer you through the terminological mire. It provides only the briefest of glimpses into the hidden depths of potential philosophical underpinnings, but it will at least let you extricate yourself from a tricky situation if you are asked to describe your research philosophy. You could say 'Well my ontology is realism, my epistemology is empiricism, and I identify as an experimental positivist using quantitative methods' and then sashay away before there are any follow-up questions.

Researcher views

Arthur, on how early career researchers should avoid wasting too much time trying to figure out their research philosophies:

(Continued)

I see with a lot of our PhD students in their very first year they are thrown into this. Like what are your ontological epistemological assumptions, all this kind of stuff, and they get bogged down in it for the first year or two, and they think it's the be-all and end-all. Yes, I think it's important to have a knowledge of that and be aware of it and consider where you lie, but you don't need to get too bogged down in it. There are far more important aspects of your PhD.

Research questions

Your research question is the central query that drives your work. It is worth considering early and often as it will guide subsequent decisions affecting how you design your study and select your research methods (Bryman, 2007). If you have a theory to test, you may need a hypothesis rather than a research question (Thomas, 2017), but in most scenarios, before choosing your research methods, you will have at least one research question. Choosing a research question can be intimidating; there are innumerable different paths your research could take (Alvesson and Sandberg, 2013). To help make your choice, your research question should satisfy three criteria:

1. It should be a question that you are passionate about answering.
2. You should have the tools or resources to attempt to answer it.
3. It should at least appear to be answerable.

You will revisit your research question regularly, and even when it seems like it has revealed its final form it will likely still require tweaking. Refining it is such an important process that it should be considered in relation to the bigger picture of your research paradigm. Your research question may change form or direction, but every time you revisit it, you will be ensuring it becomes more robust and reliable. Your research question will also be influenced by who can help you develop it. You may wish to select a topic that you can address from a unique personal perspective, but if you are working with other researchers, or you have a mentor or supervisor with expertise on the topic, it will be a collaborative process. Either way, your research question should be written clearly and concisely in the fewest words possible. There should be no implied assumptions or vague terms that could be misinterpreted. When your research question reaches a form that has no ambiguity, is specific enough to be answerable, and cannot be written more simply, it is well on its way to becoming a good research question.

Researcher views

Carolina, on frequently adjusting her research question:

You are sure you have your research question. And then it just sort of ... disappears. Like you go back to it after a few days and it just doesn't read right. I thought my supervisor

was going to get sick of me coming to them with a new research question, it was definitely annoying me! But they told me that it's normal to keep changing it. I'm happy with
the final version.

A research question can be a single overarching question, or can take the form of several
linked questions. Creswell and Clark (2017) cite examples from different studies, such as
an example of a single independent question being: 'How do different copy-and-paste
note-taking interventions affect college students' learning of Web-based text ideas?' (Igo
et al., 2008, p. 150). Examples of linked questions could be: 'What is the impact of the
Big Brothers Big Sisters program on participating youth?', 'How is the program experienced by stakeholders?', and 'How is the program implemented?' (Brady and O'Regan,
2009, p. 273). There might be a main research question, such as: 'How do young people
make educational and career decisions at the end of compulsory schooling?', followed
by a series of subsidiary questions: 'What factors do young people consider when making their choices?', 'What sources of information do they use to help their decision-
making?', and 'Which individuals are influential in shaping their choices?' (White,
2017, p. 63). Creswell and Clark (2017) also highlight how linked research questions
can determine the type of research methods needed to answer them, such as: 'Is there
a statistically significant difference in nursing student empathy, as measured by the
Interpersonal Reactivity Index (IRI), after a psychiatric nursing clinical experience?' and
'What are student perceptions of working with mentally ill clients during a psychiatric
nursing clinical experience?' (Webster, 2009, pp. 6–7). A strong study starts with strong
research questions (Tashakkori and Creswell, 2007). You can find more examples of
research questions on this book's companion website.

Research methods

Our basic research skills determine our proficiency as researchers and let us demonstrate our ability to design and implement experiments – processes we can collectively refer to as research methods. This could involve creating surveys, carrying
out interviews, computational modelling, undertaking observations, and many other
techniques (Walliman, 2017). Depending on your area of research you may have to
draw on several research methods. Rather than trying to master every method, early
career researchers who focus on a small number of complementary methods can build
up their confidence until they are experts. Persistently using the same methods can
allow us to focus on trying to replicate the results other researchers have found using
those methods. That may sound repetitive, but it will address one of the issues threat-
ening to undermine research – reproducibility (Baker, 2016). It is debatable if there is
a genuine crisis due to the number of experimental results that cannot be reproduced

(Fanelli, 2018), but it is certainly a truth universally acknowledged that a single experiment, in possession of interesting results, must be in want of several replications to
confirm its validity.

Researcher views

Genevieve, on finding enjoyment in the daily life of a researcher:

> You have to actually enjoy the day to day, whatever that involves for your subject, other-
> wise it's going to be a slog. For me, being in the lab, at a microscope, poking small things,
> moving very small volumes of liquid from one tube to another. That sums up biology
> really. Sometimes I got very bored repeating an experiment 100 times, but I also really
> enjoyed the camaraderie of working in a research group. There was a feeling of, *We're
> all in this together.*

The eventual research methods you use can be traced back to your research philosophy and your view of the world (or your view of the universe, depending on your
field of research, or your chosen philosophy, or how far back you are standing). The
general discussion on research tools often comes down to a debate between quantitative and qualitative research methods. It can be appealing to cast the entirety of
research in such black-and-white terms. On the one hand, we have the quantitative
methods usually involving measurements of *quantity* with numerical values, and presented objectively through statistical analysis, favoured by researchers of science and
underpinned by associated philosophical principles, such as realism, positivism, and
empiricism. On the other hand, we have the qualitative methods usually including
an exploration of *qualities* or values, and presented as themes through the subjective
interpretation or *lens* of the researcher, favoured by researchers of the humanities
and the arts and underpinned by philosophical principles such as nominalism, inter-
pretivism, and constructivism. In reality, it is not always that clear-cut, and many
researchers (especially social scientists) will find themselves somewhere on the research
philosophy continuum rather than at the quantitative and qualitative poles. They will
therefore be more firmly rooted in the philosophical middle-ground of pragmatism
(Biesta, 2010), meaning they will use the methodological approach that best suits
the research question being addressed (Tashakkori et al., 1998). Consequently, their
need for qualitative or quantitative research methods might change depending on
the situation, and a mixed methods approach (a combination of quantitative and
qualitative research methods) will become the most favourable option.

Quantitative analyses often involve comparing variables and looking for statistically
significant relationships (Osborne, 2008; Ong and Puteh, 2017) while qualitative
analyses may involve exploring patterns, interactions, or themes (Miles et al.,
2018). Following an existing framework is preferable, but even in objective analyses

the researcher plays a subjective role in choosing which variables to compare, or identifying the themes that emerge from the data (Braun and Clarke, 2006). One of the quickest ways to get to grips with a new research method is to learn from others. Helping another researcher to gather or analyse data in return for their guidance on a new technique is a shrewd way to gain first-hand experience and to begin establishing a network and a community of practice (Chapter 10). Once you have considered your research questions and research methods you may decide that it is time to build a comprehensive overview of the research topic you are about to start investigating. That is an indispensable skill for an early career researcher and is best performed by learning how to carry out systematic reviews of the published literature.

Systematic literature reviews

The ability to carry out robust systematic literature reviews is one of the most underrated research skills. Carrying out any type of review is a natural extension of the kind of casual research that many of us do every day – using search engines to find and explore online information. To go from commonplace searches to a more academic approach requires upgrading from a simple Google search to using something like Google Scholar which – while not without its shortcomings – is a staple of academic research (Harzing and Van der Wal, 2008; Haddaway et al., 2015). An even more important step towards conducting a basic review is to search individual databases of published academic literature (such as Scopus, Web of Science, ERIC, PubMed, or JSTOR).

Anyone can review published documents and craft a narrative that interprets the existing literature. What makes a review systematic is the use of well-defined rules and a rigorous approach that can be followed, duplicated, and built upon by other researchers (Fink, 2005). A non-systematic review of the literature might be appealing as a quick way of providing background or context to our work, but it will be of little value to the wider field. A systematic literature review, on the other hand – due to its rigour, reproducibility, and reliability – can provide a definitive assessment of a topic and help guide future work in that area. Through synthesising and presenting the available evidence on a topic, a systematic literature review can assess the overall state of a field of research and be considered an original piece of research in its own right (Gough et al., 2017).

There are guides to conducting systematic literature reviews to be found in most disciplines, for example in medicine (Khan et al., 2003), software engineering (Budgen and Brereton, 2006), social science (Papaioannou et al., 2010), pharmacy (Jesson and Lacey, 2006), information systems (Okoli and Schabram, 2010), and nursing (Cronin et al., 2008), to name but a few. Siddaway et al. (2019) provide an excellent guide to conducting systematic literature reviews that is ostensibly for psychology researchers, but is likely to be useful for researchers in almost any discipline. Four of the main steps to carrying out a systematic literature review are:

1. *Planning*. This step involves using your research question to draw up a plan of how you are going to carry out the review. At this stage you should start familiarising yourself with what has already been published on the topic and set boundaries on how you are going to search the literature – broad enough that it will be meaningful, specific enough that it will be feasible. This is also the time to choose which databases to use and the search terms that are most appropriate. Clear criteria need to be established to make definitive decisions on what will be included or excluded in the eventual analysis. For example, if you are reviewing research studies on a particular topic then you are likely to include or exclude publications based on their relevance to that topic, where and how the studies were carried out, the language of the publications, when they were published, and if they are peer-reviewed. While having a clear research question can guide your review of the literature, it is a two-way process – reviewing the literature can be an essential scoping exercise in developing a strong research question (Meadows, 2003), and as you conduct your review you may find that your research questions require tweaking.

2. *Searching*. Searching through academic research databases can be an arduous task if you have not done your due diligence at the planning stage. If, however, you begin your search armed with a list of robust search terms suitable for your chosen databases and with clear inclusion and exclusion criteria, then your searches will be more akin to following a carefully designed master plan rather than aimlessly sifting through materials. Adapting your plan, even at this stage, is acceptable as long as you record any changes. You might be overwhelmed by the sheer number of results, which could warrant tightening the focus of your search. Alternatively, you may find nothing of interest and choose to expand the scope of your search. At the end of the process you should be able to clearly and transparently describe how the search was carried out so that other researchers can replicate your work.

3. *Analysing*. Although systematic literature reviews rely on gathering secondary data, original results can be obtained through analyses of the findings of previous studies. A quantitative analysis of existing research is usually referred to as a meta-analysis (Lipsey and Wilson, 2001) but, depending on the types of studies being compared, the analysis could take a more qualitative form as either a narrative overview or a meta-synthesis (Thorne et al., 2004; Grant and Booth, 2009). If there are a large number of papers describing separate studies, for example, then a quantitative comparison across variables such as the number of participants in each study, or the countries where the studies were conducted, could be of interest. If a small number of publications are to be analysed, it might require a more qualitative investigation of the different methods and findings in those publications. As with your searches of the literature, how you analyse the materials you have gathered should not only be systematic but should be presented in as much detail as is necessary to ensure that other researchers can follow your approach and be confident of getting the same results.

4. *Synthesising*. The analysis stage allows for patterns, similarities, or gaps in the literature to be identified in the final synthesis stage. The true value of a systematic literature review is that it does not just describe what other studies have accomplished, but instead draws conclusions that are only possible by assessing the full collection of works considered. Rather than merely cataloguing the papers in a particular area, the systematic review should include a critique or a reflection that will provide new insights for the field.

This synthesis could draw a definitive line under a research topic, or potentially highlight new opportunities for future studies to build upon. When it comes to reporting and sharing your systematic literature review, following a common technique such as using a PRISMA ('Preferred Reporting Items for Systematic Reviews and Meta-Analyses') statement or flow diagram (Moher et al., 2009; Rethlefsen et al., 2021) will make your work even more accessible and useful to your field of research.

A systematic literature review template is available on this book's companion website along with sample research questions, inclusion and exclusion criteria, and PRISMA flow diagrams.

Choosing the tools to conduct the review depends on the needs of the researcher and the topic of research. Having the organisational skills to keep oversight of the review process is an advantage, and one approach is to choose software solutions designed for undertaking systematic literature reviews, such as Covidence or Rayyan (Kellermeyer et al., 2018). An alternative approach is to combine reference management software such as EndNote, Mendeley, Zotero, or BibTex with data analysis software such as NVivo or SPSS, or even a spreadsheet or collaborative writing tool such as Manubot, Excel, Overleaf, or Google Docs/Sheets (Macdonald et al., 2016; Houghton et al., 2017; Tay, 2020).

Guidance in all aspects of the review process is available from organisations dedicated to improving systematic review processes and the presentation of evidence (Tugwell et al., 2006), such as the Cochrane Collaboration (www.cochrane.org) and its sister organisation the Campbell Collaboration (www.campbellcollaboration.org). Local support in your own institution is even more beneficial. Depending on the scale of the review to be undertaken, a team-based approach involving fellow researchers could work best, while any review team will benefit from the help of an academic subject librarian, who is an ideal collaborator for a high quality systematic review (Phelps and Campbell, 2012; Bullers et al., 2018; McKeown and Ross-White, 2019).

Researcher views

Marin, on learning to carry out systematic literature reviews:

> I thought I knew all I could about systematic literature reviews until I went on a course and realised I knew very little. The librarian was my best friend when it came to getting good quality help with search terms […] I had to learn all about synthesising and analysing what I had found, why had no one mentioned that part of it before?

If you conduct a systematic literature review following the above steps it will provide an overview of the field and help identify any gaps, issues, or opportunities concerning your chosen research questions. A bonus of undertaking a systematic literature review at the start of your research journey is that it can lead to a publication early in your career which can increase opportunities for awards, grants, and employment (Pickering and Byrne, 2014). If it is a well-researched topic, your work could involve synthesising and updating the existing reviews. If there is no existing review for your topic then there is even more incentive for you to provide one. In either scenario, a well-written systematic literature review is a meaningful contribution to a field of research and so is likely to be publishable. Another benefit of writing a systematic literature review at the start of a project is that it offers a tangible way to monitor progress, as well as providing some much-needed motivation at a time when it is easy to descend into periods of unstructured reading. The systematic literature review process offers a way to explore and improve understanding of a field while having a clearly defined objective – the completion of the review itself.

Keeping track of progress

As tempting as it may seem to breeze through the basic aspects of research to get to the spicier academic skills in upcoming chapters, the importance of improving our basic research skills cannot be overstated. A common problem for early career researchers is finding the time and motivation to hone basic research skills before seeking out other academic pursuits that can seem more immediately rewarding. Developing a host of academic skills simultaneously is feasible once it is not causing our basic research skills to be neglected. The reason for the occasional dips in our desire to spend time pondering research philosophies and research questions, practising research methods, or reviewing the literature, is because it can be difficult to quantify the progress we are making. The solution is simple but is so momentous that it should be tattooed on the insides of our eyelids (or at the very least written on a post-it on our desk): Write. Up. Everything.

Writing short summaries of any advancements we have made each day, or just logging the tasks we have worked on, provides a structure for us to quantify the progress we are making. This account of our progress is not something we need to show anyone else (if an ill-advised supervisor ever asks us to provide a detailed account of everything we do each day, a more constructive alternative can usually be found – see Chapter 7), but it will become an invaluable reference for us to consult as our research advances. Cloud-based note-taking software is perfect for keeping searchable notes across different devices and can be supplemented with voice notes for when inspiration strikes on the move. Having a personal written record we can watch grow every day will provide a sense of achievement, build confidence in our abilities, and help our development as researchers (Borg, 2001; Shelton-Strong and Mynard, 2020). In Chapter 10, we will further explore the benefits of regularly reflecting on our work.

Depending on our personal taste, we may choose to keep track of our progress in a lab book, a journal, or a diary. Regardless of the form it takes, tracking progress in a written log presents a way to develop our critical thinking skills – the skills we use to assess available information and target more desirable outcomes (Halpern, 1998). A log of our research progress will throw into sharp relief the parts of our work where we feel confident, and those that need more attention. Seeing, in inescapable written form, the areas of our work where we are struggling should provide us with the necessary impetus to seek help. Discussing ideas, questions, methods, or other aspects of our work with our peers, can help us think more critically about the topics in question. If we require more guidance, that is when we call on our supervisors or other academic mentors (Chapter 7).

As we refine the written log of our progress, it could become something we want to develop into a publication (Chapter 4). Even if we do not publish any of the material, keeping a written account of our progress is a beneficial investment of our time for one more reason – practising how we write about and communicate our work is also an invaluable academic skill (which we will explore further in the coming chapters).

Summary

- Spend time considering your research philosophy and refining research questions you are passionate about. Feeling assured of your place in the field will give you confidence to develop your ideas.
- Gain experience with research methods by replicating the work of others. When you can reproduce the results of previous studies, you will be more assured in designing your own experiments.
- Practise your review skills. Become an expert at systematically searching through the published literature to assess the state of the fields you wish to investigate.
- Capture the headway you are making by keeping a written account of everything you do. Having a candid self-assessment of your development as a researcher will allow you to critically evaluate your progress.
- Improve your research skills by seeking out guidance. Basic research skills can be honed faster through collaboration and learning from others.

Successful researchers develop their skills early in their careers and continuously find ways to improve them. There are many other aspects to the role of a researcher and some early career researchers convince themselves they do not need to focus on their research because of the contributions they are making in other ways. Tread carefully down that path for there be dragons. Being a good researcher – making meaningful contributions to new knowledge – is the cornerstone of life as an academic, but it is up to us to ensure that we prioritise our research and fit our other responsibilities around it. We will see in Chapter 11 that when it comes to career progression, researchers who prioritise their research above every other component of their job, and those who seem to find ways to prioritise everything *but* their research, can have very different experiences of life as an academic researcher. Solid research skills are not only vital for any potential academic career, they are all-important transferable skills for most career paths. In Chapter 3 we shall think about the single most important skill to complement our research – academic writing.

Further reading

- Booth, A., Sutton, A., & Papaioannou, D. (2016). *Systematic Approaches to a Successful Literature Review*. London, UK: SAGE.

A comprehensive guide to carrying out systematic literature reviews.

- Creswell, J. W. & Clark, V. L. P. (2017). *Designing and Conducting Mixed Methods Research* (3rd edn). Thousand Oaks, CA: SAGE.

This book draws on examples from published studies to provide a comprehensive step-by-step guide to conducting mixed methods research.

- Jensen, E. & Laurie, C. (2016). *Doing Real Research: A Practical Guide to Social Research*. London, UK: SAGE.

An extensive guide to carrying out research that, while focusing on social research, adopts an accessible style with practical examples that will benefit researchers from any discipline.

- O'Leary, Z. (2004). *The Essential Guide to Doing Research*. London, UK: SAGE.

A companion text for conducting research that covers every aspect of the research process.

- Robson, C. (2014). *How to do a Research Project: A Guide for Undergraduate Students*. Hoboken, NJ: Wiley-Blackwell.

This book is ideal for guiding undergraduate students through their first encounters with academic research.

Resources

Further resources for this chapter can be found at: www.JosephRoche.ie/EssentialSkills

- Research Philosophy Wayfinder
- Sample Research Questions
- Systematic Literature Review Template

References

Allison, B., Hilton, A., O'Sullivan, T., & Owen, A. (1996). *Research Skills for Students: Transferable & Learning Skills*. New York, NY: Routledge.

Alvesson, M. & Sandberg, J. (2013). *Constructing Research Questions: Doing Interesting Research*. London, UK: SAGE.

Baker, M. (2016). Reproducibility crisis. *Nature, 533*(26), 353–366.

Biesta, G. (2010). Pragmatism and the philosophical foundations of mixed methods research. In A. Tashakkori & C. Teddlie (Eds.), *SAGE Handbook of Mixed Methods in Social & Behavioral Research* (pp. 95–118). Thousand Oaks, CA: SAGE.

Borg, S. (2001). The research journal: a tool for promoting and understanding researcher development. *Language Teaching Research, 5*(2), 156–177.

Brady, B. & O'Regan, C. (2009). Meeting the challenge of doing an RCT evaluation of youth mentoring in Ireland: a journey in mixed methods. *Journal of Mixed Methods Research, 3*(3), 265–280.

Braun, V. & Clarke, V. (2006). Using thematic analysis in psychology. *Qualitative Research in Psychology, 3*(2), 77–101.

Bryman, A. (2007). The research question in social research: what is its role? *International Journal of Social Research Methodology, 10*(1), 5–20.

Budgen, D. & Brereton, P. (2006). Performing systematic literature reviews in software engineering. In *Proceedings of the 28th International Conference on Software Engineering* (pp. 1051–1052). New York, NY: ACM.

Bullers, K., Howard, A. M., Hanson, A., Kearns, W. D., Orriola, J. J., Polo, R. L., & Sakmar, K. A. (2018). It takes longer than you think: librarian time spent on systematic review tasks. *Journal of the Medical Library Association, 106*(2), 198–210.

Creswell, J. W. & Clark, V. L. P. (2017). *Designing and Conducting Mixed Methods Research* (3rd edn). Thousand Oaks, CA: SAGE.

Cronin, P., Ryan, F., & Coughlan, M. (2008). Undertaking a literature review: a step-by-step approach. *British Journal of Nursing, 17*(1), 38–43.

Fanelli, D. (2018). Opinion: is science really facing a reproducibility crisis, and do we need it to? *Proceedings of the National Academy of Sciences, 115*(11), 2628–2631.

Fink, A. (2005). *Conducting Research Literature Reviews: From the Internet to Paper*. Thousand Oaks, CA: SAGE.

Gale, G. (1984). Science and the philosophers. *Nature, 312*(5994), 491–495.

Gough, D., Oliver, S., & Thomas, J. (Eds.) (2017). *An Introduction to Systematic Reviews*. London, UK: SAGE.

Grant, M. J. & Booth, A. (2009). A typology of reviews: an analysis of 14 review types and associated methodologies. *Health Information & Libraries Journal, 26*(2), 91–108.

Haddaway, N. R., Collins, A. M., Coughlin, D., & Kirk, S. (2015). The role of Google Scholar in evidence reviews and its applicability to grey literature searching. *PloS One, 10*(9), 1–17.

Halpern, D. F. (1998). Teaching critical thinking for transfer across domains: disposition, skills, structure training, and metacognitive monitoring. *American Psychologist, 53*(4), 449–455.

Harzing, A. W. K. & Van der Wal, R. (2008). Google Scholar as a new source for citation analysis. *Ethics in Science and Environmental Politics, 8*(1), 61–73.

Houghton, C., Murphy, K., Meehan, B., Thomas, J., Brooker, D., & Casey, D. (2017). From screening to synthesis: using NVivo to enhance transparency in qualitative evidence synthesis. *Journal of Clinical Nursing, 26*(5-6), 873–881.

Igo, L. B., Kiewra, K. A., & Bruning, R. (2008). Individual differences and intervention flaws: A sequential explanatory study of college students' copy-and-paste note taking. *Journal of Mixed Methods Research, 2*(2), 149–168.

Jesson, J. & Lacey, F. (2006). How to do (or not to do) a critical literature review. *Pharmacy Education, 6*(2), 139–148.

Kellermeyer, L., Harnke, B., & Knight, S. (2018). Covidence and Rayyan. *Journal of the Medical Library Association: JMLA, 106*(4), 580–583.

Khan, K. S., Kunz, R., Kleijnen, J., & Antes, G. (2003). Five steps to conducting a systematic review. *Journal of the Royal Society of Medicine, 96*(3), 118–121.

Lipsey, M. W. & Wilson, D. B. (2001). *Practical Meta-analysis*. London, UK: SAGE.

Macdonald, M., Misener, R. M., Weeks, L., & Helwig, M. (2016). Covidence vs Excel for the title and abstract review stage of a systematic review. *International Journal of Evidence-based Healthcare, 14*(4), 200–201.

McKeown, S. & Ross-White, A. (2019). Building capacity for librarian support and addressing collaboration challenges by formalizing library systematic review services. *Journal of the Medical Library Association: JMLA, 107*(3), 411–419.

Meadows, K. A. (2003). So you want to do research? Developing the research question. *British Journal of Community Nursing, 8*(9), 397–403.

Miles, M. B., Huberman, A. M., & Saldaña, J. (2018). *Qualitative Data Analysis: A Methods Sourcebook* (4th edn). Thousand Oaks, CA: SAGE.

Moher, D., Liberati, A., Tetzlaff, J., Altman, D. G., & Prisma Group (2009). Preferred reporting items for systematic reviews and meta-analyses: the PRISMA statement. *PLoS Med, 6*(7), 1–6.

Okoli, C. & Schabram, K. (2010). A guide to conducting a systematic literature review of information systems research. *Sprouts: Working Papers on Information Systems, 10*(26), 1–49.

Ong, M. H. A. & Puteh, F. (2017). Quantitative data analysis: Choosing between SPSS, PLS, and AMOS in social science research. *International Interdisciplinary Journal of Scientific Research, 3*(1), 14–25.

Osborne, J. W. (Ed.) (2008). *Best Practices in Quantitative Methods*. Thousand Oaks, CA: SAGE.

Papaioannou, D., Sutton, A., Carroll, C., Booth, A., & Wong, R. (2010). Literature searching for social science systematic reviews: consideration of a range of search techniques. *Health Information & Libraries Journal, 27*(2), 114–122.

Phelps, S. F. & Campbell, N. (2012). Commitment and trust in librarian–faculty relationships: a systematic review of the literature. *The Journal of Academic Librarianship, 38*(1), 13–19.

Pickering, C. & Byrne, J. (2014). The benefits of publishing systematic quantitative literature reviews for PhD candidates and other early career researchers. *Higher Education Research & Development, 33*(3), 534–548.

Rethlefsen, M. L., Kirtley, S., Waffenschmidt, S., Ayala, A. P., Moher, D., Page, M. J., & Koffel, J. B. (2021). PRISMA-S: an extension to the PRISMA statement for reporting literature searches in systematic reviews. *Systematic Reviews, 10*(1), 1–19.

Shelton-Strong, S. J. & Mynard, J. (2020). Promoting positive feelings and motivation for language learning: the role of a confidence-building diary. *Innovation in Language Learning and Teaching, 15*(4), 1–15.

Siddaway, A. P., Wood, A. M., & Hedges, L. V. (2019). How to do a systematic review: a best practice guide for conducting and reporting narrative reviews, meta-analyses, and meta-syntheses. *Annual Review of Psychology, 70*, 747–770.

Tashakkori, A. & Creswell, J. (2007). Exploring the nature of research questions in mixed methods research. *Journal of Mixed Methods Research, 1*(3), 207–211.

Tashakkori, A., Teddlie, C., & Teddlie, C. B. (1998). *Mixed Methodology: Combining Qualitative and Quantitative Approaches.* Thousand Oaks, CA: SAGE.

Tay, A. (2020). How to write a superb literature review. *Nature Online.* doi: 10.1038/d41586-020-03422-x

Thomas, G. (2017). *How to Do Your Research Project: A Guide for Students.* London, UK: SAGE.

Thorne, S., Jensen, L., Kearney, M. H., Noblit, G., & Sandelowski, M. (2004). Qualitative metasynthesis: reflections on methodological orientation and ideological agenda. *Qualitative Health Research, 14*(10), 1342–1365.

Tugwell, P., Petticrew, M., Robinson, V., Kristjansson, E., & Maxwell, L. (2006). Cochrane and Campbell Collaborations, and health equity. *The Lancet, 367*(9517), 1128–1130.

Walliman, N. (2017). *Research Methods: The Basics.* New York, NY: Routledge.

Webster, D. (2009). *Creative Reflective Experience: Promoting Empathy in Psychiatric Nursing.* Wilmington, DE: ProQuest Publishing.

White, P. (2017). *Developing Research Questions.* London, UK: Palgrave Macmillan.

Three
Writing

In this chapter, we will cover:

- developing writing skills
- tracking productivity and maintaining motivation
- outlining and structuring writing tasks
- drafting, editing, and the iterative writing process
- writing groups and the value of feedback.

Academic writing

You are a writer. The sooner you recognise that and either make peace with it, or – ideally – embrace it, the better. As an academic researcher, your role is not solely to gather and analyse data, but also to contribute to new knowledge by sharing your ideas and findings. Although sharing that work might include teaching, public speaking, social media, and other forms of communication (see Chapter 6 for teaching and Chapter 8 for communication and engagement), your main mode of communication will always be your writing. You might not yet think of yourself as a writer. You might know for a fact that your writing is abysmal. That is no excuse. If you take your job seriously, and you care about contributing to your field of research, and maybe even plan on making it your career, then you have a duty to improve your writing. That might sound daunting, but the good news (and the disappointing news, if you think about it too deeply) is that the bar is set dismally low – most academic writing is awful. If you make the conscious decision to become a more productive, more efficient, and more engaging writer, you will quickly rise above the status quo.

The scope of academic writing may appear vast, but the requisite skills to be a prolific writer are uncomplicated. As academic researchers we must practise our craft and to do that we need to set a writing schedule. The only difficult step is sticking to that schedule. This chapter will address the need to practise writing and embrace the different stages of the writing process to fully realise our potential as academic writers.

Reading about writing

The first step in becoming more committed to our writing is to become more committed to our reading. Reading about writing can be cathartic and stimulating. Reading about how other people approach the writing process feels like we are getting to look behind the curtain at how the magic happens, and it can be the motivation that many of us need to get started.

If reading is one of your hobbies, then you have conveniently already committed to improving your writing. The next time you are reading – be it a news article, a textbook, or a medieval fantasy novel – pay close attention to what you like about what you are reading. How does the writing capture your attention? How are the sentences and paragraphs constructed in ways that make them effortless to read? Or if you are struggling to connect with a piece of writing, then what is it about the writing that is off-putting? Recognising styles of writing that appeal to you will help you develop your own writing. Maybe you will not write your next academic paper in the style of a medieval fantasy, but the basic principle of forming word patterns that people will enjoy reading holds true whether it is academic writing, broadsheet journalism, or post-apocalyptic erotic cyberpunk.

If reading is not already a hobby of yours, but you are determined to improve your writing, a good place to start is a short text by the psychology professor Paul Silvia – *How to Write a Lot: A Practical Guide to Productive Academic Writing* (2007). It is an uncompromising and brutally effective guide to help researchers be more productive writers. A complementary companion to that book is *Air & Light & Time & Space: How Successful Academics Write* by higher education professor Helen Sword (2017). It delves into the social and emotional aspects of writing as well as including personal perspectives on writing from academics around the world. Once we recognise ourselves as writers, we need not limit our learning solely to academic writing (Antoniou and Moriarty, 2008). There are countless books about the general craft of writing, and any that can motivate us to write are invaluable. For your perusal and your motivation, there is a list of books, blogs, and other writing resources on this book's companion website.

Researcher views

Julian, on how his relationship with academic writing affected him:

> Academic writing played a huge role in my research adventure. Not due to a fondness or talent for it, but due to my own perceived ineptitude for it. A combination of perfectionism, coupled with a lack of belief in what I am trying to complete, along with some bad timing, resulted in me disembarking from my research journey … or at least, having a long layover.

Some people become addicted to self-help books and reassure themselves that as long as they are reading about self-improvement, they are taking positive action. A better approach is for us to practise our writing while reading about ways to improve it. One piece of advice that crops up in every book about writing is that to improve our writing we must practise, and to practise we must write as often as possible. Reading, too, should be part of that practice. The author Stephen King knows what it means to be a prolific writer, having published more than 60 novels, so his advice deserves our attention: 'If you want to be a writer, you must do two things above all others: read a lot and write a lot. There's no way around these two things that I'm aware of, no shortcut' (King, 2000, p. 164).

Researcher views

Isabel, on reading Stephen King's book *On Writing: A Memoir of the Craft*:

> Oh I read that book too! Someone in my lab had a copy of it and said it would help me get better at writing. Yes, it's crazy. It has lots of tips and stuff. But like the cocaine stories too … And then you're in a car crash! Ha! It was wild. Not what I was expecting. But it did make me think a lot more about how I write. I guess that's the point.

The simplest most difficult task

We need to write more, and we need to publish more. That maxim holds true for almost every academic researcher, especially those at an early stage in their careers. If you are the exception – the mythical, early career academic who is already writing and publishing prodigiously with ease – then you must find a way to maintain that level of output and continue to be a magical unicorn academic for as long as you can before you are inevitably dragged back down to the realm of human struggles alongside the rest of us. If you do not enjoy the writing process yet, then you are not alone (Kiriakos and Tienari, 2018). Even the best academics struggle with their writing and, for most, it is a constant issue. It can range from mild frustration at never quite reaching writing goals, to being the root cause of feelings of anxiety, inferiority, and dread (Cameron et al., 2009; Huerta et al., 2017; French, 2018a). Doctoral and graduate students are generally worried about their writing, and it can be the reason some choose a different career path (Thomson and Kamler, 2016; French, 2018b). We are judged on our writing (Blaxter et al., 1998; Backes-Gellner and Schlinghoff, 2010; Aprile et al., 2020). Paradoxically, we are judged not on the style, the tone, or even the quality of our writing, or at least not as much as one might think. We are judged – crudely – on whether it exists or it does not.

It is one of our enduring obligations as researchers to make sure our writing output exists. We will likely need to work on our writing, as regularly as possible, for the rest of our careers. Writing is the one academic skill that cannot be carried by the other skills in our repertoire. If we find a way to enjoy it, it will become easier, but still there will be times when it is not easy and there will be days when we do not want to write. These are the days when it is most important that we do. The bad days will likely outnumber the good days, and we do not have the luxury of waiting until we feel motivated to write. Making a writing schedule and sticking to it rigidly is the single, non-negotiable, open secret to being a more productive academic writer.

The way to stick to a writing schedule is to make sure nothing else impinges on the writing time we have scheduled for ourselves. Paul Silvia mercilessly dismantles all of the excuses (or 'specious barriers' as he labels them) we create for not sticking to our writing schedules: not having enough time, not having enough research done, not feeling inspired, or not having the right equipment – 'Equipment will never help you write a lot; only making a schedule and sticking to it will make you a productive writer' (Silvia, 2007, p. 22).

While Paul Silvia suggests that academic writing can be a 'grim business' (Silvia, 2007, p. 47), Helen Sword believes we should be cognisant of our emotions, our passion for the craft of writing, and be open to adding 'pleasure and playfulness' to our writing (Sword, 2017, p. 206). Both perspectives are true: writing is something to be enjoyed – even if just for the pleasure of creating something tangible that can be shared with others – but the *grim business* is showing up every day to commit words to paper, even when we don't feel like it. That is the skill that will define our academic writing and, if we can master it, will make our academic life immeasurably more gratifying. If, at this point, you have not already started thinking about your writing schedule, then to echo Paul Silvia's sentiment: 'This book cannot help you unless you accept the principle of scheduling, because the only way to write a lot is to write regularly, regardless of whether you feel like writing' (Silvia, 2007, pp. 27–28).

Ruthlessly protect your writing time. The longer you spend working as an academic researcher, the more tasks and responsibilities that will mysteriously and surreptitiously become part of your job. There is usually less immediate pressure to write, and it can be easier to spend our time replying to emails, scheduling meetings, preparing to teach classes, or doing any of the countless tasks that can quickly fill the day of an academic researcher (Grant and Knowles, 2000). The literary scholar Lisa Surridge rails against this phenomenon by strategically procrastinating on her teaching preparation to prioritise academic writing: 'I play chicken with my classes – because it's easy to let your research go during term time, but you know you won't walk into a class under-prepared' (Sword, 2017, p. 186). In Chapter 6, we will address managing teaching schedules, but Lisa Surridge's commitment to prioritising academic writing is admirable. If even teaching – what many of us see as our most direct and powerful way to help others fulfil their potential – can occasionally be a lower priority than academic writing, then clearly nothing can be higher.

Researcher views

Celeste, on finding motivation to write:

> It was a big problem for me. I don't enjoy writing. So for me to sit down and actually write, I tend to find that difficult. Unless someone put me under pressure and told me this is the deadline, you need to have it done by then, I wouldn't do it, to be honest.

Write every day

One of the great teachers of writing, William Zinsser, insists that we practise writing every day: 'You learn to write by writing. It's a truism, but what makes it a truism is that it's true. The only way to learn to write is to force yourself to produce a certain number of words on a regular basis' (1976, p. 49). Set yourself an amount of time to write and the number of words that you would like to reach each day. Thirty minutes should be the minimum and two hours is as much as anyone needs if they are writing every day. If you write 300–500 words every day, you will not only feel smugly productive, but you will also be writing more than the vast majority of your peers.

Write for short periods each day rather than waiting for that fabled perfect time to write (Bolker, 1998). Those spells that appear blissfully free on our calendars – the weekend, the semester break, the holidays – are mirages. By the time we reach those shimmering oases of calm we will have just as many excuses for not writing as we do now. The insistence that we will do our writing in intense periods of 'binge writing' (Kellogg, 1999), when we finally have time to *really* focus on it, is a myth that many of us tell ourselves early (and sometimes much later) in our careers. We need to be honest with ourselves about how much we are actually writing and, as with a lot of the skills in this book, the only way to do that is to monitor our progress.

Researcher views

Carolina, on only being able to focus on academic writing when there was no one else around:

> I had to wait for everyone to leave the office before I could write. Even the tiniest distraction during the day and I would do anything else other than writing. But as soon as everyone went home it was like the elves and the shoemaker. And a few hours later I would have written a few thousand words. I was the elves, obviously.

The psychology professor Robert Boice has long advocated for improving academic writing through having a schedule and monitoring progress (Boice, 1990). As researchers, if we are unhappy with our writing output, we already have all the tools we need to address the problem. We can experiment, gather data, and look for patterns. Most of us think we are writing more than we are until we start tracking the days we write, the time we spend writing, and the number of words we have written. It can be startling to see how low those numbers are when we first confront them, but once we do, we have established a baseline, as well as all the motivation we need to set about trying to improve them. By continuously monitoring our writing habits we can explore every facet of our relationship with writing and easily gather data to explain fluctuations in our productivity (Craswell and Poore, 2012). What time of the day is most productive for writing? Where is the best location to write? Which days of the week are the most challenging when it comes to accommodating writing time? Helen Sword has demonstrated that the writing practices of prolific academic writers are incredibly varied and the 'write every day!' mantra may not work for everyone (Sword, 2016, p. 312). Each of us needs to reflect on our own writing habits, address the factors that are affecting our writing, and start sticking to our writing schedule.

There is a template spreadsheet available on this book's companion website that I use to doggedly record the days when I write, how much time I spend writing, the number of words I write, and the writing tasks I am working on. This spreadsheet is modelled on Paul Silvia's version (Silvia, 2007) which was instrumental in dramatically increasing my academic writing output. Within five years I went from having virtually no writing output to having the most peer-reviewed publications in my department during that time. There are mitigating factors that make that less impressive than it sounds – I became the most prolific academic writer in my department only because my colleagues who were out-publishing me over that period both left to take up more senior (and more lucrative) positions in other universities. They are outstanding researchers, but it is no coincidence that the most prolific academic writers were considered the top candidates for prestigious senior academic positions. Keep that in mind for when we consider career progression in Chapter 11.

A first draft and an ever-improving outline

For many researchers, the most arduous part of academic writing is making a start. A blank page or screen staring back at us can be paralysing, but luckily, we can protect ourselves by relying on the power of *drafting*. All we really need to begin writing is a cursory outline to help guide us in our main objective – producing a *truly underwhelming* first draft. Managing our expectations is key at this stage and we should not be disappointed by feeble first efforts. Most of us cannot produce engaging prose on command (or, as the first draft of this sentence read: 'We are not great at writing good words when we want to.' Yikes). You only need your first draft to bring you to your second draft (and the third, and so on, through as many drafts as are needed) so that the iterative process of writing can improve your work every time.

If you are really embarrassed by your first draft, then no one needs to see it, and you can improve it until it is ready to share. You can still call it your 'first draft' when you do eventually share it and no one will ever know that it took you five iterations just to reach that point. Even the best writers in the world force themselves to get their first draft down on paper so they can see how much work it needs. The novelist Anne Lamott pointedly refers to them as 'shitty first drafts' and taps into the uncertainty we all face when she says: 'Very few writers really know what they are doing until they've done it' (Lamott, 1994, p. 50).

We choose what we classify as academic writing. It could be a research grant application, a policy briefing, a report on an experiment, an abstract for a conference presentation, a course syllabus, or simply writing up our research progress, as suggested in Chapter 2. If you are really brave, you could start writing with no idea of what you are going to write about or where it is going, but most of us need to have an idea and an outline. In Chapter 4, we will look at the different kinds of publications you might consider, but a good place to start is an academic paper. The academic paper is the staple currency of academic writing. It is also a rudimentary indicator of academic development and so it is never too early to start writing that first paper. If there are no external factors influencing the development of the paper – such as supervisors, co-authors, or funders – then you have the freedom to explore your ideas. If you do not have an idea for a paper, you could write about some of the aspects of research mentioned in Chapter 2: your research philosophy, your research methods, or a review of your research topic.

It can be tempting to start by diving straight into writing the first section of the paper but having a well-considered and coherent outline is paramount. A paper, like most things we write, is essentially a narrative and should have some form of beginning, middle, and end. Lay out your outline using working titles of the main sections. Most papers need an introduction, some background details or context, a methods section, results, some discussion, and conclusions. Expand the outline by planning how each of those sections could comprise several subsections, and estimate word counts for each subsection. This has the twofold advantage of, firstly, giving you a sense of the overall length of the paper and, secondly, dividing the paper into more manageable units of required writing.

Having an outline that effectively serves as the *Table of Contents* of your paper lets you pick and choose which subsections to work on with the confidence that they will fit into the larger structure. The outline of your paper (or report, or book chapter, or any other writing assignment) is a guide, but it is not set in stone, and you are not beholden to it. As you draft the different sections and subsections, you may find you need to move, add, or remove sections. You may have overestimated or underestimated the word count you predicted for some sections, and they may need to be merged or split accordingly. Changing and updating your outline is normal and helps you to maintain an overview of the paper. The drafting stage is where you can experiment, make mistakes, and entertain all your creative ideas.

When you start your allocated writing time each day, choose a section or subsection of the paper and begin freewriting: writing your thoughts as they come to you (Elbow, 1998; Li, 2007). The academic journal editor Roger Watson maintains that we cannot draft and edit at the same time and advises getting the words written in any way we can, before fixing them at the editing stage: 'If you are writing and can't think of the right word (e.g. for elephant) don't worry – write (big animal long nose) and move on – come back later and get the correct term. Write, don't edit; otherwise you lose flow' (Watson, 2015). Getting into a creative flow with our writing is something that freewriting can stimulate but for many academic researchers, especially in the early stages of developing writing skills, that state of flow may not arrive.

One of the most famous ways to ensure productive writing spurts without depending on creative flows is through the pomodoro technique, which involves using a kitchen timer (which may or may not happen to be shaped like a tomato/pomodoro) to measure 25-minute intervals of writing time (Cirillo, 2018). If you find yourself in creative flow, you might write for two hours, barely noticing the passage of time. What is more likely is that you might have to motivate yourself to write for 25 minutes by promising yourself the reward of a short five-minute break to stand up, stretch your legs, and forage for snacks before starting the next pomodoro. It takes discipline to keep to those five-minute breaks, so emails, messages, or other distractions should be postponed until the end of the allotted writing period.

At the beginning of your quest to be a more prolific writer, do not worry unduly about the inherent quality or value of what you are writing – there will be plenty of time to think about that during the editing process. What is most important at the drafting stage is fiercely guarding your writing time and cultivating the discipline to write regardless of your circumstances. Freewriting can be done anywhere, at any time, with a computer, a mobile device, or a pen and paper. Draft chapters of this book were written on the bus with the iPhone Notes app during 30-minute commutes to work.

Editing

The editing process ensures our work progresses from being just writing to being writing of quality. As William Zinsser reminds us: 'Rewriting is the essence of writing well: it's where the game is won or lost,' and he goes on to point out how difficult that can be to accept: 'We all have an emotional equity in our first draft, we can't believe that it wasn't born perfect. But the odds are close to 100 percent that it wasn't' (Zinsser, 1976, p. 83). Once we begin the editing process, the game really is afoot and we can now add our personality and style, finessing our initial words and polishing them until they shine. Writing scholars Rowena Murray and Sarah Moore describe this iterative nature of writing and how it 'is the manifestation of your professional learning journey and it is (or at least it should be) a continuous process involving reflection, improvement, development, progress and fulfilment of various types and in varying measures' (Murray and Moore, 2006, p. 5).

Unlike the rush of the drafting process, which is often a scramble to get the words on the page as quickly and clumsily as possible, the editing stage is when we can relax and work steadily through each word, sentence, and paragraph – rewriting our text until it starts to form something we can be proud of. There is no need to solely trust ourselves with this step and we should invite our family, friends, and colleagues to offer their perspectives and to help with proofreading (Huff, 1999; Gray, 2005). As we approach the final draft (or what we hope is the final draft but is, in all likelihood, going to be three drafts away from our final draft) we have no excuse for basic errors persisting in our text. By the time our writing ends up with a journal editor or is sent for peer-review (Chapter 4), readers should be focused on what we are saying, not distracted by the standard of our writing. The author and punctuation advocate Lynne Truss captures how some of us feel when we are sent work to review that still contains basic errors: 'No matter that you have a PhD and have read all of Henry James twice. If you still persist in writing, "Good food at its best", you deserve to be struck by lightning, hacked up on the spot and buried in an unmarked grave' (Truss, 2003, p. 43).

If you feel the need to brush up on the basics of grammar and punctuation, it will prove a worthwhile investment of your time. As well as Lynne Truss's irreverent take on the correct use of language, the linguist and popular science author Steven Pinker provides a scientific view of writing that serves many writers as their modern-day style guide (Pinker, 2014). A more vintage option is a succinct and invaluable book on the basics of writing by the author E. B. White. Most known for writing hugely popular children's books, White turned the coursebook of his teacher William Strunk Jr. into the quintessential writer's guide, *The Elements of Style* (White and Strunk, 1959), which is worthy of inclusion on every writer's bookshelf.

The distinction between the indulgence of the first draft and the careful refinement required in subsequent drafts is made clear by the prolific author Umberto Eco: 'write everything that comes into your head, but only in the first draft' (Eco, 2015, p. 151). That advice comes from an English translation of a book he wrote in the 1970s called *Come si fa una tesi di Laurea* (How to write a thesis) before he shot to fame as an award-winning novelist. It is full of sensible recommendations, such as: 'You are not Proust. Do not write long sentences. If they come into your head, write them, but then break them down' (Eco, 2015, p. 147). Making sentences less complicated is likely to be a common recommendation you will hear as you seek to improve your academic writing (Mewburn et al., 2019). Do not be surprised to see your words dramatically cut by editors, and for your writing to be much enhanced as a result. Becoming a better writer involves learning how to apply that ferocity of word-cutting to our own work.

Researcher views

Henrietta, on mentoring research students' academic writing:

> It is a tricky thing nowadays to find the line between being honest and giving critical and constructive feedback, but also not hurting their feelings where they go and tell everyone that you're a terrible person and harsh.

You can display the full, magnificent, and wondrous range of your vocabulary if your chosen words fit and do not alienate your readers (Smith, 1994). Do not feel obliged to saturate your work with academic jargon just because other academic writers do. As you are editing, keep asking yourself if what you have written can be expressed more clearly, with fewer words or sentences, using simpler language. It is appropriate to leave the final sentiment on editing to William Strunk. The gendered language is indicative of the fact that it was written more than 100 years ago in his original coursebook, long before E. B. White's re-examination of the text, but the advice itself remains undiminished: 'Vigorous writing is concise. A sentence should contain no unnecessary words, a paragraph no unnecessary sentences, for the same reason that a drawing should have no unnecessary lines and a machine no unnecessary parts. This requires not that the writer make all his sentences short, or that he avoid all detail and treat his subjects only in outline, but that every word tell' (White and Strunk, 1959, p. 23).

Writing groups

Having a writing schedule and monitoring progress will result in most of us seeing an increase in our writing output, but creating an environment where we are held accountable to people other than ourselves is one of the most reliable ways to dramatically escalate writing productivity (Boice, 1990). Writing groups emerged from university literary societies in the eighteenth century (Gere, 1987) and the education scholars Claire Aitchison and Cally Guerin define them as 'situations where more than two people come together to work on their writing in a sustained way, over repeated gatherings, for doing, discussing or sharing their writing for agreed purposes' (Aitchison and Guerin, 2014, p. 7). A writing group can include peers, colleagues, or friends who meet up regularly (in person or online) to work on their writing in a structured but social setting. Writing groups can be supportive environments where we discuss the highs and lows of the writing experience with people who are acutely aware of what we are going through. If you are the type of person who sometimes feels that academic writing can be an isolating or lonely experience, a writing group could have a positive impact on your relationship with writing (Mattsson et al., 2020). For early career academics, the time spent in a writing group is not only precious in terms of writing output, but can have profound benefits for many aspects of their work (Lee and Boud, 2003).

Some writing groups focus on productivity, impose strict rules, and expect members to write for the majority of their time together. This is especially helpful for researchers who are struggling with the golden rule of safeguarding their writing time at all costs. Having scheduled meetings with a writing group can ensure that at least those allocated writing periods will be protected. Other groups spend less time writing and focus more on motivation and support. This format is more akin to a *writers' group* (rather than a *writing group*), where members are expected to write in their own time and share samples of their work before meetings so that most of the meeting time can be spent providing constructive feedback to each other.

Researchers who assess their peers' writing, provide feedback, and in turn receive feedback from peers on their own writing, find the process to be 'time consuming, intellectually challenging and socially uncomfortable' but also 'effective in improving the quality of their own subsequent written work and developing other transferable skills' (Topping et al., 2000, p. 163). Peer feedback can be particularly daunting for those who are not writing in their first language, but it can be even more valuable (Hyland, 2004; Paltridge and Starfield, 2007). Critiquing others' work in writing groups can be as instructive to our writing skills as receiving critical feedback on our own writing (Saunders, 1989; Aitchison, 2009). Although immersive writing retreats are widely regarded as being one of the most constructive ways to incorporate peer-learning into writing (Moore, 2003; Murray and Newton, 2009), the infrequency of such retreats makes them not as useful for early career researchers who benefit from the regular feedback that comes with writing groups.

Even if your writing group is the kind that puts emphasis on spending as much time as possible writing, taking a few minutes to set out writing goals at the start of each session and to reflect on them at the end is a rewarding exercise. Writing groups can foster a sense of community stemming from a shared love of writing, a shared anxiety about writing, or something in between. Camaraderie naturally grows in spaces of constructive critique and encouragement. If you want to join an academic writing group, you should first check if there are any existing groups you could join within your department or faculty. If you cannot find a group, you may consider establishing your own. There are no definitive rules for setting up a writing group, but Aitchison and Guerin (2014) offer a range of perspectives from different scholars and researchers who have explored the benefits of forming and running academic writing groups and have plenty of advice around the practicalities and potential pitfalls. A sample format and agenda template for setting up and running a writing group is available on this book's companion website.

Researcher views

Tessa, on establishing a writing group:

> We formed a writing group. That was a really big piece for me. This was like three or four years ago now, and we still keep that up [...] We use a modified version of the pomodoro technique and, at the beginning of every meeting, everyone that is there says just generally what their goals are for the day. And we always make it really clear that it is not for someone to feel judged if they do or don't make those goals. But just for you to think about what is it *I want to do* and *Let me just say it out loud* so at least you know you'll try to hold yourself accountable [...] I don't think I would have finished my dissertation, at least not when I did, without that group and without that process.

Summary

- Read habitually. What you are reading does not really matter once you are critiquing it in relation to how you write.
- Keep a schedule and stick to it. This deceptively simple-sounding task is the key to increasing your writing output.
- Write often – every day if you can – and track your output. If there is one self-assessment you cannot afford to hide from in research, it is being honest with yourself about how much and how often you are writing.
- Embrace the iterative process of writing. Initially, it might feel like you are constantly rewriting, but after working through the stages of outlining, drafting, editing, cutting, and proofing, you will start to see the results. Your first draft will not be perfect, but your final draft will sparkle.
- Share your writing and actively seek feedback. Whether it be from friends, loved ones, supervisors, or writing groups – the more opinions you gather on your work, the more your writing will improve.

Writing is such an important academic skill that there is no way for us to ignore it. We must embrace it and develop it until it is a skill we can rely on, or we will struggle with a substantial portion of our work as academic researchers. As mentioned at the start of this chapter, the general calibre of academic writing is not high. Even if our writing ability is poor by every reliable measure we can think of, if we follow the suggestions in this chapter and commit to improving, we can easily reach and surpass the quality of standard academic writing. We might even find ourselves enjoying writing, and if that happens, we are well on our way to becoming distinguished academic researchers. Next, we need to decide what we are going to write and what to do with it once it is written. Set a course for Chapter 4, where we will explore the murky depths of academic publishing.

Further reading

- Aitchison, C. & Guerin, C. (Eds.) (2014). *Writing Groups for Doctoral Education and Beyond: Innovations in Practice and Theory*. London, UK: Routledge.

An edited collection of perspectives on writing groups written by scholars who recognise the value that writing groups can bring to early career researchers.

- Boice, R. (1990). *Professors as Writers: A Self-help Guide to Productive Writing*. Stillwater, OK: New Forums Press.

This book highlights the importance of keeping a writing schedule and being honest with ourselves and others about our writing output. It is a key reference of many other academic writing books, including most of the books on this list.

- Murray, R. (2002). *How to Write a Thesis*. Berkshire, UK: McGraw-Hill Education.

Rowena Murray is one of the most trusted voices on this topic. If you are looking for a quaint but wonderfully impudent take on the process, see Umberto Eco's book of the same name.

- Silvia, P. J. (2007). *How to Write a Lot: A Practical Guide to Productive Academic Writing*. Washington, DC: American Psychological Association.

This book is succinct and takes no prisoners. It is often described by early career researchers as the book that has had the biggest impact on their writing.

- Sword, H. (2017). *Air & Light & Time & Space: How Successful Academics Write*. Cambridge, MA: Harvard University Press.

A thoughtful and considered examination of academic writing packed with perspectives from exemplary academic writers.

Resources

Further resources for this chapter can be found at: www.JosephRoche.ie/EssentialSkills

- List of Writing Resources
- Writing Tracking Spreadsheet Template
- Writing Group Format and Agenda Template

References

Aitchison, C. (2009). Writing groups for doctoral education. *Studies in Higher Education, 34*(8), 905–916.

Aitchison, C. & Guerin, C. (Eds.) (2014). *Writing Groups for Doctoral Education and Beyond: Innovations in Practice and Theory*. London, UK: Routledge.

Antoniou, M. & Moriarty, J. (2008). What can academic writers learn from creative writers? Developing guidance and support for lecturers in higher education. *Teaching in Higher Education, 13*(2), 157–167.

Aprile, K. T., Ellem, P., & Lole, L. (2020). Publish, perish, or pursue? Early career academics' perspectives on demands for research productivity in regional universities. *Higher Education Research & Development, 40*(4), 1–15.

Backes-Gellner, U. & Schlinghoff, A. (2010). Career incentives and 'publish or perish' in German and US universities. *European Education, 42*(3), 26–52.

Blaxter, L., Hughes, C., & Tight, M. (1998). Writing on academic careers. *Studies in Higher Education, 23*(3), 281–295.

Boice, R. (1990). *Professors as Writers: A Self-help Guide to Productive Writing*. Stillwater, OK: New Forums Press.

Bolker, J. (1998). *Writing Your Dissertation in Fifteen Minutes a Day: A Guide to Starting, Revising, and Finishing Your Doctoral Thesis*. New York, NY: Henry Holt and Company.

Cameron, J., Nairn, K., & Higgins, J. (2009). Demystifying academic writing: reflections on emotions, know-how and academic identity. *Journal of Geography in Higher Education, 33*(2), 269–284.

Cirillo, F. (2018). *The Pomodoro Technique: The Acclaimed Time Management System that Has Transformed How We Work*. New York, NY: Currency.

Craswell, G. & Poore, M. (2012). *Writing for Academic Success* (2nd edn). London, UK: SAGE.

Eco, U. (2015). *How to Write a Thesis*. Boston, MA: MIT Press.

Elbow, P. (1998). *Writing with Power: Techniques for Mastering the Writing Process* (2nd edn). Oxford, UK: Oxford University Press.

French, A. (2018a). Anxiety, confusion and the affective domain: why should subject lecturers acknowledge the social and emotional aspects of writing development processes? *Journal of Academic Writing, 8*(2), 202–211.

French, A. (2018b). 'Fail better': reconsidering the role of struggle and failure in academic writing development in higher education. *Innovations in Education and Teaching International, 55*(4), 408–416.

Gere, A. R. (1987). *Writing Groups: History, Theory and Implications*. Carbondale, IL: Southern Illinois University Press.

Grant, B. & Knowles, S. (2000). Flights of imagination: Academic women be(com)ing writers. *International Journal for Academic Development, 5*(1), 6–19.

Gray, T. (2005). *Publish & Flourish: Become a Prolific Scholar*. Las Cruces, NM: New Mexico State University.

Huerta, M., Goodson, P., Beigi, M., & Chlup, D. (2017). Graduate students as academic writers: writing anxiety, self-efficacy and emotional intelligence. *Higher Education Research & Development, 36*(4), 716–729.

Huff, A. S. (1999). *Writing for Scholarly Publication*. London, UK: SAGE.

Hyland, K. (2004). *Second Language Writing*. Cambridge, UK: Cambridge University Press.

Kellogg, R. T. (1999). *The Psychology of Writing*. New York, NY: Oxford University Press.

King, S. (2000). *On Writing: A Memoir of the Craft*. New York, NY: Scribner.

Kiriakos, C. M. & Tienari, J. (2018). Academic writing as love. *Management Learning, 49*(3), 263–277.

Lamott, A. (1994). *Bird by Bird: Some Instructions on Writing and Life*. New York, NY: Pantheon Books.

Lee, A. & Boud, D. (2003). Writing groups, change and academic identity: research development as local practice. *Studies in Higher Education, 28*(2), 187–200.

Li, L. Y. (2007). Exploring the use of focused freewriting in developing academic writing. *Journal of University Teaching & Learning Practice, 4*(1), 40–53.

Mattsson, J., Brandin, E. K., & Hult, A. K. (2020). Get a room! How writing groups aid the development of junior academics' writing practice and writer identity. *Journal of Academic Writing, 10*(1), 59–74.

Mewburn, I., Firth, K., & Lehmann, S. (2019). *How to Fix your Academic Writing Trouble: A Practical Guide*. London, UK: Open University Press.

Moore, S. (2003). Writers' retreats for academics: exploring and increasing the motivation to write. *Journal of Further and Higher Education, 27*(3), 333–342.

Murray, R. & Moore, S. (2006). *The Handbook of Academic Writing: A Fresh Approach.* Berkshire, UK: McGraw-Hill Education.

Murray, R. & Newton, M. (2009). Writing retreat as structured intervention: margin or mainstream? *Higher Education Research & Development, 28*(5), 541–553.

Paltridge, B. & Starfield, S. (2007). *Thesis and Dissertation Writing in a Second Language: A Handbook for Supervisors.* New York, NY: Routledge.

Pinker, S. (2014). *The Sense of Style: The Thinking Person's Guide to Writing in the 21st Century.* New York, NY: Penguin Books.

Saunders, W. M. (1989). Collaborative writing tasks and peer interaction. *International Journal of Educational Research, 13*(1), 101–112.

Silvia, P. J. (2007). *How to Write a Lot: A Practical Guide to Productive Academic Writing.* Washington, DC: American Psychological Association.

Smith, F. (1994). *Writing and the Writer* (2nd edn). Hillside, NJ: Lawrence Erlbaum Associates.

Sword, H. (2016). 'Write every day!': a mantra dismantled. *International Journal for Academic Development, 21*(4), 312–322.

Sword, H. (2017). *Air & Light & Time & Space: How Successful Academics Write.* Cambridge, MA: Harvard University Press.

Thomson, P. & Kamler, B. (2016). *Detox your Writing: Strategies for Doctoral Researchers.* New York, US: Routledge.

Topping, K. J., Smith, E. F., Swanson, I., & Elliot, A. (2000). Formative peer assessment of academic writing between postgraduate students. *Assessment & Evaluation in Higher Education, 25*(2), 149–169.

Truss, L. (2003). *Eats, Shoots & Leaves: The Zero Tolerance Approach to Punctuation.* London: Profile Books.

Watson, R. (2015). How to get published in an academic journal: top tips from editors. *The Guardian,* 3 January. Available at: www.theguardian.com/education/2015/jan/03/how-to-get-published-in-an-academic-journal-top-tips-from-editors (accessed 30 September 2021).

White, E. B. & Strunk, W. (1959). *The Elements of Style.* New York, NY: Macmillan.

Zinsser, W. (1976). *On Writing Well: The Classic Guide to Writing Nonfiction.* New York, NY: HarperCollins.

Four

Publishing

In this chapter, we will cover:

- the importance of published work
- the dark side of academic publishing
- navigating the publishing process
- basic article types and outlines
- strategies for dealing with submissions, revisions, and rejections.

Proclaiming our work

Publishing our academic writing can feel like a game we are expected to play. It *should* be an enjoyable game, and it can be, if we come to terms with there being no winners, the rules constantly changing, no one knowing how to play, and the people running the game trying to make us feel like they did not want us to play in the first place. Academic publishing is central to research and to our own development as researchers, yet it is rarely taught in universities. Our peers, supervisors, mentors, and anyone who could help us learn the rules of the game are likely wrestling with the publishing process themselves. In this chapter, we will explore that process and learn why navigating it is a skill we must develop. We will assess the problematic nature of academic publishing and see that to circumvent its many hazards we need to be resourceful and resilient.

The fundamental academic mantra

'Publish or perish' is the most common hyperbolic phrase used to scare early career researchers. The worst part is that it is not entirely wrong. To be clear, whether we live or die is not determined by our ability to convince sceptical academics that our work deserves to be included in their collected volumes of written ideas. A failure to publish will not kill us. It can, however, kill our chances of winning a grant application, landing an academic job, or securing a promotion.

There is an expectation that early career researchers will publish their work. New knowledge and discoveries warrant sharing. More cynically, researchers can feel pressure to publish because some universities receive funding based on the publication rates of their academic staff. Consequently, academic promotion can be very difficult without a good publication record (McGrail et al., 2006). Teaching and contributing to the academic community should be taken into consideration in job applications and discussions of tenure, but publishing in well-known journals provides academics with internationally recognised bargaining chips for career progression (Jepsen et al., 2014).

For better or worse, published works remain the principal measure of academic development, and when it comes to the publish or perish mantra, 'few aphorisms enjoy more familiarity within our academic community' (De Rond and Miller, 2005, p. 322).

The importance placed on this flawed principle in the life of an academic has many detractors but until a better system emerges, 'survival in academia depends on publications in refereed journals' (Frey, 2003, p. 205). Many feel that the pressure to publish decreases the value of the research itself, with researchers scrambling to get their work into journals as quickly as possible, without taking the time needed to develop and nurture their ideas (Rawat and Meena, 2014; Sarewitz, 2016). Even the overall value of publishing in perceived prestigious journals is debatable (Starbuck, 2005) and the need to showcase ground-breaking work in such journals could be a contributing factor to issues of reproducibility in research (as mentioned in Chapter 2), putting us on the path to a potential crisis (Baker, 2016) or even a revolution (Fanelli, 2018) in how research is conducted.

As we will see in Chapter 12, academic research can be a stressful endeavour, and using the dreaded publish or perish mantra to apply more pressure is not helpful to early career researchers. To prevent that phrase causing us undue anxiety, we should focus on developing our publishing skills early in our careers (Pinheiro et al., 2014; Horta and Santos, 2016).

Researcher views

Genevieve, on the need to publish papers during a PhD:

> If I could repeat the whole thing, I would think about the work in terms of what papers it's going to produce, not in terms of how it's going to look in a thesis. I think it's a different mindset and if you think about that from the start, then the actual work that you do is different. I wish I had been more strategic [...] really thinking carefully about what I was spending my energy on.

Bigger than the music industry

Before wading into the publishing process, it is worth considering the state of the academic publishing industry and the obscene amounts of money it generates. Global revenue for academic publishing is estimated to be in excess of €20 billion, which makes it similar in scale to the music industry, but far more profitable (Buranyi, 2017). That should give us pause for thought. Almost everyone can relate to music, as that industry is virtually inescapable, but what causes a relatively niche industry like academic publishing to grow to a similar size? The answer is an illogical but lucrative business model.

Papers published in academic journals rely on 'peer review' – a formal process through which researchers evaluate each other's work, ensure the 'correctness of procedures', and 'establish the plausibility of results' (Chubin and Hackett, 1990, p. 2). A standard publisher pays writers and editors to create content as well as paying marketing, printing, and distribution costs. In academic publishing, however, the researcher produces the content free of charge, often indirectly paid for by the taxpayer through the form of research grants, and willingly provides it to the journal. The academic journal then requests senior academics to review the content pro bono, which they do out of an obligation to ensure the robustness of the peer-review system. The reviewers can recommend that the journal rejects the paper, or they can request that the authors make changes to it. This slow process can be especially challenging for early career researchers under pressure to publish as quickly as possible (Powell, 2016). The journal then publishes the final product (one of the few parts of the process where it can incur actual costs) and sells it back to their main audience who created it for them in the first place: universities and researchers (Van Noorden, 2013). This uniquely advantageous business model ensures the largest academic publishing companies can have higher profit margins than the likes of Apple, Google, or Amazon (Buranyi, 2017).

The problematic nature of academic publishing is not surprising given its seeds were sown in the middle of the twentieth century by the eventual media mogul and fraudster Robert Maxwell (Clarke, 1993). Since then, it has grown to be an indecently profitable industry, with dividends that are difficult to accurately ascertain. The fees that journals charge to access their articles have risen faster than inflation but 'the prices that campus libraries actually pay to buy journals are generally hidden by the nondisclosure agreements that they sign', meaning that 'the true costs that publishers incur to produce their journals are not widely known' (Van Noorden, 2013, p. 427). This system has long been criticised, with the economist and academic Brun Frey describing it as 'intellectual prostitution' with researchers having to choose between 'slavishly following the demands made by anonymous referees who have no property rights to the journals they advise' or withdrawing their paper, in which case 'the author has the gratification of keeping his intellectual purity, but time has been lost and the chance of a university career vanishes' (Frey, 2003, pp. 205–207).

Researcher views

Celeste, on trying to publish a paper in journals with high open access charges:

> There are some journals that I would read, and I think the paper would be a good fit for, but the price is just so expensive that we can't justify it, because the lab doesn't have that much money set aside for publishing.

Some journals offer free access to their papers by charging the authors a once-off 'open access' fee (Swan and Brown, 2004; Björk, 2017). The benefits of having their work more widely read and not hidden behind paywalls are obvious, but the exorbitant costs can make the process even more challenging for researchers (Larivière and Sugimoto, 2018). Inevitably, the lure of juicy profit margins in an industry already struggling with transparency, caught the attention of predatory publishers. These sham journals offer suspiciously fast publication routes, creating scams 'to dupe researchers, especially those inexperienced in scholarly communication' (Beall, 2012, p. 179). Predatory journals demand a much lower fee for open access publishing, while masquerading as adhering to the accepted standards of the peer-review process. In reality, 'the goal of predatory open-access publishers is to exploit this model by charging the fee without providing all the expected publishing services' (Butler, 2013, p. 433). Worryingly, not all researchers who participate in these scams are unwitting victims. Some succumb to the pressure of needing to publish and willingly submit their work to bogus journals (Kolata, 2017; Kurt, 2018).

Researcher views

Hannah, on predatory publishers:

> You can spot them. They sound like scams. Although the first one did make me think. I had my first paper published the day before and I got this email and it was all *Dear [Hannah], we would be honoured if you would submit your paper to our prestigious journal ... Blah blah blah ...* I was so confused I thought I was supposed to do another paper. But then a few people told me that as soon as you get something published you get all these dodgy emails trying to get you to pay to have a paper published.

In keeping with an industry that was, at least initially, shaped by Robert Maxwell, the attempts to fix it are frequently tainted by scandal. The librarian Jeffrey Beall maintained an infamous blacklist of predatory publishers to help researchers identify thousands of open-access journals that he felt exploited or deceived authors by charging publishing fees without maintaining the expected standards of peer review and editing services. The appropriateness of maintaining such a list was argued from both sides (Beall, 2015; Berger and Cirasella, 2015; Buschman, 2020) but it inspired renewed efforts to combat predatory publishing (Grudniewicz et al., 2019; Kakamad et al., 2020). After some powerful publishers found themselves on the list, the legal ramifications for Beall (and his employers) resulted in his list being unceremoniously removed (Silver, 2017).

Financially ruinous legal battles are the chief weapons of powerful academic publishers. One of the early advocates for online open access, the programmer and activist Aaron Swartz (who worked on the development of creative commons licences and the social news site *Reddit*), was facing the prospect of bankruptcy and prison for downloading large numbers of academic papers with the intent to share them publicly, when he took his own life at 26 years of age (Swartz, 2008; Sims, 2011; Poulsen, 2013). The current 'Robin Hood' of academic publishing is the computer programmer Alexandra Elbakyan, who maintains a website that allows people to circumvent publishers' paywalls and gives free access to millions of research publications. For her efforts, she 'risks having to pay many millions of dollars in damages, and potentially spending time in jail' while also being named by *Nature* as one of the most important people in science due to her efforts to make research more accessible (Van Noorden, 2016, p. 513). It can be a frustratingly complicated and troublesome industry for early career researchers, and we need to have the protection of a master plan before charging into the academic publishing melee.

A plan for navigating the publishing process

Despite the vexing state of the industry itself, academic publishing can be an enjoyable process, especially if we treat it like a strategic game that requires us to consider our moves in advance. To play the game and survive unscathed, we need a plan to guide us. A publication plan helps us 'to think strategically about the kinds of writing that are necessary to build a career and become known in one or more chosen fields', as well as being 'a timetable for writing based on a realistic appraisal of what is possible' (Thomson and Kamler, 2012, p. 164).

Having a publication plan ensures our work reaches appropriate audiences and reserves our most important and impactful papers for the highest quality journals. It also provides us with a clear strategy for dealing with revisions and rejections. When we establish ourselves as published researchers, we will begin to receive invitations to co-author papers, join research collaborations, and contribute to book chapters. We cannot accept every academic invitation that lands in our inboxes, so a publication plan helps us decide which opportunities best align with our publishing goals.

The publication plan should be a living document that we consult and update regularly and use to inform our decisions when publishing becomes perplexing. It can be a spreadsheet, or a simple table in a document, but it needs to have a range of information for each planned publication including working titles, topics, type of publications, key messages, intended audiences (including relevant conferences), word limits, targeted journals (ranked by prestige), links to other work, current status, and an all-important timeline. A template to use as a starting point is available on this book's companion website.

Along with the timeline, the other vital element of the publication plan is the list of journals to target for each paper, in order of preference. There is a dizzying array of academic journals to choose from, so determining an appropriate list requires some deliberation (Silvia, 2015). When you find a journal you think could be suitable, consider if the key message of your paper fits the aims and scope of that journal. If the journal's target audience and options for open access match how you want your work to be shared, then the journal is worth considering. Before selecting the journal for inclusion in your publication plan, and to avoid predatory publishers, try to answer the following three questions:

1. Have you already come across the journal in your research?
2. Do your colleagues or supervisor recommend the journal?
3. Does the journal have a website with recent publications and easy-to-find contact details for its editors?

If you are still unsure about the credibility of the journal you can check if it is part of the Committee on Publication Ethics (www.publicationethics.org), if it is indexed in a well-known journal database like Scopus (www.scopus.com), if it is on an open access group list (www.oaspa.org, www.doaj.org), or if it can be found using a journal ranking tool like Scimago (www.scimagojr.com). Once you are convinced that the journal is reputable, then you can set about considering the layout and format of your paper.

Basic paper layout

Given that our published words represent our most valuable professional assets, we need to account for every scrap of writing we produce. Editing skills, described in Chapter 3, will be our primary tools for taking the raw materials of any unpublished writing we have generated and fashioning them into something we can fit into our publication plan. This strategy should *only* be used for work that has not yet been published – reusing material we have already published would constitute self-plagiarism and would undermine our credibility and integrity as researchers (Bretag and Mahmud, 2009; Karabag and Berggren, 2012).

Appraise everything you have written that is eligible for repurposing – starting with the written account of your progress described in Chapter 2. Maybe a summary you wrote while doing background reading on a topic could form the basis of a short review, maybe a list of queries you have about a well-known experiment could be extended into a critique, or maybe your research notes could become a study protocol. If you completed any coursework that required the submission of assignments, once those assignments have been graded and the final marks returned, you can also develop those assignments into publishable work (Hayter, 2021).

The main type of publication is the journal article. While there are other types of publications such as conference proceedings papers (publications that arise from conference presentations), book chapters, professional reports, or other forms of non-academic publications, the peer-reviewed journal article is the most valuable. It is generally considered to be more prestigious than conference papers, which in turn are considered more important than conference posters and any non peer-reviewed output. Book chapters can be a special case in some disciplines, especially in the humanities, where a chapter in a well-known volume could be held in high esteem, but in most cases a peer-reviewed article in a good journal is the chief publication because it should be held to the most rigorous standards. Journal articles are more difficult to get published, and this makes them more valuable.

A basic research paper usually has an introduction, a methods section, findings, a discussion, and conclusions. Depending on your field, and the type of paper you are writing, there may be other common sections. The sections highlighted below are presented in more depth in the basic paper outline template available on this book's companion website:

- *Title and abstract.* Before you start drafting your paper, choose the simplest title that sums up what you want the paper to be about. Once you have a complete draft, you can choose a more interesting or informative title. The abstract should be left until the end. While it is usually only a 100–300 word overview, the abstract is worth careful consideration as it will be the most read part of your paper.
- *Introduction and background.* The introduction should include a short history of the topic that begins with an accessible outline of the research area before detailing the specifics of the topic in question.
- *Literature review.* You have a responsibility to your readers to ensure that you present an overview of the topic by identifying, critiquing, and connecting the most important papers in the field.
- *Purpose of paper (research questions).* This should be short and succinct, and should be clear in your mind before you start working on the paper outline.
- *Method.* This section should be as easy-to-follow as possible so that whenever your work is published, other researchers in the field can emulate what you have done. As was discussed in Chapter 2, you may choose to use your research philosophy to explain the theoretical framework underpinning your methodological decisions, your choice of research methods, or any inherent limitations.
- *Analysis and findings.* If you have a large number of tables, graphs, or figures to choose from, include only the ones needed to provide a representative overview of what has been discovered.
- *Discussion.* The discussion section is where you interpret the findings presented in the previous section and describe them in relation to the overall context you provided at the start of the paper. If you included research questions in the introductory sections of your paper, then the discussion section is where you attempt to answer them.
- *Conclusion.* The last few paragraphs should succinctly sum up what the paper has contributed to the field as well as suggestions for future work in the area.

All kinds of articles

The empirical research article – a paper sharing the methods and results of an experiment or study – is the most common type of peer-reviewed journal article. Such publications are essential, but for early career researchers it can be a daunting and time-consuming endeavour to exclusively publish original research. If the data collection or analysis steps are onerous, then reaching the publication stage can feel like a faraway goal, making it more sensible to have a publication plan that is not solely based on empirical research articles. Widening our perspectives when it comes to article types can make us better writers and, crucially, lead to faster publications. It also helps avoid the temptation of 'salami-slicing' – sneakily cutting up parts of our studies to submit them in different papers rather than providing the complete results in a single paper (Tolsgaard et al., 2019).

It is normal to build on our previous work, but we must be clear in each paper (and in our correspondence with journal editors) when the work we are presenting is just one aspect of a wider study that is being undertaken. A more noble reason for splitting our work between publications is if a paper is becoming too long. A short paper in a good journal is better than a long paper in a bad journal. There are occasions when a long article (more than 12,000 words) might be needed to definitively describe a topic but, in general, short articles (less than 6,000 words) are better for everyone and are more likely to be read.

If journals offer to publish a range of different article types it is because they value them, and while they might be inundated with original empirical research articles, some of the other article types could be underrepresented. For early career researchers finding their feet with publishing, targeting some of the other article types listed below could present faster routes to having more work published:

- *Systematic literature review.* Without needing any original data, a comprehensive review of a topic can be presented, as described in Chapter 2.
- *Case study.* This can be a short paper providing an overview of a specific event, experimental method, or situation that will be of interest to the journal's audience as a useful or instructive example.
- *Evaluation, tool, methods, protocol, or framework.* Some journals publish short and detailed descriptions of a specific topic or resource that might be of practical interest to other researchers.
- *Commentary, perspective, or position paper.* These kinds of articles are generally informed viewpoints on a specific area, such as something of national or international interest like a policy recommendation or a position on advocacy. Some journals request a comprehensive position that draws extensively on existing work. Other journals might recognise researchers' professional experience and accept something more akin to an opinion piece.
- *Letter or critique.* If we have a minor but valuable point to make, then this format could save us from needlessly stretching it into something longer. Some journals accept letters from researchers sharing early announcements from a key study before writing up the results in a longer-form paper. Other journals encourage researchers to use letters to tackle controversial topics.
- *Book review.* If we are enamoured with a recently published book that is benefiting our work, we could consider writing a review so that other researchers might avail of it too.

- *Conference review.* Committing to reviewing a conference can motivate us to explore the history and context of the conference, aid us in our efforts to connect with other delegates, and give us the confidence to immerse ourselves in the conference (described further in Chapter 10).

The submission process

Armed with a paper draft and a plan for targeting a selection of journals, we can begin the submission process in earnest by carefully inspecting the submission guidelines for the first journal on our list and adhering to them rigidly. No matter what the guidelines request – word limits, expected structure, referencing conventions, accepted language style, figure and table formats – if we follow the guidelines, we ensure the editors and reviewers can only critique the content of our paper and not the technicalities of the submission. If our paper is not considered for publication by the first journal we target, we must adapt it to match the formatting guidelines of our second preference journal, and so on, as we make our way down our list.

The cover letter to the journal editor is often neglected as a mere formality of the submission process, but its importance should not be underestimated. It need only be a single page and, as with any important piece of writing, it should be proofread by some of our trusted friends or colleagues before being sent. There are four features of a good cover letter:

1. The letter should address the journal editor with a greeting and a polite but clear statement of how we wish our paper to be considered for publication in their journal. We should double-check the spelling of their name and ensure their titles are correct.
2. Next comes the decisive middle paragraph: our motivation for choosing this specific journal and a convincing case as to how our paper aligns with the scope of the journal, builds on or references previous publications in the journal, and why readers of the journal will find our paper interesting.
3. We can then recommend several potential referees. This can be uncomfortable for early career researchers new to the field, but it is important to help the editorial team to understand what kind of researcher we feel would be appropriate to review our work, even if the editors ultimately decide to choose different reviewers (Grimm, 2005).
4. The letter should end with a short statement of integrity, declaring any conflicts of interest and confirming that the paper is original and is not currently under consideration in any other journals. Finally, we can thank the editor for considering the paper and provide them with appropriate contact details.

A template cover letter is available on this book's companion website.

A noble quest for revisions and rejections

Once we submit our article there is no way of knowing how long it will take before we receive a response. The general rule is that it will take between one and three months, and if we have not heard anything after four months, we can politely contact the journal requesting an update (Kitchin and Fuller, 2005). It is a slow process, but once we have accepted that the academic publishing game is inherently flawed, and have decided to play along anyway, then we cannot be frustrated with the editors and journal staff for doing their job. Finding the right reviewers and inviting them to provide reviews within a reasonable timeframe can be a complicated process, while the reviewers themselves are usually volunteering their time out of a sense of professional obligation. Most journals have online platforms where we can check the status of our paper whenever we start to fret that it may have been lost or forgotten. Once our paper is under review, it is the ideal time to start working on the next paper. As we get more efficient, we should have several papers at different stages of the review process at all times.

If the decision we finally receive is that we should resubmit the paper after addressing minor or major revisions recommended by the reviewers, that is an outcome worth celebrating. Even if the reviewers have requested a large number of revisions, the fact that the paper has not been rejected outright means the journal is open to publishing it in some form. Given how much effort has been invested in our paper at that stage, we owe it to ourselves, and to any co-authors, to complete the revision process and resubmit the paper in a timely manner – that paper is far closer to being published than any of our unsubmitted works.

We should not consider any of the requested revisions as a personal assessment of our abilities. It is likely that the peer review process was blind, and it should give us pride that the reviewers took such an interest in our work that they felt it could be further improved. When we work on the revised version of the paper, every single suggested revision should be addressed (Bourne, 2005). We can do this by creating a table with all the requested revisions itemised beside methodical descriptions of how each revision has been addressed in the revised version of the paper. When submitting the revised version of the paper, the table of revisions can be included in our letter to the editor – which is even more important than the cover letter with the original submission. If we can convincingly address every issue that has been highlighted by the reviewers, there is a good chance our paper will be published (Murray, 2005). If it is impossible to carry out a requested change then we can contact the editor and put forward a case for not carrying out that revision or seek alternative options for addressing it. Only if a compromise cannot be reached should we consider the final resort of not submitting a revised version of the paper and beginning the submission process again with a different journal.

If the decision from the journal is that our paper should not be published it can be disheartening, but it should not be unexpected. Rejections are normal for researchers (Bourne, 2005). Although it always stings, if the goal is to become a well published researcher, rejected papers need to be accepted as an inevitable part of the process. When we receive a rejection from a journal, we should quietly put it to one side for an hour, a day, a week, or – depending on our level of self-esteem at that time – however long it takes before we can look objectively at the feedback (Hartley, 2008). We should then consider what we can learn from the journal's decision and decide if we will submit our paper to the next journal on our list with some minor tweaks and format updates, or if the feedback has convinced us to carry out more substantial improvements (Donovan, 2007).

Usually, we submit our papers to the more prestigious journals first and work our way down the list in our publication plan. However, we may find that after taking feedback on board from a journal rejection, the subsequent version of our paper is more impressive than we had originally expected. In that case, it may be appropriate to submit the paper to a journal of even higher standing. The publishing game can be gruelling and there is nothing shameful or petty about taking satisfaction from seeing a paper published in a journal that is more prestigious than the journal that originally passed on it.

Researcher views

Arthur, on starting an academic post with no publications, before going on to publish prolifically:

> I was still at a point where I had no papers published. And I had gone to the stage with a couple of rejections that I thought that I would actually never get a paper published [...] And then I got one over the line. And from there, then you kind of start to see. It's like a monkey off your back. You kind of see how it's done. You see the process involved. You see how you need to respond to reviewers' comments. You get more confidence. You can see that there is a process and it does require patience.

Summary

- Steel yourself for the struggle of academic publishing. It is a serious business with real-world career repercussions, but sometimes treating it like a game is the best way to win.
- Develop a publication plan. This will provide a clear overview of what you are working on, where it will be published, and how it aligns with your goals as a researcher.
- Be strategic with your publications. Determine the best options for publishing your work and consider the full range of article types open to you.
- Navigate the stages of paper preparation, submission, revision, and resubmission with diligence and boundless optimism.
- Accept rejections as part of the publishing process. Even if something you have written did not find a home where you originally intended, you are still one step closer to it being published somewhere.

Running the gauntlet of academic publishing can be as demanding as it is maddening, but it is not without its rewards. There are few better ways to build confidence in our academic abilities than seeing our words published in a reputable journal. It is also a fitting tribute, considering the hours of effort invested in both carrying out the research and then writing about it. As well as providing personal validation, publishing papers also lends academic credibility to all of our professional duties, and is critical for career progression (Chapter 11). Another indispensable academic skill that will benefit from our prowess in academic writing and publishing is the ability to secure funding for our research. Don your robes, clutch your lantern, and descend into the dark arts of grantsmanship in Chapter 5.

Further reading

- Hartley, J. (2008). *Academic Writing and Publishing: A Practical Handbook*. New York, NY: Routledge.

This book gives astute attention to some of the overlooked details of academic publishing with whole chapters on choosing titles, selecting keywords, listing authors, and writing acknowledgements.

- Kitchin, R. & Fuller, D. (2005). *The Academic's Guide to Publishing*. London, UK: SAGE.

The many ways in which our research can be published and shared are covered in detail in this book.

- Murray, R. (2009). *Writing for Academic Journals*. Berkshire, UK: McGraw-Hill Education.

This book provides practical and detailed advice on how we should go about the process of submitting our papers to academic journals.

- Silvia, P. J. (2015). *Write It Up: Practical Strategies for Writing and Publishing Journal Articles*. Washington, DC: American Psychological Association.

From an author who cropped up regularly in relation to academic writing in Chapter 3, this book dispenses similarly pragmatic and concise advice, this time on the publishing process.

- Thomson, P. & Kamler, B. (2012). *Writing for Peer Reviewed Journals: Strategies for Getting Published.* New York, NY: Routledge.

Covering both the theoretical and practical aspects, this book takes a long-term and sustainable view of academic publishing.

Resources

Further resources for this chapter can be found at: www.JosephRoche.ie/EssentialSkills

- Publication Plan Template
- Basic Paper Outline Template
- Cover Letter to Journal Editor Template

References

Baker, M. (2016). Is there a reproducibility crisis? *Nature, 533*(7604), 452–455.

Beall, J. (2012). Predatory publishers are corrupting open access. *Nature, 489*(7415), 179.

Beall, J. (2015). Response to 'Beyond Beall's List'. *College & Research Libraries News, 76*(6), 340–341.

Berger, M. & Cirasella, J. (2015). Beyond Beall's list: better understanding predatory publishers. *College & Research Libraries News, 76*(3), 132–135.

Björk, B. C. (2017). Gold, green, and black open access. *Learned Publishing, 30*(2), 173–175.

Bourne, P. E. (2005). Ten simple rules for getting published. *PLoS Computational Biology, 1*(5), e57, 341–342.

Bretag, T. & Mahmud, S. (2009). Self-plagiarism or appropriate textual re-use? *Journal of Academic Ethics, 7*(3), 193–205.

Buranyi, S. (2017). Is the staggeringly profitable business of scientific publishing bad for science? *The Guardian*, 27 June. Available at: www.theguardian.com/science/2017/jun/27/profitable-business-scientific-publishing-bad-for-science (accessed 30 September 2021).

Buschman, J. (2020). A political sociology of the Beall's list affair. *The Library Quarterly, 90*(3), 298–313.

Butler, D. (2013). The dark side of publishing. *Nature, 495*(7442), 433–435.

Chubin, D. E. & Hackett, E. J. (1990). *Peerless Science: Peer Review and US Science Policy.* Albany, NY: SUNY Press.

Clarke, T. (1993). Case study: Robert Maxwell: master of corporate malfeasance. *Corporate Governance: An International Review, 1*(3), 141–151.

De Rond, M. & Miller, A. N. (2005). Publish or perish: bane or boon of academic life? *Journal of Management Inquiry*, *14*(4), 321–329.

Donovan, S. K. (2007). The importance of resubmitting rejected papers. *Journal of Scholarly Publishing*, *38*(3), 151–155.

Fanelli, D. (2018). Opinion: Is science really facing a reproducibility crisis, and do we need it to? *Proceedings of the National Academy of Sciences*, *115*(11), 2628–2631.

Frey, B. S. (2003). Publishing as prostitution? Choosing between one's own ideas and academic success. *Public Choice*, *116*(1–2), 205–223.

Grimm, D. (2005). Suggesting or excluding reviewers can help get your paper published. *Science*, *309*(5743), 1974.

Grudniewicz, A., Moher, D., Cobey, K. D., Bryson, G. L., Cukier, S., Allen, K., ... & Lalu, M. M. (2019). Predatory journals: no definition, no defence. *Nature*, *576*(7786), 210–212.

Hartley, J. (2008). *Academic Writing and Publishing: A Practical Handbook*. New York, NY: Routledge.

Hayter, M. (2021). Writing for publication: turning assignments into publishable works. In K. Holland & R. Watson (Eds.), *Writing for Publication in Nursing and Healthcare: Getting it Right* (pp. 122–143). New York, NY: John Wiley & Sons Ltd.

Horta, H. & Santos, J. M. (2016). The impact of publishing during PhD studies on career research publication, visibility, and collaborations. *Research in Higher Education*, *57*(1), 28–50.

Jepsen, D. M., Sun, J. J. M., Budhwar, P. S., Klehe, U. C., Krausert, A., Raghuram, S., & Valcour, M. (2014). International academic careers: personal reflections. *The International Journal of Human Resource Management*, *25*(10), 1309–1326.

Kakamad, F. H., Mohammed, S. H., Najar, K. A., Qadr, G. A., Ahmed, J. O., Mohammed, K. K., ... & Hassan, H. A. (2020). Kscien's list: a new strategy to discourage predatory journals and publishers. *International Journal of Surgery Open*, *23*(1), 54–56.

Karabag, S. F. & Berggren, C. (2012). Retraction, dishonesty and plagiarism: Analysis of a crucial issue for academic publishing, and the inadequate responses from leading journals in economics and management disciplines. *Journal of Applied Economics and Business Research*, *2*(3), 172–183.

Kitchin, R. & Fuller, D. (2005). *The Academic's Guide to Publishing*. London, UK: SAGE.

Kolata, G. (2017). Many academics are eager to publish in worthless journals. *New York Times*, 30 October. Available at: www.nytimes.com/2017/10/30/science/predatory-journals-academics.html

Kurt, S. (2018). Why do authors publish in predatory journals? *Learned Publishing*, *31*(2), 141–147.

Larivière, V. & Sugimoto, C. R. (2018). Do authors comply with mandates for open access? *Nature*, *562*(7728), 483–486.

McGrail, M. R., Rickard, C. M., & Jones, R. (2006). Publish or perish: a systematic review of interventions to increase academic publication rates. *Higher Education Research & Development*, *25*(1), 19–35.

Murray, R. (2005). *Writing for Academic Journals*. Berkshire, UK: McGraw-Hill Education.

Pinheiro, D., Melkers, J., & Youtie, J. (2014). Learning to play the game: Student publishing as an indicator of future scholarly success. *Technological Forecasting and Social Change, 81*(1), 56–66.

Poulsen, K. (2013). Aaron Swartz, coder and activist, dead at 26. *Wired*, 1 December. Available at: www.wired.com/2013/01/aaron-swartz/ (accessed 30 September 2021).

Powell, K. (2016). Does it take too long to publish research? *Nature News, 530*(7589), 148–151.

Rawat, S. & Meena, S. (2014). Publish or perish: where are we heading?. *Journal of Research in Medical Sciences: The Official Journal of Isfahan University of Medical Sciences, 19*(2), 87.

Sarewitz, D. (2016). The pressure to publish pushes down quality. *Nature News, 533*(7602), 147.

Silver, A. (2017). Controversial website that lists 'predatory' publishers shuts down. *Nature*. doi:10.1038/nature.2017.21328

Silvia, P. J. (2015). *Write It Up: Practical Strategies for Writing and Publishing Journal Articles*. Washington, DC: American Psychological Association.

Sims, N. (2011). Library licensing and criminal law: The Aaron Swartz case. *College & Research Libraries News, 72*(9), 534–537.

Starbuck, W. H. (2005). How much better are the most-prestigious journals? The statistics of academic publication. *Organization Science, 16*(2), 180–200.

Swan, A. & Brown, S. (2004). Authors and open access publishing. *Learned Publishing, 17*(3), 219–224.

Swartz, A. (2008). *Guerilla Open Access Manifesto*. Available at: https://archive.org/stream/GuerillaOpenAccessManifesto/Goamjuly2008_djvu.txt (accessed 30 September 2021).

Thomson, P. & Kamler, B. (2012). *Writing for Peer Reviewed Journals: Strategies for Getting Published*. New York, NY: Routledge.

Tolsgaard, M. G., Ellaway, R., Woods, N., & Norman, G. (2019). Salami-slicing and plagiarism: how should we respond? *Advances in Health Sciences Education, 24*(1), 3–14.

Van Noorden, R. (2013). The true cost of science publishing. *Nature, 495*(7442), 426–429.

Van Noorden, R. (2016). Paper Pirate. Ten people who mattered this year. *Nature, 540*(7634), 512–513.

Five
Funding

In this chapter, we will cover:

- the importance of securing research funding
- finding a mentor to develop grant-writing skills
- best practice for designing a grant application
- developing a funding plan
- learning from experience and coping with rejections.

'Grantsmanship'

The skill required to win funding for our research is sometimes referred to as 'grantsmanship' (Kraicer, 1997, p. 1). This makes it sound like an artisanal craft and, in many ways, it is, although it can sometimes feel more like a dark art that will only reveal its inner workings to us in exchange for our souls. Grantsmanship also sounds like a 'throwback term, harkening to an earlier era', and Ellen Gorsevski, a professor of rhetoric, points out that 'grantswomanship' should be just as pervasive (Gorsevski, 2016, p. 46). The difficulty in naming the skill is only the tip of the iceberg when it comes to winning research funding. As with many indispensable academic skills, it is rarely taught to early career researchers – arguably those who need it most (Kleinfelder et al., 2003; Koppelman and Holloway, 2012; Cunningham, 2020).

Securing funding provides us with the freedom to lead our own research projects (Gitlin et al., 2020), and is vital to our academic reputations. When we are successful with grant applications, it not only demonstrates that we are competent researchers, but that our ideas are fundable. For many universities and research institutions, this can be an essential requirement for recruitment and promotions (Berry, 2010; Hilton and Leukefeld, 2019). In this chapter, we will sharpen our skills as grant-writers, with strategies for improving our chances of winning research funding.

Mo' money mo' problems

As their careers progress, researchers are expected to seek funding to develop and implement their own projects, even at universities where funds are also raised through student fees, government support, sponsorship, or endowments. The resources and prestige that come with research funding are paramount to academic career progression (Berry, 2010; Locke et al., 2013). Such funding is often sought from specific research funding agencies and awarded through competitive evaluation processes (Auranen and Nieminen, 2010).

Researcher views

Anne, on how research funding can impact the work a researcher can do:

> We needed very specific equipment. And with very little funding, it was really difficult. An experiment that people would have done in five minutes, we spent sometimes two days or even more just doing this particular experiment. And then I went to a different lab, in Germany, where they had all the funding and all the equipment and I could really just experience the difference.

Research funding was initially administered through peer-review processes similar to those that govern academic publishing (described in Chapter 4). In time, these processes evolved to become far more complex: 'From those humble beginnings, the "peer review of proposals" became a hydra-headed juggernaut [...] totally unstoppable even by the thoughtful protests of many senior science policy savants' (Roy, 1985, p. 74). It has long had its critics (Cole et al., 1981; Porter, 2005; Fang and Casadevall, 2016), but as funding soared, the influence of the review process also grew. It not only affects research itself (Himanen et al., 2009; Bloch et al., 2014; Laudel and Gläser, 2014), but the formation of subsequent research policy (Braun, 1998; Smith, 2010), and our understanding of how funding mechanisms impact the overall production of knowledge remains 'fragmented at best' (Laudel, 2006, p. 490).

It is not unusual for large-scale research funding programmes to have success rates as low as 25%, dropping to less than 10% for the most over-subscribed research areas (Bourne and Chalupa, 2006; Sohn, 2020). This propagates fiercely competitive circumstances for early career researchers: 'Shrinking university budgets cause researchers to rely increasingly on this external funding of research projects, placing them in a resource environment that is characterised by scarcity, competition, and continuous evaluation' (Laudel, 2006, p. 489). Demonstrating a successful track record in securing research funding is often a prerequisite for recruitment, tenure, or promotion applications (Wooley, 2004; Griffith et al., 2006). Through this fierce competition however, new and valuable professional skills are gained. The most obvious benefit is in improving how we communicate our research, but invaluable experience can also be found in learning how to prepare budgets, estimating the cost of every part of the research project, designing appropriate work packages, tasks, milestones, and deliverables for the project, and fitting it all into a realistic timeline (Coley and Scheinberg, 2016).

When targeting our first funding opportunities, no grant is too small. Whether it is a €5 million project or a €500 project, we use the same set of skills. Even if the sums of money are modest to begin with, the ability to win funding of any kind, coupled with our growing experience of successfully administering such grants, demonstrates our potential. With every small research grant we win, we become better equipped to target larger funding opportunities.

Always two there are ... a master and an apprentice

We do not need to learn the skill of grant-writing alone. We can read about grant-writing, we can attend workshops, and we can make slow progress by ourselves, but a more efficient alternative is to learn from someone with experience. Keeping our 'artisanal craft' metaphor, the time-honoured tradition of composing grant applications is best preserved when it is passed down from elder maven to novice apprentice. Successful grant-writers often cite finding a mentor as one of the most crucial parts of the process (Boyer and Cockriel, 2001; Liu et al., 2016).

If we accept that the fastest way to become a proficient grant-writer is through the hands-on experience of helping a master grant-writer fashion a proposal, we are faced with two critical steps: first, finding, and second, convincing an expert grant-writer to be our mentor. If identifying suitable mentors is proving challenging, research development officers and financial administrators can be the most knowledgeable people in our institutions from whom to seek advice (Chapter 9). Institutional websites can also be used to compare staff profiles and find the academics who routinely secure funding, coordinate multiple research projects, and have a large network of collaborators.

Researcher views

Nora, on choosing supervisors and collaborators based on their track record at securing research funding:

> It's better to work in a research group that has money. You can tell the ones that are successful because they have loads of people working for them. That's where you want to be – there will always be people winning research grants and you never have to worry.

Once we have a shortlist of potential grant-writing mentors, asking them to share their secrets to consistently winning grants may not be the most fruitful course of action. They may struggle to explain their process and may not even know which specific aspects are contributing to their success. The best way to learn is to work together through the various stages of the grant-writing process – identifying funding opportunities, designing proposals, preparing content, managing submissions, and dealing with the eventual outcomes. Most importantly, working with successful grant-writers allows us to learn their most indispensable strategy – how they cope with unsuccessful applications. We can ask a mentor to help us with our own funding application, or offer to assist them with their next big proposal. A template email to use as a starting point in contacting a potential mentor is available on this book's companion website.

Adapt to the funding call

Writing the application itself is only one component of grant-writing. Identifying funding opportunities, gathering information about them, and seeking feedback after the application has been evaluated are just as fundamental. Most funding opportunities come with guidelines, requirements, or templates to follow. We ignore them at our peril. Writing a grant application without adhering to what the funders are looking for is the all-time classic blunder made by novice grant-writers. We should design grant applications by starting with the text of the funding call and adapting our ideas accordingly, not the other way around. We can still be true to our vision while shaping our application to meet the funder's wishes, but if we ignore the guidelines and submit something that does not fit the call, our application may not even be considered (Bordage and Dawson, 2003).

Adapting to the funding call is not always easy. When we find a funding call that seems suitable for one of our favourite research ideas it can be tempting to immediately begin writing a proposal for our dream project, hoping (irrationally) it will be what the funders are seeking. It may come as an unpleasant surprise when our application is rejected for not demonstrating sufficient alignment with the scope of the call. A more reliable approach is to gather as much information about the funding call as we can and scrutinise the funder's expectations. If the funding call text is ambiguous, it may require some reading between the lines (and possibly contacting the funders – discussed below) but, with the guidance of our mentor, we should be able to determine the kind of project the funding agency wishes to support (Clarke and Fox, 2007).

From that starting point, we can slowly draft an outline of what a 'perfect proposal' for that funding call should look like. Next, we start bringing our specific research goals and ideas into the proposal, using our (or our mentor's) research objectives and ideas to add originality, novelty, and innovation to what is already a proposal that fits everything the funders are looking for. When we first see the outline of our 'perfect proposal', we might worry our work is not suitable for that funding call after all. This is the point when we should remind ourselves that the most successful grant-writers are the ones who always find a way to adapt their work to fit the call.

Researcher views

Séamus, on making sure to write grant applications that adhere to the funding call:

> Understand the mindset and the motivations of the people that hold the purse strings. Think of it like asking contractors to quote you for a kitchen renovation. If someone quotes for a bathroom, even if it is the world's most perfect bathroom, they are not getting the job as that is not what you asked for.

A well-written grant application is clear, concise, and captures the attention of the reader (Boyack et al., 2018). The tone should be persuasive and confident, even if it is our first foray into grant-writing. We need to convince the reader that our idea is perfect for the funding call and that we should be the ones to carry out the proposed work. Although some studies of successful grants have shown that proposals are more likely to be successful if they have 'greater verbal output, more complex writing structures, and increased verbal certainty' (Markowitz, 2019, p. 279), in general, avoid jargon and acronyms. Our writing and editing skills (Chapter 3) are vital to winning grant applications: 'good writing will not save bad ideas, but bad writing can kill good ones' (Kraicer, 1997, p .1).

We should seek feedback on our draft applications, just as we would for our draft research articles. Before submitting an application, it should run the gauntlet of friends and colleagues. Having people with different backgrounds review our proposals is especially valuable. A colleague or mentor may be better qualified to judge the technical aspects of the work, but a friend or family member with no connection to the topic can gauge if a proposal is easy to read. We should strongly consider editing and improving any part of a proposal that is subsequently highlighted as being confusing or arduous to read. If more than one of our informal reviewers highlight the same part, it becomes non-negotiable and must be addressed. This process also determines our grant-writing deadlines. If our feedback team needs several weeks to carry out their assessment, then we adjust our writing schedules (Chapter 3) to ensure we have a full draft ready several weeks before the submission deadline.

In the final draft, there is no excuse for spelling mistakes, grammatical errors, or exceeding word/page limits. Anything that is not pristine and professional will make the evaluators think that we ran out of time, or did not care – neither of which is an impression we want to make. If we have the freedom to be creative with the format, we can use pictures, diagrams, tables, or lists to make the proposal easier to read (Pequegnat et al., 2011). The evaluators will likely have a scoring rubric to assess how well the proposal addresses the critical points of the funding call (Hug and Aeschbach, 2020). If we have done our due diligence, we should be able to highlight (using italics or bold text) where each point is addressed in our proposal, so the evaluators do not have to search for them. The evaluators may have many proposals to assess and might not read our full proposal in one sitting. If they are quickly checking whether it addresses all the call criteria, we should make their job as easy as possible.

Funding plans

Without a plan, our dreams of getting funded remain just dreams. A funding plan, like the publication plan described in Chapter 4, connects our overall objectives as researchers with the specific goals needed to achieve them (Cronan and Deckard, 2012). It can be a basic table or an elaborate spreadsheet but, whatever form it takes, our funding plan should serve as an overview of how we expect to fund our research. It can be as long-term as a five-year plan if necessary, but at a minimum it should show where we will be focusing our grant-writing efforts for a period of 18 months. If the specific grants are unknown, we can outline the type of funding opportunities we want to target in terms of budget and scope. To help you get started, a template funding plan is available on this book's companion website.

The first step in populating a funding plan is to identify as many funding opportunities as possible. Our mentors can advise us, but we should also seek out funding calls ourselves. If there is a research development or research support office available to us, the staff in such places are usually the best people to provide this kind of guidance. They can point us towards relevant websites, mailing lists, or other resources, and may even be able to share examples of previously funded grant applications.

When designing our funding plan, we might consider the controversial concept of 'bootlegging' our research. Bootlegging means that a portion of the work 'must be essentially done before the grant is awarded and [...] the funds are then used for the next phase of the research program' (Bourne and Chalupa, 2006, p. 59). This is contentious because it means spending some of the grant resources working on a new idea – an idea related to the one that we were originally funded to work on but that might not be developed enough to be taken seriously or that may require some preliminary proof-of-concept work. If we secure funding for this new idea, we will already have completed a portion of the work (having 'bootlegged' it in the previous grant), so the extra time and resources can be used to start bootlegging our next big idea – perpetuating a cycle as old as the craft of grant-writing itself. It is not a process that sits comfortably with everyone, but bootlegging has always been widespread among researchers trying to survive in a competitive system: 'New ideas suffered because they were "too new" for external funding and recurrent funding was insufficient: a way out was to test new ideas by either bootlegging or using the equipment of colleagues, and then apply for external grants' (Laudel, 2006, p. 490).

Researcher views

Henrietta, on the need to be strategic with funding applications:

> The only way to survive is to have competitive ideas and to compromise, because the funding will go to certain subjects and to whatever is popular [...] We can't just write proposals about the stuff that we love and are interested in. We have to listen to what is being funded. We have to understand what will get us enough money to pay our mortgage and our bills.

Having put time and effort into developing a strong proposal, it does not deserve to be neglected while we wait to hear the outcome of the evaluation process. As with the experience of publishing papers described in Chapter 4, many of our funding applications will be unsuccessful. Unlike paper publishing processes, there are not always rules prohibiting us from submitting similar grant applications to different funders to increase the chances of one of them being successful. Our funding plan can be created by overlapping, stacking, or recycling applications. Rather than trying to write completely different proposals for each funding call, we can reuse much of the same material for each application: 'Successful grant proposal writers use a pre-prepared archive of information and related data' (Gorsevski, 2016, p. 54).

Communicating with funders

Establishing contact with funding agencies is a wise choice (Bailey, 1985; Olwell, 2015). The people who serve as 'gatekeepers' for funding calls may offer advice and suggestions not found in the call text or supporting documents. We should always ask the gatekeepers a question, even if receiving an answer is not critical. Simply seeking confirmation of our eligibility to apply is a chance to get a brief description of our proposal seen by someone involved in administering the funding. They might provide a generic reply or choose not to comment. There is a chance, however, that they might notice a reason why our proposal is not suitable for the funding call, saving us the effort of needlessly preparing and submitting an ineligible application, or they may even offer advice on how to steer our idea in a direction that is more likely to be funded. If it is a small funding agency, that gatekeeper could even have a role on the panel reviewing the applications, and if their experience of communicating with us has been that we are enthusiastic, capable, polite, and easy to work with, then subconsciously they may already think of us as fundable. A template email for contacting gatekeepers is available on this book's companion website.

If we use our funding plan appropriately, we should be seeking funding from multiple sources. Some funders may wish to know if we have applied for funding elsewhere, which is unlikely to count against us, as it demonstrates that we believe in our ideas and are prepared to work hard to ensure they are funded. If we happen to be more successful than expected with our applications, and the timing of the funding cycles aligns in such a way that we are awarded multiple grants at the same time, we could find ourselves in a situation where we have more than one funding agency supporting the same work. This is almost always a positive situation. Even if some of the funders involved have an issue with our project having multiple sources of support, we can usually commit to using the extra funding to extend the scope, duration, or potential impact of the work. If a funding agency deems our idea worthy of funding, they will be glad to see their views validated by other funding agencies. If one of the funding agencies will not award the grant while there is another funding stream for the project, then we should discuss our options with the funders involved and simply choose the grant that is more lucrative or prestigious. Not being able to accept a grant because it is incompatible with a bigger and better grant is perhaps the most palatable reason for missing out on funding.

Any correspondence with funders should be conducted in a polite and professional manner. Even when dealing with rejections, we should never lower ourselves to complaining about their decisions or sending angry or rude responses. Not only is that never appropriate, but the gatekeepers are the least deserving of criticism in the grant-funding process and are people we will likely need to reconnect with regarding future applications. Anyone can be charming when they have just been awarded funding, but the mark of a good researcher is when they conduct themselves with dignified grace even when their applications are unsuccessful.

Standing on the shoulders of grant rejections

It may seem pessimistic to focus on rejections in the final section (for the second chapter running), but how we cope with such apparent knock-backs will define us as researchers. Most grant applications are rejected. If our sole reason for writing and submitting a grant application is to win funding, then we will be setting ourselves up to be disappointed. Famously, the molecular biologist Carol Greider had a grant application rejected on the same day she won her Nobel prize, a situation she described as: 'Even on the day when you win the Nobel prize, sceptics may question whether you really know what you're doing' (Sohn, 2020, p. 134).

The hardest part of the grant-writing process is coping with rejections. Robert Sternberg, a professor of human development, has won millions of dollars of research funding throughout his career, but in his book on writing successful grant proposals he says: 'there were some years that I seemed to have the golden touch in getting grants and other years in which everything I touched seemed to turn to lead [...] That is the first lesson you need to learn about securing research grants, the grant-getting process is uncertain' (Sternberg, 2014, p. 3). There have been attempts to remove the perceived stigma that could be associated with rejected grant applications by providing open repositories to share both successful and unsuccessful proposals (for example, the 'Open Grants' website: www.ogrants.org).

Researcher views

Carlos, on the frustrations of having funding applications rejected:

> They keep moving the goalposts. You think you have cracked it and then the next year the exact same funding call will give you feedback that makes it sound like they didn't read the proposal and just didn't get it.

Instead of dwelling on the outcomes of funding applications, we should embrace the grant-writing process for the right reasons. It represents a chance for us to develop our ideas (Falk, 2011), no matter how crazy and quirky (i.e., 'innovative' and 'novel') they are. Learning how to describe the importance of our research clearly and convincingly, and its potential impact for society, will bolster other tasks such as writing papers, engaging public audiences, and applying for jobs (Chapter 3, Chapter 8, and Chapter 11, respectively).

Successful grant-writers receive more rejections than most, and that is the secret to their success – they have become so efficient in the grant-writing process that they are perpetually applying (von Hippel and von Hippel, 2015). Continually submitting applications is vital to maintaining motivation: 'A good way of keeping hope on your side is to make sure you never get down to your last idea, application or rejection letter. If you keep some overlap between your research grant applications you need never let yourself get back to square one' (Aldridge and Derrington, 2012, p. 38).

Every time a grant application is rejected, we should look at how it can be improved, using a process similar to how we deal with publication rejections (see Chapter 4); once the initial sting of rejection has subsided, we should revisit the outcome objectively and, where possible, seek feedback from the funder, which could be crucial to improving future applications. Reusing, recycling, and strengthening our applications so that we can resubmit improved versions is all part of the process. Each rejection takes us closer to being funded, as well as developing another critical academic skill – persevering even when things are not going our way.

Summary

- Find a mentor. You will learn the art of grant-writing faster from an expert.
- Design your proposal around the text of the funding call. The key to winning grants is aligning your ideas with what the funders are seeking to support.

- Create a funding plan. Keep sight of the direction you want your research to take, and which funding opportunities will help get you there.
- Contact the gatekeepers. Gather as much information as possible about the funding call before applying, and seek feedback afterwards — especially when your applications are unsuccessful.
- Apply for funding incessantly. Even when you are mostly receiving rejections, build on that experience to improve and enhance your applications.

Despite the issues with how research is funded, and the constant challenge of writing successful grant applications, it *can* be an emotionally (rather than financially) rewarding process (Arlitsch, 2013). The sociologist Cynthia Carr describes how we can develop a love of grant-writing, especially when we remember we are using our research and writing skills to secure funds to make some small part of the world a better place (Carr, 2014). Once our research projects are funded, we must then learn to manage them, which we will tackle in Chapter 10. Next, after spending three chapters getting our research in order, we have the honour of thinking about how we pass on that knowledge to others. Class is in session; Chapter 6 is all about teaching.

Further reading

- Aldridge, J. & Derrington, A. M. (2012). *The Research Funding Toolkit: How to Plan and Write Successful Grant Applications*. London, UK: SAGE.

This book provides a suite of tools to pursue a variety of types of research funding.

- Berry, D. C. (2010). *Gaining Funding for Research: A Guide for Academics and Institutions*. Berkshire, UK: McGraw-Hill Education.

Putting the funding process in the wider context of academic institutions, this book gives well-informed advice on the UK research-funding environment.

- Carr, C. E. (2014). *The Nuts and Bolts of Grant Writing*. Thousand Oaks, CA: SAGE.

Several case studies presented in this book provide a more in-depth look at the specific details of grant applications.

- Gorsevski, E. W. (2016). *Writing Successful Grant Proposals*. Rotterdam, The Netherlands: Sense Publishers, Springer.

Ellen Gorsevski combines her public and private sector experiences to share her 'wee guidebook' (as she calls it) to successful grant-writing strategies – invaluable for targeting small research grants.

- Sternberg, R. J. (Ed.) (2014). *Writing Successful Grant Proposals from the Top Down and Bottom Up*. Thousand Oaks, CA: SAGE.

While this book is largely written from the perspective of the US research-funding environment, it brings together successful grant-writers from different disciplines to provide their advice on applying to some of the biggest research-funding agencies.

Resources

Further resources for this chapter can be found at: www.JosephRoche.ie/EssentialSkills

- Email to Future Grant-Writing Mentor Template
- Funding Plan Template
- Email Seeking More Clarity on Grant Template

References

Aldridge, J. & Derrington, A. M. (2012). *The Research Funding Toolkit: How to Plan and Write Successful Grant Applications*. London, UK: SAGE.

Arlitsch, K. (2013). Committing to research: librarians and grantsmanship. *Journal of Library Administration, 53*(5–6), 369–379.

Auranen, O. & Nieminen, M. (2010). University research funding and publication performance – An international comparison. *Research Policy, 39*(6), 822–834.

Bailey, A. L. (1985). So you want to get a grant: some advice from the experts. *Change: The Magazine of Higher Learning, 17*(1), 40–43.

Berry, D. C. (2010). *Gaining Funding for Research: A Guide for Academics and Institutions*. Berkshire, UK: McGraw-Hill Education.

Bloch, C., Graversen, E. K., & Pedersen, H. S. (2014). Competitive research grants and their impact on career performance. *Minerva, 52*(1), 77–96.

Bordage, G. & Dawson, B. (2003). Experimental study design and grant writing in eight steps and 28 questions. *Medical Education, 37*(4), 376–385.

Bourne, P. E. & Chalupa, L. M. (2006). Ten simple rules for getting grants. *PLoS Computational Biology, 2*(2), e12: 59–60.

Boyack, K. W., Smith, C., & Klavans, R. (2018). Toward predicting research proposal success. *Scientometrics, 114*(2), 449–461.

Boyer, P. G. & Cockriel, I. (2001). Grant performance of junior faculty across disciplines: motivators and barriers. *Journal of Research Administration, 2*(1), 19–23.

Braun, D. (1998). The role of funding agencies in the cognitive development of science. *Research Policy, 27*(8), 807–821.

Carr, C. E. (2014). *The Nuts and Bolts of Grant Writing*. Thousand Oaks, CA: SAGE.

Clarke, C. A. & Fox, S. P. (2007). *Grant Proposal Makeover: Transform your Request from No to Yes*. San Francisco, CA: John Wiley & Sons.

Cole, S., Cole, J. R., & Simon, G. A. (1981). Chance and consensus in peer review. *Science, 214*(4523), 881–886.

Coley, S. M. & Scheinberg, C. A. (2016). *Proposal Writing: Effective Grantsmanship for Funding* (4th edn). Thousand Oaks, CA: SAGE.

Cronan, M. & Deckard, L. (2012). *New Faculty Guide to Competing for Research Funding*. College Station, TX: Academic Research Funding Strategies.

Cunningham, K. (2020). Beyond boundaries: developing grant writing skills across higher education institutions. *Journal of Research Administration, 51*(2). Available at: www.srainternational.org/blogs/srai-jra1/2020/09/29/beyond-boundaries-developing-grant-writing-skills (accessed 5 October 2021).

Falk, A. (2011). Teaching grantsmanship in a nonprofit leadership class. *Journal of the Grant Professionals Association, 9*(1), 78–87.

Fang, F. C. & Casadevall, A. (2016). Research funding: The case for a modified lottery. *MBio, 7*(2), e00422-16, 1–7.

Gitlin, L., Kolanowski, A., & Lyons, K. J. (2020). *Successful Grant Writing: Strategies for Health and Human Service Professionals* (5th edn). New York, NY: Springer Publishing Company.

Gorsevski, E. W. (2016). *Writing Successful Grant Proposals*. Rotterdam, The Netherlands: Sense Publishers, Springer.

Griffith, J. D., Hart, C. L., & Goodling, M. M. (2006). Teaching grant writing with service learning. *International Journal of Teaching and Learning in Higher Education, 18*(3), 222–229.

Hilton, T. F. & Leukefeld, C. G. (2019). *Grantsmanship for New Investigators*. Cham, Switzerland: Springer International Publishing.

Himanen, L., Auranen, O., Puuska, H. M., & Nieminen, M. (2009). Influence of research funding and science policy on university research performance: a comparison of five countries. *Science and Public Policy, 36*(6), 419–430.

Hug, S. E. & Aeschbach, M. (2020). Criteria for assessing grant applications: a systematic review. *Palgrave Communications, 6*(1), 1–15.

Kleinfelder, J., Price, J. H., & Dake, J. A. (2003). Grant writing: practice and preparation of university health educators. *American Journal of Health Education, 34*(1), 47–53.

Koppelman, G. H. & Holloway, J. W. (2012). Successful grant writing. *Paediatric Respiratory Reviews, 13*(1), 63–66.

Kraicer, J. (1997). *The Art of Grantsmanship*. Strasbourg: Human Frontier Science Program.

Laudel, G. (2006). The art of getting funded: how scientists adapt to their funding conditions. *Science and Public Policy, 33*(7), 489–504.

Laudel, G. & Gläser, J. (2014). Beyond breakthrough research: epistemic properties of research and their consequences for research funding. *Research Policy, 43*(7), 1204–1216.

Locke, L. F., Spirduso, W. W., & Silverman, S. J. (2013). *Proposals That Work: A Guide for Planning Dissertations and Grant Proposals* (6th edn). Thousand Oaks, CA: SAGE.

Liu, J. C., Pynnonen, M. A., St John, M., Rosenthal, E. L., Couch, M. E., & Schmalbach, C. E. (2016). Grant-writing pearls and pitfalls: maximizing funding opportunities. *Otolaryngology – Head and Neck Surgery, 154*(2), 226–232.

Markowitz, D. M. (2019). What words are worth: National Science Foundation grant abstracts indicate award funding. *Journal of Language and Social Psychology*, 38(3), 264–282.

Olwell, R. (2015). Reach out to your program officer. *Inside Higher Ed*, 16 January. Available at: www.insidehighered.com/advice/2015/01/16/essay-need-academics-establish-close-ties-program-officers (accessed 5 October 2021).

Pequegnat, W., Stover, E. & Boyce, C.A. (2011). *How to Write a Successful Research Grant Application* (2nd edn). New York, NY: Springer Publishing.

Porter, R. (2005). What do grant reviewers really want, anyway. *Journal of Research Administration*, 36(2), 5–13.

Roy, R. (1985). Funding science: the real defects of peer review and an alternative to it. *Science, Technology, & Human Values*, 10(3), 73–81.

Smith, K. (2010). Research, policy and funding – academic treadmills and the squeeze on intellectual spaces 1. *The British Journal of Sociology*, 61(1), 176–195.

Sohn, E. (2020). Secrets to writing a winning grant. *Nature*, 577(7788), 133–135.

Sternberg, R. J. (Ed.) (2014). *Writing Successful Grant Proposals from the Top Down and Bottom Up*. Thousand Oaks, CA: SAGE.

von Hippel, T. & von Hippel, C. (2015). To apply or not to apply: a survey analysis of grant writing costs and benefits. *PloS One*, 10(3), e0118494, 1–8.

Wooley, S. F. (2004). A review committee as a way to teach grant writing skills. *Journal of Health Education*, 35(6), 366–368.

Six
Teaching

In this chapter, we will cover:

- the current state of teaching in higher education
- proactively aligning teaching and research
- the basics of course design
- assessment and technology
- creating a teaching philosophy statement.

The noblest profession

Of all the skills we develop as researchers, teaching has the greatest impact on other people. Teaching is often described as the 'noblest profession' (Goode, 1976, p. 195), and once we are confident that the core components of our work – research, academic writing, publishing, and securing funding (Chapters 2–5) – are progressing well, then we have the perfect platform from which to distinguish ourselves as university teachers. Being an educator is a fundamental aspect of life as an academic, but the first time we are tasked with the responsibility of educating university students, it can be a chastening experience. Naturally gifted teachers are exceedingly rare, but we can all improve our teaching and face our classes with confidence and enthusiasm.

In this chapter, we will look at how early career researchers can find their way into teaching, as well as the factors that determine whether they thrive or struggle. We will look at how aligning our teaching and research boosts our chances of finding appropriate teaching opportunities, as well as how to develop lectures, modules, and essential resources to demonstrate our abilities as educators.

Teaching in higher education

Fulfilling our potential as academic researchers requires balancing our teaching and research obligations. We need to spend enough time improving our abilities as educators to ensure our students are benefiting from our teaching, while also spending enough time researching, writing, and publishing to feel we are doing justice to our primary role as academic researchers. Finding a balance between those two positions – even before adding in the complications of administrative expectations (Chapter 9) – is an enduring challenge throughout our careers.

The role of universities has changed dramatically since the middle of the twentieth century. Where once they were seen as exclusive and elitist, the opening up of access to universities – known as the 'massification' of higher education – has transformed them into places of potential social mobility (Bell et al., 2009; Mok and Neubauer, 2016).

Universities now have more far-reaching roles in society and provide, at the very least, 'some form of post-secondary-school education, where 'education' signals something more than professional training' (Collini, 2012, p. 7). The education itself has increasingly been subjected to measurements of 'quality' – and what is deemed *quality* in university education is often seen differently from administrative and academic perspectives (Anderson, 2006; Blackmore, 2009).

University education has seen a gradual movement away from content-focused and teacher-centred approaches towards more learning-focused and student-oriented approaches, where the teacher and learner engage in a process of meaning-making or mutually constructed understanding (Fink, 2013; Scales, 2017). This 'constructivist' approach to higher education is deemed to prepare students to be independent lifelong learners (Lueddeke, 1999). It is within this modern university landscape that researchers, somewhat incongruously, become teachers.

Finding our way into teaching roles in universities can be relatively straightforward, although the process itself seems preposterous. Early career researchers begin their careers by proving they have the necessary qualifications or experience. That comfortingly logical state of affairs in early career progression is upended when, at a certain point, they unceremoniously find themselves in the position of having to teach. There is every possibility that they have never taught before, and up to that point may not have demonstrated any desire or ability to be educators. This becomes a central, and often panic-inducing, new direction in a fledgling academic career – the more we excel at our research, the more we will be entrusted with teaching an ever-growing number of students (Ramsden, 2003). Follow that trajectory and we will find gloomily familiar figures – renowned senior professors, leaders in their research fields, who are dreadful lecturers and educators.

Students deserve better, but it is not entirely fair to blame lecturers. Most will have learned to teach on the job. It is not their main role as academic researchers, and it is a role that some will not have sought or desired. In the absence of any formal training, when we first teach in a university, we gravitate towards teaching in the same style that was used to teach us. This is natural but ultimately not constructive; if we are trying to emulate the lecturers who taught us – who had no formal training either and who also emulated their teachers – we are propagating a system based on anecdotal experience rather than evidence-based best practice. Many universities now recommend that new academic staff undertake short teacher training courses, but these types of interventions are not always mandatory (Gibbs and Coffey, 2004; Postareff et al., 2007), resulting in situations where 'faculty members have little, if any, professional training in teaching' (Sunal et al., 2001, p. 247).

Veteran academic researchers may warn us that teaching is a secondary part of our jobs; that research should be our main concern, and that our teaching commitments should be something we suffer – limiting its infringements on our precious research time as much as possible. That may bring short-term benefits, but in the longer term, there will be repercussions. If we merely endure our teaching obligations, actively avoid them, or convince ourselves we are succeeding as educators when all evidence suggests otherwise – it is inherently unfair on our students. Equally, if we are shirking our responsibility to become better educators, then our teaching will not improve, and every time we find ourselves in a lecture hall, a classroom, or a laboratory – aware that our students are receiving an educational experience that is less than what they deserve – a feeling of guilt will gnaw at the very core of our academic being.

A healthier approach is to embrace the teaching we are required to do and use it to enrich other parts of our academic identity (McKeachie and Svinicki, 2014). The Nobel Prize-winning physicist Richard Feynman, despite being one of the most sought-after academics in the world, who could easily have justified dedicating his time solely to research, insisted that any university position he held included a teaching role. Being famously passionate about education, he believed that teaching is crucial for researchers to stay motivated, active, and creative (Feynman and Leighton, 1985).

We must prioritise our research for the sake of our academic development and our careers, but that focus on becoming a better researcher should not be to the detriment of our teaching. We also do not want to follow the well-worn path of the academics who ignore their research responsibilities by convincing themselves that their teaching obligations are all-consuming and cling to the ultimate false hope that they will find time to catch up on their research, writing, and publishing when the teaching semester ends. To protect ourselves from such situations we must align our teaching with our research.

Aligning teaching and research

Some early career researchers wait to be asked to undertake their first teaching assignment. That can pose problems if such an invitation never appears. Even if it does, the request is likely to be based around the needs of the professor or department doing the inviting, rather than the research interests of the researcher being asked to teach. Passively waiting for a teaching invitation also makes it more difficult to decline such an invitation if it arrives – an early career researcher with no teaching experience will be under more pressure to accept any teaching opportunities that arise. This can result in the subject of their first teaching experience being a topic far removed from their own area of expertise. Being *volunteered* for teaching outside of their comfort zone leads to additional work, as the early career researcher strives to get to grips with unfamiliar material. This burden, coupled with the inherent challenge of teaching for the first time, can damage their confidence and potentially start a cycle of stressful teaching experiences culminating in academic burnout (Watts and Robertson, 2011).

Researcher views

Willow, on having to teach a module at short notice on a topic she was not familiar with:

> Sometimes it's a bit like just reading a few pages ahead in the book to stay ahead of the class. I was dropped in it. No support. They should have given me an Oscar for the performance.

A more fulfilling first teaching experience can be orchestrated by proactively seeking teaching opportunities that align with our areas of research. This more deliberate approach of pitching guest lectures, workshops, or seminars on our research topic will let us build a body of teaching material that we can feel confident about. At first, it is unlikely we will have enough material to create an entire degree programme from our research, but we should have more than enough for a 20-minute seminar – and that is where to begin.

Create a short presentation that describes your research area and how you hope to contribute to the field. You will have plenty of time to polish your presentation and experiment with styles of communication (Chapter 8), so the goal should be to become comfortable presenting the material. If your department runs a seminar series, present your seminar to see what kinds of questions and comments it receives. Request as much feedback as you can from anyone who attends your seminar. If you cannot find an existing seminar series, establish an informal one with your research group or fellow researchers in your department.

As you gain more experience presenting your topic and incorporating feedback, you can expand the presentation. What is the history of the field you are working in? What are the most important ethical considerations? Which case studies are significant? All of these questions are important for researchers to ponder but might not receive appropriate consideration – until they have to teach. Grow your presentation until you can present a 50-minute lecture. It will not require as much material as it might first appear – early career researchers 'never fail to be surprised by how little they can cover in 50 minutes' (Morss and Murray, 2005, p.33). This is your *back-pocket* lecture that you are always ready to present at short notice. If a professor asks you to provide a guest lecture due to an unforeseen emergency, you can immediately offer a polished and well-rehearsed lecture on your research.

Find courses where it would make sense for you to offer your guest lecture – courses where the benefits of research-led teaching are underscored (Griffiths, 2004; Healey, 2005). Suggest your guest lecture to your supervisor, other professors in your department, and other departments on campus. For overburdened professors trying to staff a course, the offer of a self-contained guest lecture could be exactly what they are looking for. A template email to help you offer a guest lecture is available on this book's companion website. Even if a professor cannot immediately fit a guest lecture into their course, if they need an emergency lecture in future, they should remember your offer. Senior academics recognise the importance of early career teaching experience and may offer to help you tailor your guest lecture to better fit the overall context of the course. They may even offer to co-teach the material with you. Such experience should be embraced (Bell, 2001; Austin, 2002), and will help build confidence to progress from giving guest lectures to designing modules and courses.

Researcher views

Rene, on always being distracted by the students who seem less engaged:

> I always saw this one kid who was sleeping in my lectures. No matter how good my lecture was I only could see him, nothing else. I nearly said something but I found out later he has narcolepsy.

Course design

Once we have some experience presenting our polished, back-pocket lecture, we can begin designing similar lectures, and plan how they will combine to comprise a short module. From there, we can propose how a series of our modules could form the backbone of an undergraduate or postgraduate degree course. Challenging ourselves to design courses early in our academic careers not only prepares us for formal lecturing roles – it can help us to secure such roles in the first place. When early career researchers are applying for their first lecturing job, they can feel overwhelmed if they are expected to develop new modules and degree programmes (Ferman, 2002; Fry et al., 2009; Norton et al., 2013). If we are already comfortable with course design, we can seize the opportunity to create courses that align our research interests with the strategic goals of the university (Chapter 11).

Researcher views

Vanessa, on being tasked with creating an entire programme at short notice:

> I was quite anxious about developing an entire curriculum, when I had such limited teaching experience or training in how to teach properly, curriculum development, all of that. But, it was just kind of like learn as you go, what I liked best, what I took from good professors that I had in the past.

To design a module, you should start with a *module descriptor*. This is a template document provided by most higher education institutions to help their academic staff to define their teaching in a way that will be consistent with other modules across the institution. What begins as a teaching planning document for an academic staff member will eventually become the description of the module that students will use to choose their course of study. Common elements of module descriptors include:

- an overview of the content that will be covered on the module
- the duration of the module
- the structure of the module (in terms of lectures, tutorials, labs, practicals, or placements)
- the modes of teaching that will be used
- how the module will be assessed and graded
- reading lists.

The overall module, and each individual lecture, will have a set of *learning outcomes* – what students will be expected to know or be able to achieve after participating in the module (Otter, 1992). Defining the learning outcomes helps lecturers to reflect on 'the relationship between what they teach and what students do, in fact, learn' (Allan, 1996, p. 104). The assessment of our modules can then be guided by checking if the learning outcomes have been met. Throughout Europe, this structured approach to creating modules is known as the 'Bologna Process' – an agreement between cooperating countries that keeps the standards and quality of higher-education qualifications consistent and comparable (Heinze and Knill, 2008). A template module descriptor is available on this book's companion website.

When we strive for excellence in teaching, it is not limited to the ways in which we teach; it extends to how we design course content and modes of assessment. Designing a module is where we stamp our views as an educator on how we teach. We can use the process to show how we will provide 'conditions which stimulate students to think and learn, and which encourage students to take responsibility for their own learning' (Hall, 1996, p. 112). We should consider our own interpretation of learning, how we assess learning, the best ways to support our students, and the effect the teaching will have on the students 'intellectually, physically, or emotionally' (Bain, 2004, p. 49).

In designing a module, we decide if our role is conveying knowledge to our students or constructing understanding with our students (Petrie, 1990). We decide the kind of learning environment that we want to create – an impartial space, or a place where values, ethical considerations, and socioscientific issues are openly debated (Arghode et al., 2013). Addressing our personal values might seem like it could bias our teaching but, depending on the topic, it could be more responsible to clearly acknowledge our views: 'Teachers cannot avoid expressing their values: the question is whether they choose to have their values revealed explicitly or implicitly [...] classrooms can never be value-free environments; however, it is certainly important to strive for value-fair environments' (Sadler et al., 2006, p. 372).

Early in our research journeys, being a teaching assistant is a common way to gain teaching experience. Such roles can build confidence with duties such as grading assignments and running tutorials. Even more valuable, however, is the opportunity to see how a course is run from the perspective of the teachers. This can provide us with insight into the kinds of modules we hope to eventually lead ourselves. After gaining some teaching assistant experience, there is no need to continue seeking out such opportunities – focusing on guest lectures and course design will better serve our professional development (Chapter 10) and career progression (Chapter 11).

Technology and assessment

When we think of assessment, we often dwell on the anxiety-inducing examinations and end-of-semester assignments that are not easy to forget for anyone who has experienced them. This form of high-stakes assessment is, however, only one aspect of how learning is evaluated. Scholars in the field of assessment make clear distinctions between assessment *of* learning, assessment *for* learning, and assessment *as* learning (Lam, 2016).

Researcher views

Mac, on assessment strategies that suit him and his employer:

> I was dreading having to make exam questions and spend my summer grading. But the dean actually asked us if we could have less exams and so I offered to do 100% continuous assessment. I volunteered straight away. It's sweet. Everything is graded as we go. I actually get the TAs to do the grading. I haven't had to mark anything in about three years.

In recent decades, higher education institutions have begun moving away from a perceived overdependence on traditional forms of summative assessment, such as end-of-semester exams or assignments. Formative assessment – regular student-focused feedback which can be informal (low-stakes) or formal (carrying credit) – is becoming more prevalent (Yorke, 2003; Boud and Falchikov, 2007). This move towards more formative assessment reduces the focus on 'assessment for the purpose of warranting achievement' and instead provides insights for both student and teacher in the guise of 'learning-oriented assessment' (Knight, 2006, p. 442). Although these periodic interventions provide both student and teacher with more information on their performance throughout the module (Kearns, 2012), it can be intimidating for lecturers who are new to formative assessment (Bailey and Garner, 2010).

There is 'no singular curriculum model, implementation strategy, nor approach to learning [that] will suit all academic settings' (Hubball and Burt, 2004, p. 52), which is why it is so important for us to engage with the creative and reflexive opportunities afforded by using technology (Johnson and Carruthers, 2006). The most pervasive example of technology in higher education teaching is the use of virtual learning environments, such as Moodle (Costello, 2013) or Blackboard (Heaton-Shrestha et al., 2007). Almost every higher education institution has a virtual learning environment, and while they have their critics (Heirdsfield et al., 2011), such tools can make our teaching more efficient and enhance learning and assessment.

A formative assessment quiz, for example, can easily be automated with pre-programmed answers to provide students with an immediate sense of their progress on our modules. Providing such feedback 'as soon as possible [...] before the pressures of life outside the classroom [...] flood in to distract the learner's attention' are more valuable to students when they happen immediately after the learning takes place, rather than waiting weeks for feedback in the form of assignments or exam results (Brookfield, 2006, p. 185).

Another form of formative assessment, reflective journaling (Anderson, 1992; Hughes et al., 1997), can be facilitated through virtual learning environments to provide an online space for students to develop their writing. This can pave the way for more purposeful assessment opportunities such as self-assessment and peer-assessment where students (usually anonymously) review and evaluate each other's work. When combined, these forms of assessment allow students to compare how they marked their own work with how it was marked by their peers. Seeing the standard of each other's work can be instructive for students, and technology-mediated self-assessment and peer-assessment can be even more meaningful if we empower our students to help us create the grading criteria (or rubrics) for such assessments (Dochy et al., 1999; Stevens and Levi, 2005; Tong et al., 2018).

Virtual learning environments also facilitate 'flipped classroom' approaches, where multimedia lecture material is provided for students to engage with in their own time, at their own pace, so that more class time can be dedicated to what would tradition-ally be considered 'homework' (O'Flaherty and Phillips, 2015, p. 85). This makes it easier to identify the material that our students find most challenging, and provides more insight into individual learning (Fulton, 2012; Herreid and Schiller, 2013).

Technology is central to the inexorable rise of online learning, also referred to as e-learning or distance learning (Cutri and Mena, 2020; Mishra et al., 2020), which became almost ubiquitous during the COVID-19 global pandemic (Rapanta et al., 2020; Mahmood, 2021; Hofer et al., 2021). To prevent it being an isolating expe-rience for students, we should ensure a social presence in how our online lectures are taught, providing more opportunities for interactivity with teachers and fellow students (having smaller discussion groups in virtual breakout rooms, for example) to foster a sense of community (Cobb, 2009; Park and Kim, 2020). Having a blended model of synchronous (real-time) and asynchronous (offline) teaching means a wider range of student learning can be supported. Although this demonstrates the value of technology in improving equitable learning, when designing our courses to be as inclusive as possible it is worth considering that expecting students to have reliable access to technology and high-speed Internet could compound existing inequalities, sometimes referred to as *the digital divide* (Van Dijk, 2006). Often the student with the most pressing learning needs also faces the biggest challenges in accessing technology (Barraket and Scott, 2001).

Technology can increase student participation through audience response systems and mobile technology allowing students to interact with our teaching material using their phones, laptops, or other smart devices (Kay and LeSage, 2009; Stowell, 2015). Audience response systems are growing in popularity, and include Crowdpurr, Mentimeter, Poll Everywhere, Socrative, TurningPoint, and VoxVote. Poll Everywhere, for example, can facilitate class discussions by embedding interactive questions in the lecture slides, with the students' anonymously contributed answers appearing on the lecture screen in real-time (Kappers and Cutler, 2015). The students then vote on the responses until the class comes to a consensus, ensuring that they are more likely to remember the right answer when it is revealed, regardless of whether the class suggestions were correct (Lang, 2016).

This use of Poll Everywhere to 'facilitate decision making in a democratic manner' (Shon and Smith, 2011, p. 244) provides interactivity on a scale that would be almost impossible without technology. It can be equally effective stimulating discussion in small groups or facilitating feedback at public lectures with thousands of participants (Roche et al., 2016a, 2016b). It can be especially important for students who do not feel comfortable speaking out in class. For such students, seeing their anonymous contributions on the lecture screen as part of a class discussion can be empowering.

How we integrate technology, teaching, and assessment should be consistent with our overall aims as educators. To make that connection, every academic lecturer needs a teaching philosophy statement.

The teaching philosophy statement

A teaching philosophy statement is a personal reflection on our values and how we approach teaching and learning (Chism, 1998). It is generally only one or two pages long and is a rare example of an academic document that should always be written in the first-person narrative voice. The first section provides context. In my teaching philosophy statement, for example, I first describe my background before sharing my belief that my role as an educator is to help students fulfil their potential. As I delve deeper into this belief, I suggest that my teaching should provide the next generation of researchers with an understanding of their responsibilities to society, while also ensuring that they are well prepared to meet those responsibilities. I then connect my views on teaching and learning with best practice from peer-reviewed literature in the field. The different parts of a teaching philosophy statement, drawn from Schönwetter et al. (2002), can include:

- an acknowledgement of our personal context and how it has shaped our views as educators
- what we believe is the purpose of teaching and learning
- our understanding of the role of the teacher
- our understanding of the role of the student
- the methods we use to implement our belief system
- how we incorporate assessment and evaluation into our work.

A template teaching philosophy statement is available on this book's companion website.

The teaching philosophy statement should be a continually evolving document, and the reflection required to update our views and beliefs can be just as important as the final statement itself (Beatty et al., 2009). One of the most well-known models for reflection, from Brookfield (1995), is to develop our teaching philosophy by considering our work from four different perspectives (or critical lenses):

1. The perspective from the theoretical literature.
2. The perspective of our students.
3. The perspective of our colleagues.
4. Our own personal perspective.

Using such a model to regularly reflect on our teaching – and update our teaching philosophy statement accordingly – can reduce doubt and anxiety about our teaching abilities. Even the most confident teachers can find themselves questioning their abilities from time to time, especially if they receive negative feedback from students. Such occasional criticisms can be difficult to reconcile within the wider context of our teaching but using a structured model of reflection to interpret such feedback 'helps us avoid these traps of demoralization and self-laceration' (Brookfield, 1995, p. 2). This form of commitment to self-evaluation is often referred to as *reflective practice*, which we will explore further when we discuss professional development in Chapter 10.

Researcher views

Tessa, on her early experiences of teaching as a person of colour:

> That was a really interesting experience for me, because it was a teacher education programme in [that university] with 100% white students with me as the teacher, you know, trying to tell them maybe we should think about stuff like equity or things like that in your classrooms and what I maybe didn't expect was how much the population of students impacted how teaching that class felt.

Summary

- Seek opportunities to teach. Proactively pursuing the kind of teaching experience you need is far better than waiting to see what opportunities may arise.
- Align your teaching with your research. Both are critical, both demand time – the best way to avoid neglecting either is to ensure they are connected.
- Design a lecture or a seminar that you can present at short notice. Over time, build on that lecture to demonstrate how you would design a module, a course, or even a degree programme.
- Give due consideration to forms of assessment that will enrich your students' learning and make your teaching more efficient.
- Develop a teaching philosophy statement and update it regularly. This will ensure it is ready for job applications and motivate you to reflect on your teaching on an ongoing basis.

When we are tasked with teaching, it is a measure of faith in our abilities. Such responsibility should be an honour, but competing expectations in our academic roles can occasionally make teaching feel like a burden. Aligning our teaching and research, proactively seeking the right opportunities, having our teaching resources well prepared, and regularly reflecting on our practice will make teaching a more fulfilling experience. When we take pride in our teaching, we become better educators. This, in turn, will improve how we share our research in publications, how we communicate with funders, and how we engage public audiences. Teaching can take many guises, and we need to examine a specific and intense form of teaching in the next chapter – schedule a meeting in your diary, Chapter 7 deals with the supervisory relationship.

Further reading

- Boud, D. & Falchikov, N. (Eds.) (2007). *Rethinking Assessment in Higher Education: Learning for the Longer Term.* Oxford, UK: Routledge.

This book collects the views from scholars across the field of higher education assessment and provides a comprehensive overview of how to connect teaching, learning, and assessment in university environments.

- Brookfield, S. D. (2006). *The Skillful Teacher: On Technique, Trust, and Responsiveness in the Classroom.* San Francisco, CA: John Wiley & Sons.

Stephen Brookfield is a leading scholar in teaching and critical thinking and this book combines those fields to convey how skilful teachers critically reflect on their teaching and the experiences of their students.

- Fink, L. D. (2013). *Creating Significant Learning Experiences: An Integrated Approach to Designing College Courses.* San Francisco, CA: John Wiley & Sons.

Integrated course design can strengthen higher education teaching and learning and this book provides guidance on linking all of the necessary elements while prioritising student-centred learning.

- Lang, J. M. (2016). *Small Teaching: Everyday Lessons from the Science of Learning.* San Francisco, CA: John Wiley & Sons.

This book proposes small incremental changes we can make to improve our teaching – perfect for early career researchers who find themselves thrust into teaching before they feel adequately prepared.

- Tong, V. C. H., Standen, A., & Sotiriou, M. (2018). *Shaping Higher Education with Students: Ways to Connect Research and Teaching.* London, UK: UCL Press.

Researchers from a range of different disciplines showcase the benefits of connecting teaching and research while also involving students in shaping that connection.

Resources

Further resources for this chapter can be found at: www.JosephRoche.ie/EssentialSkills

- Email Template Offering Guest Lecture
- Module Descriptor Template
- Teaching Philosophy Statement Template

References

Allan, J. (1996). Learning outcomes in higher education. *Studies in Higher Education, 21*(1), 93–108.

Anderson, G. (2006). Assuring quality/resisting quality assurance: academics' responses to 'quality' in some Australian universities. *Quality in Higher Education, 12*(2), 161–173.

Anderson, J. (1992). Journal writing: the promise and the reality. *Journal of Reading, 36*(4), 304–309.

Arghode, V., Yalvac, B., & Liew, J. (2013). Teacher empathy and science education: a collective case study. *Eurasia Journal of Mathematics, Science & Technology Education, 9*(2), 89–99.

Austin, A. E. (2002). Preparing the next generation of faculty: graduate school as socialization to the academic career. *The Journal of Higher Education, 73*(1), 94–122.

Bailey, R. & Garner, M. (2010). Is the feedback in higher education assessment worth the paper it is written on? Teachers' reflections on their practices. *Teaching in Higher Education, 15*(2), 187–198.

Bain, K. (2004). *What the Best College Teachers Do*. Boston, MA: Harvard University Press.

Barraket, J. & Scott, G. (2001). Virtual equality? Equity and the use of information technology in higher education. *Australian Academic & Research Libraries, 32*(3), 204–212.

Beatty, J. E., Leigh, J. S., & Lund Dean, K. (2009). Finding our roots: an exercise for creating a personal teaching philosophy statement. *Journal of Management Education, 33*(1), 115–130.

Bell, L., Neary, M., & Stevenson, H. (2009). *The Future of Higher Education: Policy, Pedagogy and the Student Experience*. New York, NY: Continuum International Publishing Group.

Bell, M. (2001). Supported reflective practice: a programme of peer observation and feedback for academic teaching development. *International Journal for Academic Development, 6*(1), 29–39.

Blackmore, J. (2009). Academic pedagogies, quality logics and performative universities: evaluating teaching and what students want. *Studies in Higher Education, 34*(8), 857–872.

Boud, D. & Falchikov, N. (Eds.) (2007). *Rethinking Assessment in Higher Education: Learning for the Longer Term*. Oxford, UK: Routledge.

Brookfield, S. (1995). *Becoming a Critically Reflective Teacher*. San Francisco: Jossey-Bass.

Brookfield, S. D. (2006). *The Skillful Teacher: On Technique, Trust, and Responsiveness in the Classroom*. San Francisco, CA: John Wiley & Sons.

Chism, N. V. N. (1998). Developing a philosophy of teaching statement. *Essays on Teaching Excellence, 9*(3), 1–2.

Cobb, S. C. (2009). Social presence and online learning: A current view from a research perspective. *Journal of Interactive Online Learning, 8*(3), 241–254.

Collini, S. (2012). *What Are Universities For?* London, UK: Penguin.

Costello, E. (2013). Opening up to open source: looking at how Moodle was adopted in higher education. *Open Learning: The Journal of Open, Distance and e-Learning, 28*(3), 187–200.

Cutri, R. M. & Mena, J. (2020). A critical reconceptualization of faculty readiness for online teaching. *Distance Education, 41*(3), 361–380.

Dochy, F. J. R. C., Segers, M., & Sluijsmans, D. (1999). The use of self-, peer- and co-assessment in higher education: a review. *Studies in Higher Education, 24*(3), 331–350.

Ferman, T. (2002). Academic professional development practice: What lecturers find valuable. *The International Journal for Academic Development, 7*(2), 146–158.

Feynman, R. P. & Leighton, R. (1985). *'Surely You're Joking, Mr. Feynman!': Adventures of a Curious Character*. London: Random House.

Fink, L. D. (2013). *Creating Significant Learning Experiences: An Integrated Approach to Designing College Courses*. San Francisco, CA: John Wiley & Sons.

Fry, H., Ketteridge, S., & Marshall, S. (2009). *A Handbook for Teaching and Learning in Higher Education: Enhancing Academic Practice* (3rd edn). New York, NY: Routledge.

Fulton, K. (2012). Upside down and inside out: flip your classroom to improve student learning. *Learning & Leading with Technology, 39*(8), 12–17.

Gibbs, G. & Coffey, M. (2004). The impact of training of university teachers on their teaching skills, their approach to teaching and the approach to learning of their students. *Active Learning in Higher Education, 5*(1), 87–100.

Goode, D. (1976). The noblest profession in the world. *Improving College and University Teaching, 24*(4), 195.

Griffiths, R. (2004). Knowledge production and the research–teaching nexus: the case of the built environment disciplines. *Studies in Higher Education, 29*(6), 709–726.

Hall, C. (1996). Key teaching roles of a university lecturer and their integration into the quality systems of a New Zealand university. *Assessment & Evaluation in Higher Education, 21*(2), 109–120.

Healey, M. (2005). Linking research and teaching to benefit student learning. *Journal of Geography in Higher Education, 29*(2), 183–201.

Heaton-Shrestha, C., Gipps, C., Edirisingha, P., & Linsey, T. (2007). Learning and e-learning in HE: the relationship between student learning style and VLE use. *Research Papers in Education, 22*(4), 443–464.

Heinze, T. & Knill, C. (2008). Analysing the differential impact of the Bologna Process: theoretical considerations on national conditions for international policy convergence. *Higher Education, 56*(4), 493–510.

Heirdsfield, A., Walker, S., Tambyah, M., & Beutel, D. (2011). Blackboard as an online learning environment: what do teacher education students and staff think? *Australian Journal of Teacher Education, 36*(7), 1–16.

Herreid, C. F. & Schiller, N. A. (2013). Case studies and the flipped classroom. *Journal of College Science Teaching, 42*(5), 62–66.

Hofer, S. I., Nistor, N., & Scheibenzuber, C. (2021). Online teaching and learning in higher education: lessons learned in crisis situations. *Computers in Human Behavior, 121*(106789), 1–10.

Hubball, H. & Burt, H. (2004). An integrated approach to developing and implementing learning-centred curricula. *International Journal for Academic Development, 9*(1), 51–65.

Hughes, H. W., Kooy, M., & Kanevsky, L. (1997). Dialogic reflection and journaling. *The Clearing House: A Journal of Educational Strategies, Issues and Ideas, 70*(4), 187–190.

Johnson, H. & Carruthers, L. (2006). Supporting creative and reflective processes. *International Journal of Human-Computer Studies, 64*(10), 998–1030.

Kappers, W. M. & Cutler, S. L. (2015). Poll everywhere! even in the Classroom: an investigation into the impact of using Poll Everywhere in a large-lecture classroom. *Computers in Education Journal, 6*(20), 140–145.

Kay, R. H. & LeSage, A. (2009). Examining the benefits and challenges of using audience response systems: a review of the literature. *Computers & Education, 53*(3), 819–827.

Kearns, L. R. (2012). Student assessment in online learning: challenges and effective practices. *Journal of Online Learning and Teaching, 8*(3), 198–208.

Knight, P. (2006). The local practices of assessment. *Assessment & Evaluation in Higher Education, 31*(4), 435–452.

Lam, R. (2016). Assessment as learning: examining a cycle of teaching, learning, and assessment of writing in the portfolio-based classroom. *Studies in Higher Education*, *41*(11), 1900–1917.

Lang, J. M. (2016). *Small Teaching: Everyday Lessons from the Science of Learning*. San Francisco, CA: John Wiley & Sons.

Lueddeke, G. R. (1999). Toward a constructivist framework for guiding change and innovation in higher education. *The Journal of Higher Education*, *70*(3), 235–260.

Mahmood, S. (2021). Instructional strategies for online teaching in COVID-19 pandemic. *Human Behavior and Emerging Technologies*, *3*(1), 199–203.

McKeachie, W. & Svinicki, M. (2014). *Mckeachie's Teaching Tips: Strategies, Research, and Theory for College and University Teachers* (14th edn). Belmont, CA: Wadsworth Cengage Learning.

Mishra, L., Gupta, T., & Shree, A. (2020). Online teaching-learning in higher education during lockdown period of COVID-19 pandemic. *International Journal of Educational Research Open*, *1*(100012), 1–8.

Mok, K. H. & Neubauer, D. (2016). Higher education governance in crisis: a critical reflection on the massification of higher education, graduate employment and social mobility. *Journal of Education and Work*, *29*(1), 1–12.

Morss, K. & Murray, R. (2005). *Teaching at University: A Guide for Postgraduates and Researchers*. London, UK: SAGE.

Norton, L., Norton, B., & Shannon, L. (2013). Revitalising assessment design: what is holding new lecturers back? *Higher Education*, *66*(2), 233–251.

O'Flaherty, J. & Phillips, C. (2015). The use of flipped classrooms in higher education: a scoping review. *The Internet and Higher Education*, *25*(1), 85–95.

Otter, S. (1992). *Learning Outcomes in Higher Education: A Development Project Report*. London, UK: Unit for the Development of Adult Continuing Education.

Park, C. & Kim, D. G. (2020). Exploring the roles of social presence and gender difference in online learning. *Decision Sciences Journal of Innovative Education*, *18*(2), 291–312.

Petrie, H. G. (1990). Reflecting on the second wave of reform: restructuring the teaching profession. In S. L. Jacobson & J. A. Conway (Eds.), *Educational Leadership in an Age of Reform* (pp. 14–29). New York: Longman.

Postareff, L., Lindblom-Ylänne, S., & Nevgi, A. (2007). The effect of pedagogical training on teaching in higher education. *Teaching and Teacher Education*, *23*(5), 557–571.

Ramsden, P. (2003). *Learning to Teach in Higher Education* (2nd edn). New York, NY: Routledge.

Rapanta, C., Botturi, L., Goodyear, P., Guàrdia, L., & Koole, M. (2020). Online university teaching during and after the Covid-19 crisis: refocusing teacher presence and learning activity. *Postdigital Science and Education*, *2*(3), 923–945.

Roche, J., Cullen, R. J., & Ball, S. L. (2016a). The educational opportunity of a modern science show. *International Journal of Science in Society*, *8*(3), 21–30.

Roche, J., Stanley, J., & Davis, N. (2016b). Engagement with physics across diverse festival audiences. *Physics Education*, *51*(4), 1–6.

Sadler, T. D., Amirshokoohi, A., Kazempour, M., & Allspaw, K. M. (2006). Socioscience and ethics in science classrooms: Teacher perspectives and strategies. *Journal of Research in Science Teaching*, 43(4), 353–376.

Scales, P. (2017). *An Introduction to Learning and Teaching in Higher Education: Supporting Fellowship*. London, UK: Open University Press.

Schönwetter, D. J., Sokal, L., Friesen, M., & Taylor, K. L. (2002). Teaching philosophies reconsidered: a conceptual model for the development and evaluation of teaching philosophy statements. *International Journal for Academic Development*, 7(1), 83–97.

Shon, H. & Smith, L. (2011). A review of Poll Everywhere audience response system. *Journal of Technology in Human Services*, 29(3), 236–245.

Stevens, D. D. & Levi, A. J. (2005). *Introduction to Rubrics: An Assessment Tool to Save Grading Time, Convey Effective Feedback, and Promote Student Learning*. Sterling, VA: Stylus Publishing.

Stowell, J. R. (2015). Use of clickers vs. mobile devices for classroom polling. *Computers & Education*, 82, 329–334.

Sunal, D. W., Hodges, J., Sunal, C. S., Whitaker, K. W., Freeman, L. M., Edwards, L.,... & Odell, M. (2001). Teaching science in higher education: faculty professional development and barriers to change. *School Science and Mathematics*, 101(5), 246–257.

Tong, V. C. H., Standen, A., & Sotiriou, M. (2018). *Shaping Higher Education with Students: Ways to Connect Research and Teaching*. London, UK: UCL Press.

Van Dijk, J. A. (2006). Digital divide research, achievements and shortcomings. *Poetics*, 34(4–5), 221–235.

Watts, J. & Robertson, N. (2011). Burnout in university teaching staff: a systematic literature review. *Educational Research*, 53(1), 33–50.

Yorke, M. (2003). Formative assessment in higher education: moves towards theory and the enhancement of pedagogic practice. *Higher Education*, 45(4), 477–501.

Seven

Supervision

In this chapter, we will cover:

- doctoral research supervision
- finding and communicating with a supervisor
- maintaining effective supervisory relationships
- planning and monitoring progress
- the value of gaining supervision experience.

The supervisory relationship

The relationships we build and maintain with supervisors can have far-reaching effects on our careers and professional development. Good supervision can help early career researchers achieve their full academic potential, while a poor supervisory relationship can have a detrimental effect on career progression and personal wellbeing. In this chapter, we will explore research supervision, especially doctoral research, and how to find potential supervisors. We will see the importance of planning and monitoring progress, and how to establish a productive supervisory relationship. Finally, we will consider the benefits of gaining experience as a supervisor and understanding the different perspectives of the supervisor and supervisee.

Doctoral supervision

Doctoral study in medieval universities was initially a process that qualified individuals to teach medicine, theology, or law. In the early nineteenth century, the philosopher and linguist Wilhelm Von Humboldt restructured the University of Berlin to become a research-led institution. The resulting Humboldtian doctoral degree became the first that focused on contributing new knowledge and understanding to a field of study. The new doctorate was open to research in any discipline, and became an award in 'the mother of all sciences' – philosophy – and was renamed as the DPhil and, subsequently, the PhD (Eley and Murray, 2009; Taylor et al., 2019).

In the nineteenth century, as PhD programmes were slowly introduced in other countries, Harvard and Yale were among the first universities to award research doctorates in the US. The advent of the First World War – and the perceived German advantage of doctoral-trained scientists – accelerated the spread of PhD programmes in the twentieth century to the point where doctoral study is now offered in many universities around the world (Wellington, 2013; Taylor et al., 2019). A PhD still constitutes the degree of 'Doctor of Philosophy' and remains one of the foremost internationally recognised research degrees (Bernstein et al., 2014).

The PhD supervisory relationship is the most formative academic relationship that an early career researcher can experience. For at least three years, a PhD supervisor serves as a guide through the critical early years of an academic research career. The supervisor in doctoral study, also referred to as an 'advisor' in some contexts (Lee, 2020), is the person, usually a more senior academic staff member, responsible for providing academic support and guidance to the supervisee (Wellington, 2010). The objective of the PhD process itself is for the student (or 'candidate') to successfully demonstrate that they have acquired the skills to conduct independent research (Rugg and Petre, 2020). Even among supervisors, however, there are differing views on the true purpose of doctoral education – from knowledge generation and skills development to academic and professional recognition (Loxley and Kearns, 2018).

Doctoral students often begin their research knowing very little about what the supervision process entails (Pole et al., 1997) and building a constructive supervisory relationship can be critical to doctoral success (Matthiesen, 2009). A strong relationship improves the likelihood of researchers completing their doctoral studies, which cannot be taken for granted considering the completion rate in Western countries can be below 60% (Ruud et al., 2018). There are many ways that poor supervision can contribute to this rate of attrition, with ethical issues (Löfström and Pyhältö, 2014), bullying (Morris, 2011), and harassment (Lee, 1998) common symptoms of problematic supervisory relationships.

Doctoral supervision has long been considered 'the most advanced level of teaching in our education system' (Connell, 1985, p. 38). An abiding issue for supervisors, however, is that they are often expected to fit doctoral supervision into their schedule for research, rather than having it formally recognised as part of their teaching schedule. The self-esteem of supervisors, and even their status within their department, can be affected by the performance of their PhD students, while the challenges they face in the supervisory relationship 'span a spectrum from the minor and episodic to the habitual and extreme' (Hockey, 1996, p. 368). The role of doctoral supervision is becoming increasingly complex (Bøgelund, 2015), and it can help to remember that, despite appearances, the supervisory relationship can be as important to the supervisor as it is to the supervisee. Maintaining a supervisory relationship requires careful deliberation from both sides.

Researcher views

Anne, on how researchers can have very different experiences with the same supervisor:

> I had an incredible relationship with my supervisor. My mate in the lab, my friend, had a terrible relationship with him. And this is the same supervisor. I had all the support from him. And it wasn't because he favoured a particular person, it just goes back to how you handle things […] I had no problem with somebody being hands-on when it came to my PhD.

(Continued)

Some people don't like it. Some people think, okay, now, I'm doing a PhD, that's my own thing, you're only there to oversee everything. He was completely hands-on, but for me, it worked out very well. So it really depends on the person.

Establishing clear communication

For some research projects, especially during undergraduate or Master's degrees, a supervisor might be assigned without the student having much say in the matter. When it comes to doctoral and postdoctoral research, however, the candidate should seize the initiative to contact potential supervisors themselves. Following the same approach used to identify academic mentors (described in Chapter 5), compile an email list of possible supervisors who broadly share your research interests and who have good track records in publishing and successful supervision. If you feel you have not had enough research experience to be sure of your specific research interests, then focus on the topics or subjects you most enjoyed during your studies up to that point.

Senior academics receive many requests from prospective candidates, so tailor each email to the specific research area of the potential supervisor you are contacting. The email should be clear, concise, and convey that you have the right attitude to thrive in their research group. Highlight your qualifications and any potential scholarships or research grants that are open to you. Early in your research career it is acceptable to describe your ideas for potential research projects in basic terms, but make your enthusiasm for research evident, and as you gain more experience, you might consider including a proposal or a research plan (discussed further in Chapter 11). A sample email template is available on this book's companion website to help you get started.

The decision to supervise a student, especially a doctoral student, will not be made lightly by any academic researcher. Often, 'supervisors need training in how to give pastoral support to their PhD students' (Hockey, 1995, p. 208), and they may not always feel equipped to deal with the challenges their students face (Hockey, 1991; Abiddin et al., 2009). Establishing a clear understanding of each other's roles is key to any successful supervisory relationship. A valuable exercise to ensure the relationship is built on mutual understanding is for the supervisor and supervisee to spend some time discussing their perceptions and expectations of their respective roles (Malfroy, 2005). A common approach is to independently adjudge who has more responsibility when it comes to selecting research topics, testing theories, designing experiments, arranging meetings, drafting and editing text, and ensuring quality (Brown and Atkins, 2002). In such an exercise, both parties complete their assessments separately and then meet to compare their answers. There will likely be differences in expectations, but confronting those differences at the start of the supervisory process will help foster an understanding of each other's perspectives.

One of the most difficult things to come to terms with in doctoral research is that there will always be some level of uncertainty. This uncertainty stems from the need to have freedom to take your research in new directions based on your evolving interpretation of the area, topic, and research questions. It can be tempting to make decisions on every aspect of the research straight away, but this can hinder your long-term progress rather than simplifying it. The role of the supervisor is to support you in finding your way to the most appropriate topics or questions, without pushing you in a specific direction or overly constraining your options. If key aspects of your PhD remain undefined after months of research, then your supervisor will help you make those decisions. Doctoral research has no fixed curriculum; communication between student and supervisor is vital for keeping track of what progress is being made and what milestones are being reached on the research journey.

You might not hear from your supervisor every day or every week, but they will advise you at critical junctures. If you are undertaking experiments or fieldwork, they will help you to develop the expertise necessary to become an independent researcher, so that you will eventually no longer need their guidance (Lovitts, 2008). Their support will be integral in helping you write up your results and submit them for publication (although Chapter 3 and Chapter 4 of this book will ensure you are not overly dependent on your supervisor in this regard). Most importantly, your supervisor will reassure you, monitor your progress, and keep you focused on completing your studies.

Researcher views

Lilly, on communicating with her supervisor:

> She can be very available when I ask her to be. But if I don't ask her to be, which sometimes I don't because I like to procrastinate, then if I send her an email, she doesn't reply for a month. I just don't chase her. When I chase her, she does reply. But she keeps telling me that I need to nag her and we just get stuck in this cycle of procrastination, nagging, not feeling like I'm being pushed enough. The quality of the connection is good, but the frequency is not very... desirable.

Managing the relationship

There are many ways to approach supervision, with different styles being necessary for different individuals at different times (Whitelock et al., 2008; Lee, 2020; Gruzdev et al., 2020). Supervisory styles range from being formal to casual, and these styles affect the social dynamic and trust between the supervisor and student (Rapoport et al., 1989; Boehe, 2016). In a supervisory relationship following a pattern of informality, meetings can be held in a relaxed fashion with all schedules and tasks agreed orally. Such an approach can reduce power dynamics, and put both student and supervisor on an equal playing field. This kind of 'supervision over coffee' (Hemer, 2012, p. 837) can help maintain a productive supervisory relationship, especially in the early stages. When challenges arise, however, a supervisory relationship might need to move into a more formal and professional pattern. This may involve creating a clear plan with a schedule of meetings, mutually endorsed, in a written agreement (Hockey, 1996). A sample schedule of meetings is available on this book's companion website and could include:

- The date, time, duration, frequency, venue, and format of the meetings.
- The records that will be kept; both parties might take notes during the meeting with an agreement that the student summarises the main points after the meeting and sends them to the supervisor. The supervisor will likely also keep a record of the meetings, to consult as needed.
- How any follow-up actions from the meeting will be implemented and monitored.
- An agreement about the responsibilities of the student and supervisor, including what the student needs to provide before the meetings, and what level of feedback the supervisor will contribute.
- A strategy for amending the agreed schedule of meetings if either party feels it is not working.

Having an agreed schedule of meetings is a good step towards maintaining a productive supervisory relationship, but the research journey will remain unpredictable. The relationship can be particularly complicated for those undertaking professional or part-time doctoral study (Evans, 2002), or non-traditional routes to obtaining their doctorates (Archbald, 2011; Alebaikan et al., 2020). One option to strengthen the supervisory support available is to enquire about the possibility of co-supervision, either at the outset, or if things become challenging along the way. It is increasingly common for PhD students to have co-supervisors (occasionally from different institutions), or sometimes a panel of supervisors, so that they can benefit from complementary styles of supervision (Douglas, 2003; Cornér et al., 2017). Although it can be frustrating if their individual advice is contradictory, having multiple supervisory opinions can help you choose the right time to conclude your research. One of the most important things to keep in mind is that it is unlikely to be a flawless or definitive piece of work, so finding ways to measure progress is crucial.

Researcher views

Reese, on having more than one supervisor:

It can be really beneficial in a lot of ways. And I think it was definitely beneficial for my PhD. Did it cause me more stress and anxiety? 100%.

A sensible method for keeping track of progress, as well as safeguarding the sanity of both the supervisor and the supervisee, is to map out a timeline for your research. There are 'very few tools to assist in doctoral supervision', which is why a timeline, when designed and implemented correctly, can be so powerful (Maxwell and Smyth, 2010, p. 421). The timeline can take many shapes, and should be adapted to a form that you find most effective. Using that timeline, you can plan how you will complete the necessary tasks and reach key milestones, such as completing data collection, publishing results, or preparing for the *PhD Viva* – an oral examination to assess the standard of the final doctoral work submitted (Share, 2016; Hodgson, 2020). A sample research timeline is available on this book's companion website.

Throughout your research journey, your supervisor will strive to help you become an independent and self-directed researcher (Gurr, 2001). They will be both your supporter and your critic – a person who will give you advice and guidance when you need direction, but who will also offer a critical consideration of your work (Manathunga, 2005b). Even when a supervisory relationship is built on solid foundations of open and honest communication, challenges can still emerge. As well as unforeseen changes in personal circumstances, the most common issues that arise are difficulties with the research itself, struggles with adapting to the research culture, or failing to work effectively with a supervisor (Manathunga, 2005a). Doctoral supervision, due to its duration, is more likely to be strained by the 'asymmetries of power inherent in postgraduate supervision' (Manathunga, 2007, p. 219).

Your supervisor should be able to steer you around most obstacles, but if issues arise relating to the supervisory relationship itself, you need not rely solely on their guidance. Doctoral research can be a more rewarding process when it is a social practice that incorporates the advice and encouragement of others (Kamler and Thomson, 2014). Asking for help is a necessary part of any research journey. Determine all the supports open to you, from graduate studies offices and student societies to individual staff members and fellow researchers in your department. Everyone has a unique experience of supervisory relationships, but no matter what kind of testing situation you encounter, it is almost certain that others have faced similar situations.

Being honest with yourself and your supervisor is key to sustaining a healthy and productive supervisory relationship. If the supervisory relationship is dysfunctional, and you have exhausted all options to improve or change things – including talking to your supervisor directly about any issues that have arisen (Kearns and Gardiner, 2011) – you have more drastic courses of action open to you. You can contact the coordinator of the PhD programme to seek a change of supervisor, or to seek permission to conclude your work without a supervisor. While not an ideal situation to be in, it is not unusual. Although academic job applications usually request a reference from a former supervisor (or co-supervisor), an alternative can usually be found. Not every supervisory relationship is constructive, and ending a relationship that is no longer functioning may be a necessary last resort.

Researcher views

Sarah, on being consoled by her supervisor after getting negative feedback for a paper:

> That was definitely the highlight of my 1,050 years doing this PhD. My supervisor, she's quite strict and she's a statistician. She's like your stereotypical statistician, emotionally as well, in terms of, you know, hugging students and stuff. And I remember how nice she was to me. She tried to comfort me saying *this is okay* and *this happens all the time* [...] It was actually a big deal because she went outside of her comfortable zone to make me feel okay.

Acquiring supervision skills

As your research journey continues, you could find yourself being called upon to supervise undergraduate projects, internships, summer students, Master's students, and eventually your own PhD students and postdoctoral researchers (Armstrong and Shanker, 1983; Shaw et al., 2013). The best way to acquire the skill of supervision is through gaining first-hand experience. Not only is supervision itself a valuable academic skill to develop, but being a supervisor will enable you to see the supervisory relationship from both perspectives and may even help you discover empathy for your own supervisor.

If you are delegated supervisory responsibilities, immerse yourself in the role and be aware of the impact a supervisor can have on students' experience of academic research. If it is their first time carrying out research, plan on having regular meetings to help them understand their research timeline and the work expected of them. Ask them to prepare a meeting agenda (that includes their questions and ideas) to share with you before the meetings, and during the meetings give them the opportunity to explain their understanding of what progress has been made and what they think the next steps should be. Novice researchers may need support developing confidence in their abilities (Greener, 2020), particularly when it comes to assimilating academic texts (Hubbard and Dunbar, 2017). Assign your students only one or two papers to read at a time and request short, structured summaries to prompt them to take notes as they read. This will also help them to start thinking about their academic writing (Chapter 3), especially if you provide them with sample theses or dissertations to illustrate the standards expected of them.

Researcher views

Celeste, on her first experience of being a supervisor, which involved supervising an undergraduate student's research project while Celeste was working on her PhD:

> I had no idea what I was doing. But she didn't know that. We got through it in the end anyway and [she] is doing a PhD herself now, so it probably wasn't so bad.

As you are supervising students, reflect on the strengths and weaknesses of the relationship you have with your own supervisor. What kind of feedback do you find most useful? How are you affected by their praise or constructive criticism? Do you prefer when you have a scheduled time to meet so that you can prepare, or do you secretly crave the pressure of dealing with 'the unannounced drop-in'? When you are planning meetings with your students, ask them to meet you in your office, in your lab, in a meeting room, in a cafe, or in a virtual meeting room. Only as a last resort should you meet them in their workspace, and if you do, make it clear when you will be making your appearance. Even if you adopt an informal and casual style of supervision, your students will prefer to have prior notice of when they will see you. People often work better when they feel relaxed, and having constant anxiety that a supervisor may appear at any moment does not create ideal working conditions (Wisker, 2012; Barry et al., 2018).

If you are tasked with supervising doctoral students, the stakes become higher, and you should do everything you can to continue improving your supervision skills. When your students are working hard, make sure to commend their efforts when they are thriving, and doubly so if they are struggling. Praise is hard to come by in academia, and we should embrace opportunities for feedback to encourage our students to fulfil their academic potential (Wang and Li, 2011). If they succeed in publishing a paper or winning a research grant, then we should applaud their work, and use it as an opportunity to challenge them to set more ambitious goals. The best supervisors expect their students (and themselves) to continuously adjust their expectations towards higher levels of academic achievement. Unsurprisingly, the biggest influence on shaping the supervisor we become is how we were ourselves supervised (Doloriert et al., 2012; Stephens, 2014). A good way to be conscious of that process is to regularly reflect on our supervision and document how we experience transitioning from the role of supervisee to that of a supervisor (Halse, 2011; Prendergast, 2016). Such documented experiences can be invaluable for other supervisors to reflect on their own practice.

Summary

- Find the right supervisor. Explore the options open to you and tailor your enquiries to the specific context of each potential supervisor you contact.
- Strive for clear communication. A strong supervisory relationship is built on regular, open, and honest communication.
- Manage the supervisory relationship. Use an agreed schedule of meetings with an indicative timeline of milestones to keep an overview of the progress being made.
- Seek advice. As you encounter challenges, discuss them with your supervisor and utilise the support systems available to you.
- Seize opportunities to supervise. As well as developing skills in guidance and management, supervising students will help you better understand your own supervisor's perspective.

Research supervision is one of the most important and demanding academic roles and can have career-long impacts on both supervisor and supervisee. Maintaining a strong supervisory relationship is not without its challenges, but with careful consideration from both sides, a productive, healthy, and ultimately successful relationship is within reach for all of us. To give ourselves the best chance of a positive relationship, we should commit to mutually agreed approaches to communication and planning. Gaining experience from supervising students ourselves, can help us empathise with our supervisors. Having covered the most intense and specific academic relationship, we can now turn our attention to broader forms of communication. In the next chapter, we will explore how to connect with different audiences.

Further reading

- Kamler, B. & Thomson, P. (2014). *Helping Doctoral Students Write: Pedagogies for Supervision*. New York, NY: Routledge.

This book combines research and writing as inextricably linked elements in successful supervision.

- Lee, A. (2020). *Successful Research Supervision: Advising Students Doing Research* (2nd edn). New York, NY: Routledge.

Drawing on a research study on effective supervision, this book details different approaches to supervision that can be adapted and combined.

- Matthiesen, J. (2009). *How to Survive Your Doctorate: What Others Don't Tell You*. London, UK: McGraw-Hill Education.

Written for doctoral students, this book is informed by student experience through illustrative case studies.

- Taylor, S., Kiley, M., & Humphrey, R. (2019). *A Handbook for Doctoral Supervisors* (2nd edn). New York, NY: Routledge.

This book provides invaluable context for the evolving role of the doctoral supervisor.

- Wellington, J. J. (2010). *Making Supervision Work for You: A Student's Guide*. London, UK: SAGE.

A guide for students that covers the main aspects of supervised research and how to maintain an effective supervisory relationship.

Resources

Further resources for this chapter can be found at: www.JosephRoche.ie/EssentialSkills

- Email to Potential Supervisor Template
- Agreed Schedule of Meetings Template
- Draft Research Timeline Template

References

Abiddin, N. Z., Hassan, A., & Ahmad, A. R. (2009). Research student supervision: an approach to good supervisory practice. *The Open Education Journal, 2*(1), 11–16.

Alebaikan, R., Bain, Y., & Cornelius, S. (2020). Experiences of distance doctoral supervision in cross-cultural teams. *Teaching in Higher Education,* 1–18.

Archbald, D. (2011). The emergence of the nontraditional doctorate: an historical overview. *New Directions for Adult and Continuing Education, 129,* 7–19.

Armstrong, M. & Shanker, V. (1983). The supervision of undergraduate research: student perceptions of the supervisor role. *Studies in Higher Education, 8*(2), 177–183.

Barry, K. M., Woods, M., Warnecke, E., Stirling, C., & Martin, A. (2018). Psychological health of doctoral candidates, study-related challenges and perceived performance. *Higher Education Research & Development, 37*(3), 468–483.

Bernstein, B. L., Evans, B., Fyffe, J., Halai, N., Hall, F. L., Jensen, H. S., ... & Ortega, S. (2014). The continuing evolution of the research doctorate. In M. Nerad & B. Evans (Eds.), *Globalization and its Impacts on the Quality of PhD Education* (pp. 5–30). Rotterdam, The Netherlands: Sense Publishers.

Boehe, D. M. (2016). Supervisory styles: a contingency framework. *Studies in Higher Education, 41*(3), 399–414.

Bøgelund, P. (2015). How supervisors perceive PhD supervision – and how they practice it. *International Journal of Doctoral Studies, 10*(1), 39–55.

Brown, G. & Atkins, M. (2002). *Effective Teaching in Higher Education.* New York, NY: Routledge.

Connell, R. W. (1985). How to supervise a PhD. *Vestes, 28*(2), 38–42.

Cornér, S., Löfström, E., & Pyhältö, K. (2017). The relationships between doctoral students' perceptions of supervision and burnout. *International Journal of Doctoral Studies, 12,* 91–106.

Doloriert, C., Sambrook, S., & Stewart, J. (2012). Power and emotion in doctoral supervision: implications for HRD. *European Journal of Training and Development, 36*(7), 732–750.

Douglas, D. (2003). Reflections on research supervision: a grounded theory case of reflective practice. *Research in Post-Compulsory Education, 8*(2), 213–230.

Eley, A. & Murray, R. (2009). *How to be an Effective Supervisor: Best Practice in Research Student Supervision.* London, UK: McGraw-Hill Education.

Evans, T. (2002). Part-time research students: are they producing knowledge where it counts? *Higher Education Research & Development, 21*(2), 155–165.

Greener, S. (2020). The novice researcher. *European Journal of Hospital Pharmacy, 27*(6), 321–322.

Gruzdev, I., Terentev, E., & Dzhafarova, Z. (2020). Superhero or hands-off supervisor? An empirical categorization of PhD supervision styles and student satisfaction in Russian universities. *Higher Education, 79*(5), 773–789.

Gurr, G. M. (2001). Negotiating the 'Rackety Bridge' – a dynamic model for aligning supervisory style with research student development. *Higher Education Research & Development, 20*(1), 81–92.

Halse, C. (2011). 'Becoming a supervisor': the impact of doctoral supervision on supervisors' learning. *Studies in Higher Education*, *36*(5), 557–570.

Hemer, S. R. (2012). Informality, power and relationships in postgraduate supervision: supervising PhD candidates over coffee. *Higher Education Research & Development*, *31*(6), 827–839.

Hockey, J. (1991). The social science PhD: a literature review. *Studies in Higher Education*, *16*(3), 319–332.

Hockey, J. (1995). Getting too close: a problem and possible solution in social science PhD supervision. *British Journal of Guidance & Counselling*, *23*(2), 199–210.

Hockey, J. (1996). A contractual solution to problems in the supervision of PhD degrees in the UK. *Studies in Higher Education*, *21*(3), 359–371.

Hodgson, D. (2020). Helping doctoral students understand PhD thesis examination expectations: a framework and a tool for supervision. *Active Learning in Higher Education, 21*(1), 51–63.

Hubbard, K. E. & Dunbar, S. D. (2017). Perceptions of scientific research literature and strategies for reading papers depend on academic career stage. *PloS One, 12*(12), e0189753, 1–16.

Kamler, B. & Thomson, P. (2014). *Helping Doctoral Students Write: Pedagogies for Supervision*. New York, NY: Routledge.

Kearns, H. & Gardiner, M. (2011). The care and maintenance of your adviser. *Nature, 469*(7331), 570.

Lee, A. (2020). *Successful Research Supervision: Advising Students Doing Research* (2nd edn). New York, NY: Routledge.

Lee, D. (1998). Sexual harassment in PhD supervision. *Gender and Education, 10*(3), 299–312.

Löfström, E. & Pyhältö, K. (2014). Ethical issues in doctoral supervision: the perspectives of PhD students in the natural and behavioral sciences. *Ethics & Behavior, 24*(3), 195–214.

Lovitts, B. E. (2008). The transition to independent research: who makes it, who doesn't, and why. *The Journal of Higher Education, 79*(3), 296–325.

Loxley, A. & Kearns, M. (2018). Finding a purpose for the doctorate? A view from the supervisors. *Studies in Higher Education, 43*(5), 826–840.

Malfroy, J. (2005). Doctoral supervision, workplace research and changing pedagogic practices. *Higher Education Research & Development, 24*(2), 165–178.

Manathunga, C. (2005a). Early warning signs in postgraduate research education: a different approach to ensuring timely completions. *Teaching in Higher Education, 10*(2), 219–233.

Manathunga, C. (2005b). The development of research supervision: 'turning the light on a private space'. *International Journal for Academic Development, 10*(1), 17–30.

Manathunga, C. (2007). Supervision as mentoring: the role of power and boundary crossing. *Studies in Continuing Education, 29*(2), 207–221.

Matthiesen, J. (2009). *How to Survive Your Doctorate: What Others Don't Tell You*. London, UK: McGraw-Hill Education.

Maxwell, T. W. & Smyth, R. (2010). Research supervision: the research management matrix. *Higher Education, 59*(4), 407–422.

Morris, S. E. (2011). Doctoral students' experiences of supervisory bullying. *Pertanika Journal of Social Sciences and Humanities, 19*(2), 547–555.

Pole, C. J., Sprokkereef, A., Burgess, R. G., & Lakin, E. (1997). Supervision of doctoral students in the natural sciences: expectations and experiences. *Assessment & Evaluation in Higher Education, 22*(1), 49–63.

Prendergast, M. (2016). The pursuit of 'balance' by a greenhorn supervisor. *International Journal of Learning, Teaching, and Educational Research, 15*(8), 14–22.

Rapoport, T., Yair, G., & Kahane, R. (1989). Tutorial relations – the dynamics of social contract and personal trust. *Interchange, 20*(1), 14–26.

Rugg, G. & Petre, M. (2020). *The Unwritten Rules of PhD Research* (3rd edn). London, UK: Open University Press.

Ruud, C. M., Saclarides, E. S., George-Jackson, C. E., & Lubienski, S. T. (2018). Tipping points: doctoral students and consideration of departure. *Journal of College Student Retention: Research, Theory & Practice, 20*(3), 286–307.

Share, M. (2016). The PhD viva: a space for academic development. *International Journal for Academic Development, 21*(3), 178–193.

Shaw, K., Holbrook, A., & Bourke, S. (2013). Student experience of final-year undergraduate research projects: an exploration of 'research preparedness'. *Studies in Higher Education, 38*(5), 711–727.

Stephens, S. (2014). The supervised as the supervisor. *Education + Training, 56*(6), 537–550.

Taylor, S., Kiley, M., & Humphrey, R. (2019). *A Handbook for Doctoral Supervisors* (2nd edn). New York, NY: Routledge.

Wang, T. & Li, L. Y. (2011). 'Tell me what to do' vs.'guide me through it': feedback experiences of international doctoral students. *Active Learning in Higher Education, 12*(2), 101–112.

Wellington, J. J. (2010). *Making Supervision Work for You: A Student's Guide*. London, UK: SAGE.

Wellington, J. (2013). Searching for 'doctorateness'. *Studies in Higher Education, 38*(10), 1490–1503.

Whitelock, D., Faulkner, D., & Miell, D. (2008). Promoting creativity in PhD supervision: tensions and dilemmas. *Thinking Skills and Creativity, 3*(2), 143–153.

Wisker, G. (2012). *The Good Supervisor: Supervising Postgraduate and Undergraduate Research for Doctoral Theses and Dissertations* (2nd edn). London, UK: Macmillan International Higher Education.

Eight
Communication and Engagement

In this chapter, we will cover:

- research impact and types of communication
- presentation styles
- legacy media
- social media
- participatory engagement and citizen science.

Finding our voice

Publishing and teaching are fundamental to being an academic researcher, but communicating our work more broadly to public audiences requires a complementary set of skills. In this chapter, we will consider public engagement and the importance of developing different styles of communication for legacy media and social media. We will also appraise the participatory forms of engagement that are becoming central to the social responsibilities of researchers.

Research impact and engaging public audiences

Our research is more likely to be seen, shared, and discussed when we improve how we communicate with public audiences. Developing complementary ways to share our work enhances our communication skills, which will have positive implications for our professional development (Chapters 10) and career progression (Chapter 11). Most institutions of higher education have mission statements that explicitly reference a responsibility to society to generate new knowledge for the greater good (Furco, 2010). This can take many forms, including community engagement, civic engagement, public service, or community service (Beere et al., 2011), extending even to activism and social justice (Overton et al., 2016; Mitchell and Soria, 2017). The responsibility to help society is entwined with how institutions of higher education gauge the impact of their research. Although there is debate over how to define research impact (Penfield et al., 2014), it usually involves cultural, political, scientific, or socioeconomic effects, and encompasses all the ways research can contribute to society outside of academic environments.

How institutions of higher education engage public audiences ranges from global communication plans to partnerships with local communities (Yamamura and Koth, 2018). Three of the most important approaches to communicating with public audiences are dissemination, conversation, and participation. Dissemination involves one-way forms of communication such as public lectures, press releases, as well as traditional media like radio, television, and newspapers. These can become two-way forms of communication when audiences have the chance to respond. Public engagement that involves academic researchers listening to their audiences and participating in some form of dialogue has become more feasible with the advent of social media, allowing academic researchers to interact directly with different audiences. The National Co-ordinating Centre for Public Engagement (NCCPE) in the UK describes public engagement as the way in which higher education institutions communicate education and research benefits with public audiences, and explicitly defines it as two-way communication that involves both sharing and listening (NCCPE, 2020). The most engaged form of communication, and sometimes the most challenging, is participation – where public audiences are not only listened to, but are empowered to contribute through co-creation, co-design, or other approaches that provide active roles in the research process.

The first thing to decide when communicating our work, is whether we know our audience. It is surprisingly common in academia for researchers to commit to public engagement without ever really understanding who their audience is, other than a nebulous notion of 'the general public'. At the very least, we should use plural terms like 'public audiences' or even 'publics' to acknowledge that there are different groups and communities we are hoping to engage. We cannot communicate with everyone using the same methods or expect each person to interact with our work in the same way, so having a target audience of 'the public' is not helpful. A better approach is to name the groups with whom we are hoping to connect. If we believe our work will be of interest to vaccine-hesitant single parents, then that is the group we should address in our public engagement work. If we are hoping our work will be of interest to inner-city school students between the ages of 8 and 12, then they are our audience, and not 'the general public'.

Other outdated terms to avoid include 'the lay person' as a way of describing someone outside of academia, or referring to public engagement work as 'outreach'. The term 'outreach' implies that communicating our research is a service we provide for people who are difficult to reach. Thinking of public audiences as being hard to reach is condescending because it suggests that they are somehow to blame for not knowing or caring about our work when, in reality, it is our responsibility to demonstrate why our research is worth caring about.

The 'deficit model' of communication is used to describe when researchers assume their role is to provide knowledge to public audiences whom they believe are *deficient* in knowledge (Trench, 2008). In disseminating our work, one-way modes of communication may occasionally be appropriate or unavoidable but, if possible, we should find ways to listen to our audiences. Learning how to connect and collaborate with different audiences results in valuable experiences and competencies, and fosters community engagement skills (Dostilio, 2017). Building on one-way dissemination approaches to communicating our work – by seeking opportunities for two-way dialogue and discussion – will help us to recognise the knowledge, experience, and expertise that public audiences can contribute to improving our research.

Researcher views

Genevieve, on communication and engagement during a PhD:

> I think there was a sentiment that it's good to do communication and engagement because grant applications want to know how you're going to communicate your findings to [*air quotes gesture*] *the public* [...] It wasn't that I was made to feel like it was a waste of my time, but there was a sense that sometimes academics are doing it as a tick-box exercise and not because of its inherent value. But I really enjoyed it. The experiences I had doing communication and public engagement events as a PhD student reminded me why I was interested in doing the PhD in the first place [...] The different perspectives that you get from talking to people who have completely different backgrounds and different experiences, those kinds of interactions really made me take a step back and be like *Yeah this subject is amazing. It's so fascinating. This is why I wanted to do this research. Because it's so cool.* And I found it very easy to forget that, when I was just in the lab all the time.

Communicating our work

Before exploring ways to facilitate discussion, dialogue, and participation, we should first be comfortable with the basics of communicating our research. Always have an 'elevator pitch' ready – a rehearsed statement that succinctly describes your research, in a few sentences, using accessible language (Palmer et al., 2019). Enlist friends and colleagues to listen to your elevator pitch and use their feedback to fine-tune a simple but engaging overview of your work. Your pitch should start with a sentence or two that introduces your area of research, leads into the main research questions, and finishes with why it is important. It should not trivialise your work, but it should use terms that are easy to understand. It should take less than 30 seconds to deliver, but will take much longer to prepare, practise, and refine. Sample research pitches are available on this book's companion website.

Once your elevator pitch is polished, you can expand each of the key points to become a five-minute talk to use whenever you are asked to describe your work in more detail. That can then be expanded further to become a public lecture (Chapter 6 describes the process of crafting and refining a robust lecture that can be presented at short notice). Unlike a lecture designed for your students, a public lecture needs to be self-contained – the audience should not require any background knowledge on the lecture topic. Rather than dealing with the constraints of how academic lectures fit into the broader learning outcomes and assessment of an academic course, public lectures allow more freedom to experiment with finding a style of communication that works best for a standalone presentation. If you are confident that your *back pocket guest lecture* (Chapter 6) is easy to understand, then it can serve as the basis for your public lecture.

Slides are not strictly necessary for public talks (or even for academic lectures), and they are one of the most abused presentation aids. When used appropriately, however, a strong slide deck can be indispensable. The slides should have as little text as possible so as not to be overly distracting (Collins, 2004), but can serve as visual cues or prompts as you speak. The audience's attention should primarily be on you and not the images on the screen. The notes under each slide (which the audience will not see when it is being presented) should contain all the information, sources, and references so that when you are preparing for your talk you can quickly refresh your memory about what you are going to say, even if you have not given the presentation for some time.

For academic lectures, you may choose to use slides that have one main point of information and a reference with an embedded link for additional reading, so that your students can use the slides (with additional lecture notes as needed) to help with their assignments and exam revision. For a public talk, you may prefer to have a single word, phrase, picture, or graphic per slide, to support each point you are making. It can be tempting to add cartoons or other mildly diverting material, but such content is not helpful in supporting learning, and simpler slides are more advisable (Mayer et al., 2008). Choose a font that is easy to read and looks professional. Never choose *Comic Sans* font unless the tone of your talk aligns with the character the font was originally designed for – *Microsoft Bob*, a digital talking dog tasked with helping children use computers (Beaumont-Thomas, 2017). Template slides for both academic lectures and public lectures are available on this book's companion website.

One of the most ubiquitous styles of presenting research to public audiences is the 'TED' approach – sharing ideas in short, intense presentations (Gallo, 2014). It is sometimes criticised for being a format that simplifies ideas to fit a preconceived structure (Romanelli et al., 2014), but the TED format is a globally recognised presentation style that is both engaging and entertaining. The temptation for some early career researchers is to copy the style of high-profile TED speakers. What connects the best talks, however, is not that the speakers all present in the same style, but that all of them have invested significant amounts of time practising and refining their talks. To make a talk look effortlessly relaxed and engaging requires hours of rehearsing, seeking feedback, and fine-tuning every detail of the presentation: 'the quality of speech performance correlated positively with [...] total preparation time, time spent preparing a visual aid, number of rehearsals for an audience, time rehearsing silently, time rehearsing out loud, number of rehearsals out loud, [...] and preparation of speaking notes' (Menzel and Carrell, 1994, p. 17).

Every public presentation deserves your best effort, but the amount of preparation time should increase in line with the size of the potential audience. Along with designing the structure of the talk, refining the content, and preparing slides, the preparation phase should be used to hone your presentation skills. Practise project-ing your voice as if you are speaking to the back row of the audience. Speak slower than you would normally, and be aware of your movements, especially hand gestures, which should be used sparingly to reinforce key points. Practice is a non-negotiable part of the process and should be harnessed to discover the style of communication that works best for you. Seek feedback and critique recordings of your practice pres-entations. You can adopt or mimic presentation styles you see in other presentations, but it is better for you and your audience if you develop a style that works for you. You do not need to look or sound like anyone else when presenting your work, you only need to find a presenting style that allows you to feel comfortable and confident.

Expect to feel nervous before speaking in front of public audiences (Holgate, 2011). It shows that you respect your audience and that your body is preparing you for the somewhat unnatural situation of having to perform in front of a crowd of expectant strangers. It becomes easier with experience, but rather than attempting to quell your nerves completely, it can be useful to expect or even welcome the adrenaline rush that comes with public speaking. Instead of trying to suppress what is a natural physiologi-cal response, it can help to recognise your increased heart-rate and the need for deeper breaths as theatrical cues – your body has started providing you with the boost you need to go present a wonderful talk.

Legacy media

Despite the arrival of two-way interactive communication facilitated by online media, legacy mass media such as newspapers, magazines, television, and radio are still promi-nent modes of communication (Christian, 2012; Langer and Gruber, 2021). As you become more established in your field of research, you will likely receive invitations to present public lectures (Gasman, 2016). You may be contacted by producers, journalists, or editors, who wish to ask you questions about your work or, more commonly, to ask you to comment on a news story where you can serve as an expert voice (LSE, 2014).

It can be daunting to discuss a topic that is outside your own research area, but you have the skills to quickly reach an appropriate level of understanding. It is entirely acceptable to inform a journalist that you are not immediately available to discuss a topic and that you need some time to be able to fully address the issue. If it is a promi-nent news story, there are probably already press releases you can digest to gain a gen-eral understanding before consulting academic sources (Arnold, 2003). Comparing press releases to the original published research can also be a helpful exercise in preparing to share your work with your own institution's communication team (Autzen, 2014).

Working with journalists can provide insight into mass media, and as you learn from your experiences, your goal should be to eventually pitch your own articles. Not only would this allow you to share your words with public audiences exactly as you would wish, but writing for different audiences can be highlighted on your resume or CV as evidence of your communication skills. If journalists or editors contact you seeking a comment about a topic that you have already written about for academic audiences, offer to write a new piece for them to consider for their publication. With print deadlines and time constraints being what they are (Fahy and Nisbet, 2011), some journalists may be keen to write the piece themselves. However, if there is a long lead-in time, and if they have a slate of other articles to work on in the meantime, it might suit them to have someone who knows the area write the first draft, saving them from having to research the topic themselves. Ensuring that the situation benefits all parties is key. If you are new to writing for public audiences and require a lot of editorial guidance to bring your writing up to the desired standard, then it might not suit the publishers. If you excel, however, and are offered a column or some form of regular writing engagement then you can discuss remuneration. This could pave the way for exploring further public writing engagements such as magazine articles, essays, and popular books (Meredith, 2010).

Higher education institutions often keep a directory of contact details for researchers and their topics so that journalists can easily reach the right person. As well as checking with your institution's communication office to see if you can be added to such a directory, you can proactively pitch articles (Wilkinson and Weitkamp, 2016). A template email for pitching an article to a newspaper is available on this book's companion website.

Radio and television interviews can be even more intimidating than public lectures. You may be eager to respond to every question, but it is crucial to take your time. Most of us tend to speak too fast in interviews, so – just like public lectures – if you feel like you are speaking a little bit slower than your normal talking speed, that is probably a good pace. Keep your answers relatively short and to the point. Always let the interviewer finish asking their question before you answer. An interview is not like a normal conversation where people interrupt each other – that quickly becomes irritating for audiences. Try not to speak over the interviewer, and if they interrupt you, it should not be taken personally – they (or the producers) may simply be worrying about the timing of the interview within the wider broadcast. Whatever is happening around you, your focus should always remain on answering the questions calmly and succinctly.

Researcher views

Mei, on having her colleagues support her before a TV interview:

> My whole group got me ready for it [...] They had a mock interview room set up and they took turns being [the interviewer]. It was still weird doing the real thing with the makeup and lights and everything but I would have been lost if I didn't spend the day before doing practice runs.

Social media, dialogue, and discussion

Once comfortable with one-way dissemination, we can challenge ourselves to develop communication skills that focus on dialogue and discussion. Social media are digital tools for sharing information and connecting with virtual communities that have dramatically changed the field of public engagement, providing an alternative to broadcasting in the form of 'narrowcasting' – where specific information is shared with individual groups (Carrigan, 2019, p. 58). Social media are relevant for academic researchers because of the opportunities they provide for sharing work and developing a wider professional network. The role of social media in public engagement can encompass connecting audiences with text, audio, or video content (podcasts or YouTube videos, for example), as well as providing virtual spaces for such engagement to take place (personal or professional websites and social networking services, such as LinkedIn and Facebook).

How we use social media in our work depends on a host of factors, such as how we hope to interact with public audiences, what we wish to achieve by doing so, and our capacity to spend time exploring the options open to us. Most researchers will use at least one or two academic services to archive their work and connect with other researchers. Sites such as Google Scholar and ResearchGate are among the most popular and can be coupled with an active ORCID ID ('Open Researcher and Contributor Identifier') to cover the basics of sharing our work online (Thelwall and Kousha, 2017). While academic social media sites are valuable, to connect with wider audiences more mainstream social media platforms are required – Twitter is popular among academics for finding like-minded researchers, connecting with potential collaborators, and seeking out employment opportunities (Veletsianos, 2012; Stewart, 2015).

While setting up a social media account is painless, cultivating an online presence that attracts people to interact with us takes time and effort. Researchers often become frustrated with how long it takes to develop a following, and if they have not engaged with social media before, the sheer number of different options can be overwhelming. Establishing a shared account for a research group can provide a way for colleagues to develop their social media skills and learn from each other while sharing the burden of maintaining an online presence. Blogging – continually updating short, online, self-publications – is one of the most useful forms of public engagement through social media (Kouper, 2010), and is ideal for sharing engagement duties in a research group. Maintaining a blog provides an outlet for developing writing and communication skills in a controlled digital environment (Guerin et al., 2015).

Some researchers discover that they are not only good at communicating their research, but that they enjoy it more than the research itself. If we hope to someday work in communications, that is no bad thing, but if we want to be credible researchers, we must ensure that our communication commitments are not taking up the time we should be spending researching, writing, and publishing. Developing a social media presence for our work, giving public talks, and speaking on behalf of our discipline through mass media are all important ways to improve our communication skills. Beyond that, we should only engage such communication channels when we have something to say. Senior, tenured academics with years of research credibility safely stored in the peer-review bank can dedicate some of their time to media work without it affecting their credentials. For an early career researcher, however, the distracting and sometimes addictive appeal of being in the public eye can be a dangerous siren song.

Researcher views

Quinn, on researchers spending more time on social media than on their research:

> I see my supervisor on Twitter talking about lots of things but he hasn't published a paper in six years. He just likes the attention I guess but we worry people will find out and ask him if he is drawing his salary just to sit on Twitter all day and not do any research or help his students.

To resist the temptation of spending valuable research time engaging the media, a healthier pattern of communication is to focus on our research first, and only when we have meaningful research outputs to share should we ramp up the amount of time we invest in communicating our work. Producing an academic publication from material we have already communicated through public channels is not easy or efficient. Instead, having our work first appear in a book or an academic journal starts the communication cycle from the point of strongest academic credibility. Once published, we can discuss our work in any public forum we choose – from websites, print media, radio and television broadcasts; to in-person events like public lectures, panels, seminars, workshops, and festivals. These can all be supported directly or indirectly through an extensive array of social media platforms. We do not need to be active across every platform and should prioritise being active solely on the social media platforms that best suit our needs (Carrigan, 2019).

Democratising research

When we have progressed beyond the basic levels of disseminating our work through one-way mass media, and have become comfortable with dialogue and discussion through social media, the next level of engagement to target is *participation*. Participatory research is when we no longer just share our findings, but instead find ways to listen to relevant audiences so that they can help shape our research.

The methods of participation can be varied (Rowe and Frewer, 2005), from citizen assemblies (Devaney et al., 2020) to indigenous research (Chilisa, 2020). Participatory approaches can include providing public information, establishing community partnerships, or facilitating opportunities for participating in different aspects of the research process (Barker, 2004).

Participatory research can take unique forms in certain fields, such as 'public and patient involvement' in healthcare (Barham, 2011), but the most well-known collective term is 'citizen science'. Although already a field so broad that it is difficult to define (Eitzel et al., 2017), citizen science generally pertains to the involvement of non-professionals in the research process and has grown rapidly to include academic journals, conferences, global associations, and large-scale projects around the world (Roche and Davis, 2017a; Vohland et al., 2020).

Public engagement through citizen science can be self-taught, but it can be potentially transformative to develop those skills in a cohort of fellow learners through the growing number of courses and professional learning opportunities available through higher education institutions (Trench and Miller, 2012; Baram-Tsabari and Lewenstein, 2017). There are times when public engagement may not be easy, or even appropriate (Stilgoe et al., 2014), with ongoing challenges surrounding societal trust in research expertise (Kahan, 2010; Roche and Davis, 2017b; Wright, 2020). For participatory approaches – more than any other kind of public engagement – it is worthwhile considering professional development or training to become better equipped to deal with the unforeseen challenges that can arise when public audiences contribute to research (Blackstock et al., 2007).

Participatory forms of public engagement empower citizens to take more active roles in research, from understanding and deliberating research decisions to active forms of protest and resistance (Davies and Horst, 2016). As universities aim to 'incorporate the needs of the local and broader community into higher education's academic priorities' (Furco, 2010, p. 377), public engagement can lay the groundwork for more democratic approaches to research. By making research more open, accessible, and democratic we can restore trust in researchers to tackle the most pressing challenges facing society (Roche et al., 2020).

Researcher views

Summer, on engaging with the communities involved in her research:

> I was doing most of my work with vulnerable populations and I think I never accounted for the actions and time it takes to reciprocate and give back to the communities I was working with. I think institutions, departments, and researchers seldomly account for enough resources for giving back to their research subjects […] We should always find ways to contribute directly (not abstractly) to the communities that are part of our research.

Summary

- Determine your audiences. Ensure you are using the right forms of communication to engage the groups and communities that can benefit from your research.
- Experiment with presentation styles. Try communicating your research in different ways until you find a style you are comfortable with that is both professional and accessible.
- Consider dissemination as a gateway to dialogue. Sharing research through mass media may begin as a one-way approach to communication, but following it up with efforts to listen to your audiences can foster constructive conversations.
- Cultivate a social media presence that works for you. Online platforms should be used in ways that benefit your research without becoming a burden.
- Aspire to participatory approaches. Finding ways for different audiences and communities to engage in your research is rife with complications, but it has the potential to be the most valuable and rewarding aspect of being an academic researcher.

Communicating our research and finding ways to engage public audiences has benefits beyond the obvious attraction of increasing the impact of our research. Connecting with diverse communities, and learning from them, can be professionally satisfying and improve our understanding of the impact of our work. Striving to contribute to the greater good of society through our work as academic researchers can also provide an enormous sense of purpose and pride – the importance of which cannot be overstated in an academic life that can, at times, be as isolating as it is challenging. As we will see in Chapters 10 and 11, developing a range of communication skills will serve us well in our professional development and on most career paths we consider. Before then, we must tackle the most stimulating, fascinating, and captivating part of any academic job – administration. Sarcasm aside, administrative tasks are an unavoidable component of life as an academic researcher, so let us efficiently, and hopefully painlessly, embrace our administrative responsibilities in the next chapter.

Further reading

- Beere, C. A., Votruba, J. C., & Wells, G. W. (2011). *Becoming an Engaged Campus: A Practical Guide for Institutionalizing Public Engagement*. San Francisco, CA: John Wiley & Sons.

This book describes the many approaches that can be taken to creating a university environment that both supports and sustains public engagement.

- Carrigan, M. (2019). *Social Media for Academics*. London, UK: SAGE.

The definitive guide to social media for academic researchers at any stage of experience with online engagement.

- Gasman, M. (2016). *Academics Going Public: How to Write and Speak Beyond Academe*. New York, NY: Routledge.

This edited volume offers advice on faculty members becoming more engaged with public audiences and covers key issues such as strategies for coping with controversy and backlash.

- Meredith, D. (2010). *Explaining Research: How to Reach Key Audiences to Advance Your Work*. New York, NY: Oxford University Press.

This communications guidebook comprehensively covers the challenges of improving communication within academia, connecting with public audiences, and engaging the media.

- Wilkinson, C. & Weitkamp, E. (2016). *Creative Research Communication: Theory and Practice*. Manchester, UK: Manchester University Press.

Science communication scholars Clare Wilkinson and Emma Weitkamp explore the theoretical, practical, and ethical considerations necessary for effective research communication.

Resources

Further resources for this chapter can be found at: www.JosephRoche.ie/EssentialSkills

- Research Elevator Pitch Samples
- Lecture Slides Template
- Email Template Pitching Newspaper Article

References

Arnold, K. (2003). Journals, the press, and press releases: a cozy relationship. *Science Editor, 26*(3), 82–84.

Autzen, C. (2014). Press releases – the new trend in science communication. *Journal of Science Communication, 13*(3), C02.

Baram-Tsabari, A. & Lewenstein, B. V. (2017). Science communication training: what are we trying to teach? *International Journal of Science Education, Part B, 7*(3), 285–300.

Barham, L. (2011). Public and patient involvement at the UK National Institute for Health and Clinical Excellence. *The Patient: Patient-Centered Outcomes Research, 4*(1), 1–10.

Barker, D. (2004). The scholarship of engagement: a taxonomy of five emerging practices. *Journal of Higher Education Outreach and Engagement, 9*(2), 123–137.

Beaumont-Thomas, B. (2017). How we made the typeface Comic Sans. *The Guardian*, 28 March. Available at: www.theguardian.com/artanddesign/2017/mar/28/how-we-made-font-comic-sans-typography (accessed 6 October 2021).

Beere, C. A., Votruba, J. C., & Wells, G. W. (2011). *Becoming an Engaged Campus: A Practical Guide for Institutionalizing Public Engagement*. San Francisco, CA: John Wiley & Sons.

Blackstock, K. L., Kelly, G., & Horsey, B. (2007). Developing and applying a framework to evaluate participatory research for sustainability. *Ecological Economics, 60*(4), 726–742.

Carrigan, M. (2019). *Social Media for Academics*. London, UK: SAGE.

Chilisa, B. (2020). *Indigenous Research Methodologies* (2nd edn). London, UK: SAGE.

Christian, A. J. (2012). The web as television reimagined? Online networks and the pursuit of legacy media. *Journal of Communication Inquiry, 36*(4), 340–356.

Collins, J. (2004). Education techniques for lifelong learning: giving a PowerPoint presentation: the art of communicating effectively. *Radiographics, 24*(4), 1185–1192.

Davies, S. R. & Horst, M. (2016). *Science Communication: Culture, Identity and Citizenship*. London UK: Palgrave Macmillan.

Devaney, L., Torney, D., Brereton, P., & Coleman, M. (2020). Ireland's citizens' assembly on climate change: lessons for deliberative public engagement and communication. *Environmental Communication, 14*(2), 141–146.

Dostilio, L. D. (2017). *The Community Engagement Professional in Higher Education: A Competency Model for an Emerging Field*. Sterling, VA: Stylus Publishing.

Eitzel, M. V., Cappadonna, J. L., Santos-Lang, C., Duerr, R. E., Virapongse, A., West, S. E., ... & Jiang, Q. (2017). Citizen Science terminology matters: exploring key terms. *Citizen Science: Theory and Practice, 2*(1), 1–20.

Fahy, D. & Nisbet, M. C. (2011). The science journalist online: shifting roles and emerging practices. *Journalism, 12*(7), 778–793.

Furco, A. (2010). The engaged campus: toward a comprehensive approach to public engagement. *British Journal of Educational Studies, 58*(4), 375–390.

Gallo, C. (2014). *Talk Like TED: The 9 Public-speaking Secrets of the World's Top Minds*. London, UK: St. Martin's Press.

Gasman, M. (2016). *Academics Going Public: How to Write and Speak Beyond Academe*. New York, NY: Routledge.

Guerin, C., Carter, S., & Aitchison, C. (2015). Blogging as community of practice: lessons for academic development? *International Journal for Academic Development, 20*(3), 212–223.

Holgate, S. A. (2011). Presenting science for the anxiety averse. *Science*. DOI: 10.1126/science.caredit.a1100052

Kahan, D. (2010). Fixing the communications failure. *Nature, 463*(7279), 296–297.

Kouper, I. (2010). Science blogs and public engagement with science: practices, challenges, and opportunities. *Journal of Science Communication, 9*(1), A02.

Langer, A. I. & Gruber, J. B. (2021). Political agenda setting in the hybrid media system: why legacy media still matter a great deal. *The International Journal of Press/Politics, 26*(2), 313–340.

LSE GV314 Group (2014). Scholars on air: academics and the broadcast media in Britain. *British Politics, 9*(4), 363–384.

Mayer, R. E., Griffith, E., Jurkowitz, I. T., & Rothman, D. (2008). Increased interestingness of extraneous details in a multimedia science presentation leads to decreased learning. *Journal of Experimental Psychology: Applied, 14*(4), 329–339.

Menzel, K. E. & Carrell, L. J. (1994). The relationship between preparation and performance in public speaking. *Communication Education, 43*(1), 17–26.

Meredith, D. (2010). *Explaining Research: How to Reach Key Audiences to Advance Your Work*. New York, NY: Oxford University Press.

Mitchell, T. D. & Soria, K. M. (Eds.) (2017). *Educating for Citizenship and Social Justice: Practices for Community Engagement at Research Universities*. London UK: Palgrave Macmillan.

NCCPE (2020). *What is Public Engagement?* National Co-ordinating Centre for Public Engagement. Available at: www.publicengagement.ac.uk/about-engagement/what-public-engagement (accessed 6 October 2021).

Overton, B., Pasque, P. A., & Brukhardt, J. C. (2016). *Engaged Research and Practice: Higher Education and the Pursuit of the Public Good*. Sterling, VA: Stylus Publishing, LLC.

Palmer, J., Owens, S., & Doubleday, R. (2019). Perfecting the 'Elevator Pitch'? Expert advice as locally-situated boundary work. *Science and Public Policy, 46*(2), 244–253.

Penfield, T., Baker, M. J., Scoble, R., & Wykes, M. C. (2014). Assessment, evaluations, and definitions of research impact: a review. *Research Evaluation, 23*(1), 21–32.

Roche, J. & Davis, N. (2017a). Citizen science: an emerging professional field united in truth-seeking. *Journal of Science Communication, 16*(04), R01.

Roche, J. & Davis, N. (2017b). Should the science communication community play a role in political activism? *Journal of Science Communication, 16*(01), L01.

Roche, J., Bell, L., Galvão, C., Golumbic, Y. N., Kloetzer, L., Knoben, N., ... & Winter, S. (2020). Citizen science, education, and learning: challenges and opportunities. *Frontiers in Sociology, 5*(613814), 1–10.

Romanelli, F., Cain, J., & McNamara, P. J. (2014). Should TED talks be teaching us something? *American Journal of Pharmaceutical Education, 78*(6), 1–3.

Rowe, G. & Frewer, L. J. (2005). A typology of public engagement mechanisms. *Science, Technology, & Human Values, 30*(2), 251–290.

Stewart, B. (2015). Open to influence: what counts as academic influence in scholarly networked Twitter participation. *Learning, Media and Technology, 40*(3), 287–309.

Stilgoe, J., Lock, S. J., & Wilsdon, J. (2014). Why should we promote public engagement with science? *Public Understanding of Science, 23*(1), 4–15.

Thelwall, M. & Kousha, K. (2017). ResearchGate versus Google Scholar: which finds more early citations? *Scientometrics, 112*(2), 1125–1131.

Trench, B. (2008). Towards an analytical framework of science communication models. In D. Cheng, M. Claessens, N. R. J. Gascoigne, J. Metcalfe, B. Schiele, & S. Shi (Eds.), *Communicating Science in Social Contexts: New Models, New Practices* (pp. 119–135). Dordrecht, The Netherlands: Springer.

Trench, B. & Miller, S. (2012). Policies and practices in supporting scientists' public communication through training. *Science and Public Policy, 39*(6), 722–731.

Veletsianos, G. (2012). Higher education scholars' participation and practices on Twitter. *Journal of Computer Assisted Learning, 28*(4), 336–349.

Vohland, K., Land-Zandstra, A., Ceccaroni, L., Lemmens, R., Perelló, J., Ponti, M., ... & Wagenknecht, K. (2020). *The Science of Citizen Science*. Cham, Switzerland: Springer Nature.

Wilkinson, C. & Weitkamp, E. (2016). *Creative Research Communication: Theory and Practice*. Manchester, UK: Manchester University Press.

Wright, D. B. (2020). Improving trust in research: supporting claims with evidence. *Open Education Studies, 2*(1), 1–8.

Yamamura, E. K. & Koth, K. (2018). *Place-based Community Engagement in Higher Education: A Strategy to Transform Universities and Communities*. Sterling, VA: Stylus Publishing, LLC.

Nine
Administration

In this chapter, we will cover:

- administrative tasks and the importance of teamwork
- time management
- strategies for managing administrative tasks more efficiently
- scheduling and prioritising
- opportunities arising from administration.

The least loved part of the job

Academic posts generally involve three core components: research, teaching, and administration (Houston et al., 2006; Brendel and Cornett-Murtada, 2019). Of the three, administration (sometimes referred to as 'service') is usually the part that is most ill-defined and ill-favoured. Administration can include a variety of voluntary and obligatory tasks. In this chapter, we will interpret the administrative part of the academic researcher's job as being the tasks and responsibilities we are expected to carry out for our department or university. Some of the duties often considered voluntary 'service' to our research communities are too important to be combined with obligatory administrative tasks, and are instead tackled separately in other chapters: applying for research grants (Chapter 5), designing and assessing courses (Chapter 6), supervising students (Chapter 7), engaging public audiences (Chapter 8), and attending conferences (Chapter 10).

The vast majority of academic researchers enjoy research or teaching or – ideally – both. There are, however, a select few who love the administrative parts of their job the most. While such colleagues are to be cherished, it is important to observe them for any additional strange behaviour: for example, if they do not need to breathe, or if they accidentally mention their undercover mission to gather information for their home planet. Other than arousing suspicion about whether they do, in fact, come in peace, those who relish administrative tasks probably only differ from the rest of us in having figured out how to do their administrative work so efficiently that it brings them satisfaction. Improving efficiency will be central to the advice in this chapter, along with nurturing good time management skills, communicating with our administrative teams, dealing with emails and meetings, and structuring our workloads based on our priorities. Building on these foundations, we should remain open to the potential bombshell that administrative tasks might lead us to new career frontiers we wish to explore.

Becoming a team player

A tired trope in any university is that academics loathe administration, despite it being a key part of their job. A common workload distribution for new academic staff is that in a typical five-day working week, two days should be devoted to research, two to teaching, and one to administration (Kyvik, 2013). In reality, the various duties of the role will never fit neatly into a system of designated days (Soliman and Soliman, 1997; Kenny and Fluck, 2014). It is important, therefore, to know how much time we are *expected* to spend on each part of the job, and compare it to what is actually happening on a daily basis.

Teaching is timetabled, making it the part of the job that should be easiest to quantify, but research and administration can find themselves in direct competition for our time. Research is more fundamental to our job, but without anyone checking on our day-to-day progress, it is easy to postpone focusing on our research with few short-term repercussions. Administration, on the other hand, can flood our email inboxes every day, relentlessly vying for our attention. Some academic researchers blame their administrative workloads when they are not making as much progress with their research as they would wish (Miller, 2019). Shirking from our administrative duties to focus on our research, however, is not an option – our colleagues depend on our contributions as much as we depend on theirs.

If we find administrative work encroaching on our research time, it is our responsibility to come up with a solution. There is either an issue with how many administrative responsibilities we have been assigned – which can be brought up with management to make sure that there has been a fair distribution of administrative work among everyone on the team – or else we must learn how to manage our administrative work more efficiently so that it does not demand an unreasonable amount of time.

In many institutions, there can be a social divide between administrative and academic staff (Bess and Dee, 2014). Prominent or unspoken hierarchies can result in research and teaching receiving precedence, with full-time administrators having fewer opportunities for recognition or reward. This inequity can influence staff members' relationships with their work. Academics, knowing that any research they do outside of their expected working hours will eventually benefit their career, sometimes treat the role like a vocation or a calling. Administrators, without the incentive of having research outputs to bring additional commendations to their work, may be more inclined to treat their positions as regular '9 to 5' jobs (although they too face longer working hours as a consequence of perennial understaffing in higher education environments). The differences in the roles can be further exacerbated by salary scales and promotion opportunities.

There may be more fundamental differences between academic and administrative staff at senior management level, but for early career researchers, nurturing a strong working relationship with everyone on the administrative team is key to good administration. Some academics resent administrative staff (Ginsberg, 2011) and make their work more difficult by not seeking help from them, ignoring them, overruling them, or even mistreating them through rude or condescending behaviour. In such cases, it is no wonder that administrators might be wary when working with new academic staff members. We can address this by being open and empathetic in our communication as soon as we become members of a new administrative team (Macfarlane, 2007).

Researcher views

Henrietta, on carefully choosing the members of your team:

> If you hear someone shouting in a conference call in the office next door, maybe don't invite them to be a team member.

Encouraging teamwork, communication, and support in our administrative roles will help us become more productive and efficient colleagues. Administrative teams usually have experienced full-time administrators who can guide us through our first administrative responsibilities. As researchers, we are not expected to have the same skills as full-time administrators, and it is perfectly reasonable to seek their advice. Our administrative colleagues are likely to respond with patience and support to such genuine attempts to contribute to the team. For some researchers, 'help' seems to be the hardest word, so there is a template email available on this book's companion website to use when help is needed.

Managing our time

To deal with our administrative tasks as efficiently as possible, we need to manage our time appropriately. Time management is a skill that has long been seen as crucial in higher education institutions, for both students and staff (Lay and Schouwenburg, 1993; Wolters et al., 2017). Although accounting for all of our time might require a broader approach, like 'life management' (Robison, 2013, p. 3), good time management skills can reduce the amount of time we spend on administration, and improve our efficiency in every facet of our work (Ames, 2019). As with research (Chapter 2) and writing (Chapter 3), the best way to improve efficiency in administration is to keep an overview of how we are spending our time. We can do that the old-fashioned way with a pen and paper, or by using an online personal calendar to populate our schedule (Feddern-Bekcan, 2008).

Unlike our research – which has no real upper limit in terms of how much time we can invest in it – we should be able to determine how much administration we need to do and how long it takes. If it is not already described in our contract or job description, then there is even more reason to categorise and itemise how we spend our time so that our administrative workload can be completely quantified. Once we have oversight of everything we spend our time working on, we can prioritise what is important to achieving our goals (Clark and Sousa, 2018). For an early career researcher, those priorities will be research and writing. We should structure our working day so that the part of the day when we are most alert and productive is when we give our full attention to those priorities. After that, we can address our administrative tasks, which may feel like carrying out maintenance rather than working towards our goals. Finally, we should record the progress that we have made and update our plans for the next day accordingly – essentially managing our time management (Badiru et al., 2016).

Structuring our working day to ensure a significant amount of time is spent on high-priority tasks that take us closer to achieving our research and career objectives protects us from the phantom scourge forever haunting academics – feeling unproductive. It is unrealistic, however, to hope to spend all day every day working at our highest levels of productivity (Schwartz, 2013). Some people work best in the early morning tranquillity, or the peace of the wee hours, while others peak in the afternoon (Knight and Mather, 2013). Finding our most productive times of the day takes some trial and error, but once we know when we work best it is easier to schedule our day around those periods.

During every working day we experience lulls in our motivation and productivity, and these moments are when we should allot time to tasks that are still important, but do not necessarily directly advance our priorities, and which may not require us to perform at our most productive best – administrative tasks such as reading and replying to emails, making work-related calls, updating meeting schedules, completing reports, and anything else we deem administrative work. These are the types of tasks that may need to be addressed every day, and can easily expand to fill our time, so by restricting them to designated periods during the day we can ensure they are not encroaching on our most productive periods. Imposing such constraints on administrative tasks also compels us to look for more efficient ways to complete them.

Researcher views

Sarah, on balancing her part-time PhD with a full-time job:

> I wake up at five and the first chunk of the day is my PhD work and then I do my job. Then I can enjoy the evening. Because if I don't do it in the morning, and get that crap out of the way as soon as possible, it will be in the back of my mind for the rest of the day. And in the evening, if I'm too tired to do it, I'll feel very guilty and I can't handle the guilt […] It's like *Okay, I'm going to do two hours a day for four days and then that's good enough.* But to convince yourself that a certain amount of work is good enough, so that you feel that you're okay and you've done as much as you could … it's really, really difficult.

An ongoing battle for efficiency

To improve our efficiency, we must analyse our workloads to identify what is taking up more time than it should, before experimenting with strategies to speed things up. Any simple repetitive task that regularly takes time should be a candidate for streamlining or even automation. If a significant amount of your time is spent collecting or accessing the same kinds of information, then tabulating that data in secure online spreadsheets which can be maintained and updated by you and your team will quicken your workflow. If a specific type of report or calculation is often required from those spreadsheets, then finding a basic formula or macro that can automate your most common actions will simplify the process (Alexander and Walkenbach, 2017). It may demand some experimenting with formulas, or searching online to find relevant examples, but if it results in turning a regular time-consuming task into the click of a button, you are dramatically improving your efficiency.

Researcher views

Reese, on managing her time effectively during her PhD:

> I start with just sitting down, making a list. I come in at the beginning of the day and make a list of what I wanted to do […] As soon as I got [results] I would organise them in such a format that they could go directly into my thesis. So I was always planning ahead towards putting it into my thesis, even if it was three years from now, or the next day, everything was done in such a way that it wasn't being done twice.

Where our administrative duties will most likely try to break free from their allotted time is in the omnipresent workhorse of online communication – email (Berghel, 1997). As we will see in Chapter 12, academic stress can have serious implications for our health, and email is often touted as a key contributor (Jerejian et al., 2013). The expectation to regularly check and reply to emails as part of our jobs can start to feel, paradoxically, like it is distracting us from doing our jobs (Gill, 2010). That distraction can be both frustrating and addictive, and while the advice for academic researchers struggling with email-induced stress is usually to check email only once per day, that can be just as stressful if we are always confronted with an overflowing inbox.

Being vigilant to incoming emails (or similar kinds of messages or modes of communication) throughout the day means that we are not giving our full attention to more important work. Constant vigilance is a good strategy for fighting evil, but it does not help anyone who is trying to be more productive (Jackson et al., 2003; Gomez, 2017). A better approach is to assign the task of addressing your email inbox to the periods when you are at your least productive (in my case, this directly corresponds to when

I am most hungry). If you have finished working on a high-priority task because lunch is approaching, this might be a perfect moment to quickly browse your emails, dismiss those not needing a response, write succinct responses to those that do, and flag any important messages that will require more considered replies later.

As the end of your working day approaches, set yourself a fixed amount of time to reply to as many emails as you can before you finish for the day. Always tackle them in order of importance; if it takes you a few days to reply to the emails that you deemed less urgent, you can take comfort from having not invested any of your productive energy in those emails. You can apologise for tardy replies if needed, but most people working in higher education institutions understand that there is an overabundance of email. If you find yourself writing the same kinds of emails repeatedly – such as providing details of a course you are running – keep a template response that you can copy, paste, and tweak as needed. This will not only save you time but will result in your email replies being more consistent.

If you are going to be away from your email for an extended period, spend some time setting up an 'out-of-office' automated response (Cherak, 2020). In that message, there is no need to promise that you will reply to each email on your return – simply indicate a date when you hope to be able to check your email again and, if appropriate, provide alternative contact details for a person or people who may be able to help while you are away. If you find your emails are intruding on your prioritised research and writing time, consider turning on your out-of-office reply for a day or two each week and see if that makes you more efficient with your work. A template for an automated out-of-office email reply is available on this book's companion website.

Researcher views

Byron, on the cyclical nature of replying to emails:

> Emails kill me. I let them all pile up and then send a million replies. And instead of being rewarded for all that work, all of those people send you more emails. It never ends.

Being present

As well as the abundance of emails, another mainstay of administration is the ever-increasing number of meetings (Luong and Rogelberg, 2005). We should use our schedule to determine which meetings are most important and if it is practical for us to attend. If our meeting schedules cause administrative work to impinge on our research time, then we need to stand down from some recurring meetings or reach an understanding with the meeting organisers that we may not always be available to attend. Most colleagues recognise the challenge of attending meetings and it is accept-able to choose between meetings based on their importance or urgency at that time. If we update our meeting schedule regularly, we can politely provide meeting organisers with plenty of notice when we are unable to attend their meetings.

If we coordinate a course, a programme, or a project, then it is our responsibility to oversee the efficient scheduling and running of meetings. We should always ask ourselves if a meeting is necessary – if it is just a way for information to be shared, then perhaps that information could be shared over email with a follow-up commu-nication to remind any committee members if their input is needed by a certain date. Such a scenario does not help with the issue of email overload, but we are at least spar-ing our colleagues an unnecessary meeting and the associated scheduling challenges (Shin and Higa, 2005; Rogelberg et al., 2007).

Researcher views

Hannah, on making project coordinators feel guilty about bringing people together for unnec-essary gatherings:

> I say it every time. It drives [them] mad. Just as they are getting really into it, I'll go, dead-pan, *Couldn't this meeting have been an email?*, and you can actually see them die inside.

When we need to regularly check-in with our teams, short informal meetings are helpful, especially when there is no pressure to attend every meeting. We should only schedule formal meetings with our colleagues if their verbal input is needed (Francisco, 2007). In that case, we can circulate an agenda (open to additions from everyone attending the meeting) in advance, along with a clear idea of the purpose of the meeting including what it may achieve, or what problem it might solve (Boudett and City, 2014). A sample meeting agenda template is available on this book's com-panion website.

Over the course of a semester, the number of students seeking to meet with us can swell, to the point where it may feel like there is not enough time to meet with all of them. If scheduling individual meetings becomes impractical, then we can set office hours (either in-person or in a virtual environment), which are set times during the week when students can visit to seek advice (Pfund et al., 2013). To help our students help each other, we can set up an online discussion board for each class where stu-dents can post questions and answers before deciding if they need to bring a question to our office (such virtual learning environments are discussed in Chapter 6). Class discussion boards require minimal maintenance, and if something crops up repeat-edly it can be addressed in a class email or lecture (Suler, 2004).

When our research, teaching, and administration tasks start to pile up, it is easy for us to feel flustered. Although it is not necessarily a bad thing for our colleagues to be aware when we are struggling (Chapter 12), that does not extend to our students. Conveying how busy we are to our students only makes them feel bad about taking up our time (Nunn, 2018). When our students come to us seeking advice, we should not dwell on our workload or how busy we are – that is our burden, not theirs. Our sole focus in that moment should be on helping them to fulfil their academic potential.

Poisoned chalice or blessing in disguise?

Most higher education institutions guarantee 'academic freedom', granting researchers the privilege of being able to investigate, analyse, and publish work on any topic we choose (Karran, 2007, p. 289). We may wish to focus on one area of research throughout our careers, or to expand our research to other disciplines – interpreting one discipline through the lens of another, combining disciplines, or transcending disciplinary boundaries – in multidisciplinary, interdisciplinary, or transdisciplinary approaches (Alvargonzález, 2011). As we saw in Chapter 6, teaching and research are integral parts of an academic job and so finding ways for them to align and overlap means that spending time on one can benefit the other. Administration is also an integral part of the job ... so is it crazy to consider trying to align our administrative work with our research? Yes, it is. The good news, however, is that in an academic role 'crazy' is only one or two compelling arguments away from being considered 'creative' or 'innovative'.

Aligning our administrative tasks and our research requires flexibility (Spurling, 2015). If we are already teaching a module associated with our research area, then we may consider evaluating the teaching methods and assessment used on that module (Saroyan and Amundsen, 2001). For any new module or programmes we implement, we could study how they are administered and their impact on students, staff, and the wider institution (Bird, 2017). We could gather data showing how academics in our fields of research adapt to leadership roles, or how the research grants for our disciplines are administered (Kulakowski and Chronister, 2006). As with any area of research, we can publish our findings – academic journals span administrative topics such as operations (Cheng, 1993), policy (Harvey and Kosman, 2014), and leadership (Inman, 2011). As well as the personal benefits of aligning two fundamental parts of the job, having staff within a university conduct research on its administration can improve the overall effectiveness of the institution (Shattock, 2003).

While working as academic researchers, there is a chance we may consider (or be politely asked to consider) becoming academic administrators. There are a lot of things to weigh-up before making such a decision. After spending time carving out a professional identity as an academic researcher, it may feel uncomfortable leaving that behind. Becoming a full-time administrator would see our research output decline and our teaching hours dwindle or disappear. It is possible to spend some time in administration and move back into research, but it will certainly slow our progress as academic researchers. Conversely, it might prove an enticing opportunity for researchers seeking change or a fresh start. The changing nature of higher education means that there are plenty of opportunities for administrators to move within and between institutions (Gander et al., 2014). The change in career direction could also be seen as a promotion, with potential salary implications to contemplate (salary negotiations are tackled in Chapter 11).

If you decide to consider an administrative leadership position, you can start preparing for such a role while still an academic researcher. Most academics serve on several committees; volunteering to chair one could be a way to explore your administrative leadership capabilities in a relatively low-stakes environment before taking on more demanding leadership roles. Speaking to different kinds of administrators about their jobs could be instructive, as the role of an administrative leader or manager can mean being responsible for strategy and finance (Smith, 2011), as well as managing human resources and institutional governance (Powers and Schloss, 2017). Even if you do not find any administrators who have a similar background or career path as you, do not let that deter you – bringing fresh perspectives to administrative leadership could benefit both you and your university (Kezar and Lester, 2011).

Summary

- Communicate with everyone on the administrative team. Good administration needs everyone to play their part, and open communication is key, regardless of whether you are seeking help or providing support.
- Quantify your administrative workload. Keep a record of how much time you are spending on your core responsibilities so that you can identify any tasks that are taking up an unreasonable amount of your time.
- Improve efficiency. Automating repetitive tasks and finding strategies to reduce the most time-consuming duties will make you a more effective administrator.
- Keep a schedule that reflects your priorities. Determine how much time is being taken up by emails and meetings and ensure that your research goals are not being compromised.
- Consider the opportunities that administrative work provides. Becoming more involved in administration may facilitate you moving your research, or even your career, in an interesting new direction.

Administrative service is the least glamorous aspect of the life of an academic researcher. However, once we have determined how it fits within our overall priorities, appropriately structured our workload, and established more efficient ways of communicating and scheduling, administration is not nearly as off-putting as its reputation would have us believe. One way or another, it has to be addressed; it is part of the job and needs to be embraced for the sake of our professional development. In the next chapter, we will explore just how professional development can help us fulfil our potential and become accomplished academic researchers.

Further reading

- Ames, K. (2019). *Time Management for Academic Impact: Controlling Teaching Treadmills and Tornadoes*. New York, NY: Routledge.

This book provides an overview of the kinds of work faced by academic staff and demonstrates how good time management skills can lead to academics being more productive and having increased confidence in their roles.

- Bess, J. L. & Dee, J. R. (2014). *Bridging the Divide between Faculty and Administration: A Guide to Understanding Conflict in the Academy*. New York, NY: Routledge.

A detailed look at the tension and conflict between academic and administrative teams in higher education institutions, with strategies designed for a range of situations.

- Gander, M., Moyes, H., & Sabzalieva, E. (2014). *Managing your Career in Higher Education Administration*. New York, NY: Palgrave Macmillan.

This guide is written for administrators and professional service staff in higher education institutions and draws on case studies to illustrate the landscape of university administration careers.

- Kulakowski, E. C. & Chronister, L. U. (2006). *Research Administration and Management*. Sudbury, MA: Jones & Bartlett Publishers.

The easiest way for an academic researcher to find their way into senior administration and management is to consider research administration. This book collects the perspectives of experienced administrators and covers historical, infrastructural, practical, technological, and legal aspects of research administration.

- Powers, K. & Schloss, P. J. (2017). *Organization and Administration in Higher Education*. New York, NY: Taylor & Francis.

An edited volume that covers every aspect of achieving institutional excellence through effective and efficient management.

Resources

Further resources for this chapter can be found at: www.JosephRoche.ie/EssentialSkills

- Administrator Help Request Email Template
- Out-of-office Email Reply Template
- Meeting Agenda Template

References

Alexander, M. & Walkenbach, J. (2017). *Excel Macros*. Hoboken, NJ: John Wiley & Sons.

Alvargonzález, D. (2011). Multidisciplinarity, interdisciplinarity, transdisciplinarity, and the sciences. *International Studies in the Philosophy of Science, 25*(4), 387–403.

Ames, K. (2019). *Time Management for Academic Impact: Controlling Teaching Treadmills and Tornadoes*. New York, NY: Routledge.

Badiru, A. B., Rusnock, C. F., & Valencia, V. V. (2016). *Project Management for Research: A Guide for Graduate Students*. Boca Raton, FL: CRC Press Taylor & Francis.

Berghel, H. (1997). Email – The good, the bad, and the ugly. *Communications of the ACM, 40*(4), 11–15.

Bess, J. L. & Dee, J. R. (2014). *Bridging the Divide between Faculty and Administration: A Guide to Understanding Conflict in the Academy*. New York, NY: Routledge.

Bird, E. L. (2017). Student and staff perceptions of the international postgraduate student experience: a qualitative study of a UK university. *Journal of International Students, 7*(2), 329–346.

Boudett, K. P. & City, E. A. (2014). *Meeting Wise: Making the Most of Collaborative Time for Educators*. Boston, MA: Harvard Education Press.

Brendel, W. & Cornett-Murtada, V. (2019). Professors practicing mindfulness: an action research study on transformed teaching, research, and service. *Journal of Transformative Education, 17*(1), 4–23.

Cheng, T. E. (1993). Operations research and higher education administration. *Journal of Educational Administration, 31*(1), 77–90.

Cherak, S. (2020). Out of office replies and what they can say about you. *Nature, 578*(7793), 179–181.

Clark, A. & Sousa, B. (2018). *How to be a Happy Academic: A Guide to Being Effective in Research, Writing and Teaching*. London, UK: SAGE.

Feddern-Bekcan, T. (2008). Google calendar. *Journal of the Medical Library Association: JMLA, 96*(4), 394–395.

Francisco, J. M. (2007). How to create and facilitate meetings that matter. *The Information Management Journal, 41*(6), 54–58.

Gander, M., Moyes, H., & Sabzalieva, E. (2014). *Managing your Career in Higher Education Administration*. New York, NY: Palgrave Macmillan.

Gill, R. (2010). Breaking the silence: the hidden injuries of the neoliberal university. In R. Ryan-Flood & R. Gill (Eds.), *Secrecy and Silence in the Research Process: Feminist Reflections* (1st edn) (pp. 1–17). London, UK: Routledge.

Ginsberg, B. (2011). *The Fall of the Faculty*. New York, NY: Oxford University Press.

Gomez, A. (2017). *The Email Warrior: How to Clear your Inbox and Keep it that Way*. Richmond Hill, ON, Canada: Saturn Books.

Harvey, M. & Kosman, B. (2014). A model for higher education policy review: the case study of an assessment policy. *Journal of Higher Education Policy and Management, 36*(1), 88–98.

Houston, D., Meyer, L. H., & Paewai, S. (2006). Academic staff workloads and job satisfaction: expectations and values in academe. *Journal of Higher Education Policy and Management, 28*(1), 17–30.

Inman, M. (2011). The journey to leadership for academics in higher education. *Educational Management Administration & Leadership, 39*(2), 228–241.

Jackson, T., Dawson, R., & Wilson, D. (2003). Reducing the effect of email interruptions on employees. *International Journal of Information Management, 23*(1), 55–65.

Jerejian, A. C., Reid, C., & Rees, C. S. (2013). The contribution of email volume, email management strategies and propensity to worry in predicting email stress among academics. *Computers in Human Behavior, 29*(3), 991–996.

Karran, T. (2007). Academic freedom in Europe: a preliminary comparative analysis. *Higher Education Policy, 20*(3), 289–313.

Kenny, J. D. & Fluck, A. E. (2014). The effectiveness of academic workload models in an institution: a staff perspective. *Journal of Higher Education Policy and Management, 36*(6), 585–602.

Kezar, A. & Lester, J. (2011). *Enhancing Campus Capacity for Leadership: An Examination of Grassroots Leaders in Higher Education.* Stanford, CA: Stanford University Press.

Knight, M. & Mather, M. (2013). Look out – it's your off-peak time of day! Time of day matters more for alerting than for orienting or executive attention. *Experimental Aging Research, 39*(3), 305–321.

Kulakowski, E. C. & Chronister, L. U. (2006). *Research Administration and Management.* Sudbury, MA: Jones & Bartlett Publishers.

Kyvik, S. (2013). Academic workload and working time: retrospective perceptions versus time-series data. *Higher Education Quarterly, 67*(1), 2–14.

Lay, C. H. & Schouwenburg, H. C. (1993). Trait procrastination, time management. *Journal of Social Behavior and Personality, 8*(4), 647–662.

Luong, A. & Rogelberg, S. G. (2005). Meetings and more meetings: the relationship between meeting load and the daily well-being of employees. *Group Dynamics: Theory, Research, and Practice, 9*(1), 58–67.

Macfarlane, B. (2007). *The Academic Citizen: The Virtue of Service in University Life.* New York, NY: Routledge.

Miller, J. (2019). Where does the time go? An academic workload case study at an Australian university. *Journal of Higher Education Policy and Management, 41*(6), 633–645.

Nunn, L. M. (2018). *33 Simple Strategies for Faculty: A Week-By-Week Resource for Teaching First-Year and First-Generation Students.* New Brunswick, NJ: Rutgers University Press.

Pfund, R., Rogan, J., Burnham, B., & Norcross, J. (2013). Is the professor in? Faculty presence during office hours. *College Student Journal, 47*(3), 524–528.

Powers, K. & Schloss, P. J. (2017). *Organization and Administration in Higher Education.* New York, NY: Taylor & Francis.

Robison, S. (2013). *The Peak Performing Professor: A Practical Guide to Productivity and Happiness.* San Francisco, CA: Jossey-Bass.

Rogelberg, S. G., Scott, C., & Kello, J. (2007). The science and fiction of meetings. *MIT Sloan Management Review, 48*(2), 18–21.

Saroyan, A. & Amundsen, C. (2001). Evaluating university teaching: time to take stock. *Assessment & Evaluation in Higher Education, 26*(4), 341–353.

Schwartz, T. (2013). Relax! You'll be more productive. *The New York Times*, 10 February. Available at: www.nytimes.com/2013/02/10/opinion/sunday/relax-youll-be-more-productive.html (accessed 4 April 2021).

Shattock, M. (2003). Research, administration and university management: what can research contribute to policy? In R. Begg (Ed.), *The Dialogue between Higher Education Research and Practice* (pp. 55–66). Dordrecht, The Netherlands: Springer.

Shin, B. & Higa, K. (2005). Meeting scheduling: face-to-face, automatic scheduler, and email based coordination. *Journal of Organizational Computing and Electronic Commerce, 15*(2), 137–159.

Smith, D. O. (2011). *Managing the Research University*. New York, NY: Oxford University Press.

Soliman, I. & Soliman, H. (1997). Academic workload and quality. *Assessment & Evaluation in Higher Education, 22*(2), 135–157.

Spurling, N. (2015). Differential experiences of time in academic work: how qualities of time are made in practice. *Time & Society, 24*(3), 367–389.

Suler, J. (2004). In class and online: using discussion boards in teaching. *CyberPsychology & Behavior, 7*(4), 395–401.

Wolters, C. A., Won, S., & Hussain, M. (2017). Examining the relations of time management and procrastination within a model of self-regulated learning. *Metacognition and Learning, 12*(3), 381–399.

Ten

Professional Development

In this chapter, we will cover:

- project management
- academic conferences
- networking
- communities of practice
- reflective practice.

Fulfilling potential

Developing academic research skills is not a challenge that has a fixed endpoint. Even when we are proficient at researching, writing, publishing, teaching, supervising, and administration – while also winning research grants and engaging public audiences with our work – our journeys are not complete. We have, however, given ourselves an excellent platform from which to fulfil our potential as academic researchers. The European Commission, within its charter for researchers and code of conduct for the recruitment of researchers, suggests that 'researchers at all career stages should seek to continually improve themselves by regularly updating and expanding their skills and competencies' (European Commission, 2005, p. 15).

In this chapter, we will move beyond the core set of skills that every early career researcher needs, and focus on how to gain experience that will build our confidence and enhance our expertise. We will look at the fundamentals of good project management to make sure we are doing justice to the work we are tasked with leading. We will consider academic conferences, which not only allow us to showcase our skills, but are vital to career progression, especially when coupled with the professional witchcraft that is academic networking. Finally, we will explore communities of practice and the benefits of regularly reflecting on our own professional learning.

Managing projects

Learning how to manage projects is an essential skill for academic researchers, both in terms of productivity and, crucially, maintaining their sanity. As soon as one of our research grant applications is awarded, we will have to manage the budget, coordinate any staff hired to work on the project, and oversee project reporting. By improving our project management skills, we will become more efficient at planning and implementing all aspects of our research (Badiru et al., 2016). If our projects are designed following the advice in Chapter 5, it should be a relatively straightforward process to address the requirements of the funding call while also achieving our research objectives.

Even if we are tasked with managing a project that we did not design, or that is not research-oriented, the basics of good project management are still defined by clear planning and sensible management of our resources.

Efficient project planning begins with setting an overall aim for the project. This is usually a general statement of what it *should* achieve, followed by a set of objectives that state more explicitly *how* that aim will be achieved. A set of measurable outputs and outcomes will allow you to ascertain if these objectives are being reached. The outputs are the tangible results of the project, and can include papers, reports, books, workshops, or any other products, services, or events developed through the project. Outcomes are the effects or impacts of the project, and can include changes in attitudes, understanding or behaviours, raising awareness of an issue, or any other kind of consequence or legacy of the project.

Once those high-level aspects of the project are in place, the specifics of how the project will be implemented need to be fleshed out. Large-scale research projects – mirroring the approach of the European Commission, which funds 'the world's biggest multinational research programme' (Abbott, 2020, p. 371) – are usually broken up into individual but interconnected units of work called 'work packages'. While these work packages need to function in tandem for the project to be a success, they also grant a level of autonomy within the project so that different people or organisations can lead separate work packages and the individual tasks within them.

As well as these self-contained tasks, the work packages usually include milestones and deliverables. The milestones provide a way of indicating when a certain point of the project has been reached, and can be as general as a research study concluding, or as specific as a targeted number of events being reached. The project outputs are typically called deliverables, or the deliverables can sometimes be reports describing the outputs. Capturing all of this in a project plan is crucial in order to keep oversight of the project, and to ensure that everyone on the team knows when the work they are responsible for needs to be completed and how it will fit into the timeline of the overall project. One of the most common tools used for project planning is a Gantt Chart – a template of which is available on this book's companion website.

Having a Gantt Chart in place is beneficial, but it is only the first step in efficiently managing our project (Maylor, 2001). The administration skills from Chapter 9 – time-management, communication, teamwork, scheduling meetings, prioritisation, and monitoring progress – are essential to running a successful project. Assembling the right team, however, may be the most critical aspect of all (Bush and Hattery, 1956; Salas, 2015; Gibert et al., 2017). University-based projects may require internal staff recruitment or an external process. Either way, taking the time to recruit top candidates is key; having a capable, motivated team is the best way to ensure a project will succeed.

We should aim to hire individuals who complement the team rather than solely recruiting people with similar backgrounds, skills, or experiences. It may initially feel disconcerting to hire someone with a different skill set, who might be more experienced and capable than us in certain areas, but it will strengthen professional learning within the team. If we have confidence in our staff to complete their tasks more efficiently than we could, it will help us resist the urge to micromanage (Mochal and Mochal, 2011). A successful project manager trusts their team to take responsibility and be accountable for their own decisions. If we gain experience in team-building, self-governance, improving efficiency, conflict-resolution, and managing risk, we may find ourselves being tasked with other kinds of management, such as overseeing a course, a programme, or a department.

Researcher views

Ivar, on the rewards of being involved in research projects:

> One of the best parts of the job is working on research projects. You meet lots of new people, get to travel to exotic places for project meetings ... and sometimes the work is interesting too!

Conferencing

Along with publications and public engagement events, one of the main avenues for sharing research project results is through academic conferences. Academic conferences bring researchers together – usually for several days – to discuss their research through a programme of presentations, workshops, keynote addresses, and social events. Large scale academic conferences can have thousands of attendees, under a broad research theme, while smaller conferences – sometimes referred to as 'symposia' or 'colloquia' – may focus on more specific research topics. The primary goal of modern academic conferences is for scholars to interact with their peers, so as to remain productive and creative (Coser, 1997), although they also serve to support 'professional socialization, the reproduction of academic status hierarchies, and the legitimation of new subfields' (Gross and Fleming, 2011, p. 153).

The academic conference has its roots in the earliest gatherings of scholars communicating their ideas. It evolved from Ancient Greek symposia, and eighteenth-century coffee houses and French Salons, through to the formation of learned bodies like the Royal Society, and the modern-day incarnation of 'a formal meeting based on intellectual communication' (Nicolson, 2017, p. 6). For early career researchers, academic conferences are a rite of passage. While publishing our research gives it credibility, presenting it at academic conferences increases our visibility and can generate career opportunities (Leahey, 2007; Kriwy et al., 2013). Attending conferences helps us meet new colleagues in our fields of research and may boost our chances of subsequent collaborations and publications (Campos et al., 2018).

National conferences are wise to attend early in our studies, but as we progress, we should aim to attend the most noteworthy international conferences in our fields. Choose the conferences attended by the most high-profile researchers in your field – those whose work you admire and cite in your own research. A supervisor or mentor can help identify such conferences as – similar to the predatory journals described in Chapter 4 – there are predatory conference organisers who dupe researchers into paying for sham events (Cobey et al., 2017). Academic researchers generally apply to present their work at conferences by submitting papers – in full or as short abstracts – which are accepted or declined following a peer-review process. As mentioned in Chapter 4, having a paper published in a conference proceedings – a collected volume of the papers presented at a conference – does not carry as much academic value as a peer-reviewed journal article. Even though having a paper accepted at a prestigious conference can be a competitive process, your strategy should be to submit a paper that draws on work you have recently published in a journal article – adding a new perspective or building on the content of that paper. If you do not have a suitable publication to draw from, then you should submit a paper that is an early version of a journal article you hope to publish, keeping the main results and conclusion for that article rather than squandering them on a conference proceedings paper that will not be read as widely.

The two most common conference presentation formats are talks and posters. If given the option, either before or after submitting your conference paper, always choose presenting a talk over presenting a poster. The conference paper will be a stepping stone towards an eventual journal article, and the talk will give you valuable experience speaking in front of an academic audience. A conference poster, on the other hand, is a less constructive use of your time and will not be of much value to you outside of the conference itself. If presenting posters is unavoidable early in your research career, only spend as much time creating them as it takes to make them look adequately professional. An academic poster template – with guidelines on what to include and what to avoid – is available on this book's companion website.

Academic conferences have always been helpful places for delegates to expand their professional networks (Egri, 1992). They are also inherently odd. Conferences can serve as a microcosm of everything that is wonderful and terrible about working in academic research. Seeing hordes of excited researchers proudly sharing their work is a sight to behold and the enthusiasm can be infectious. For some people, however, conferences can be intimidating and uncomfortable, and at their worst can be outright unpleasant, distressing, or discriminatory (Settles and O'Connor, 2014; Biggs et al., 2018).

Conferences can be environments where problematic academic hierarchies are reinforced; senior researchers are likely to get more recognition and plaudits for their work even if it is identical to that of a more junior colleague. This 'Matthew effect' (named after a biblical reference loosely interpreted as those 'who have' being rewarded and the 'have-nots' receiving nothing) is even worse for women in research – sometimes referred to as the 'Matilda effect' – with women being less likely than men to receive due recognition for their work (Rossiter, 1993).

Researcher views

Nadine, on how uncomfortable she felt at her first academic conference:

> I stood at my poster and no one came near me. It was awful. I felt like I was on show and I wasn't sure if I should be trying to make eye contact so that people would come over [...] Eventually a guy came over and he wasn't interested in my poster at all. I really wanted to leave but they told us we had to stay beside our posters.

Historically, a key problem with academic conferences has been their reliance on being in-person events, with the associated travel requirements posing financial and geographical barriers for many researchers (Timperley et al., 2020). When the kind of casual international travel associated with conference attendance became impossible due to the COVID-19 global pandemic in 2020, long-running academic conferences were either cancelled, postponed, or reinvented as virtual conferences. Although hosting academic conferences online raises issues around accommodating different time zones, and compounds the digital divide (Chapter 6), the improved accessibility, coupled with the reduced environmental impact, mean that virtual academic conferences are here to stay and are only going to become more popular (Klöwer et al., 2020). Despite its troublesome past, the future of the academic conference has the potential to be 'rooted in sustainability, equitability and inclusion' (Niner et al., 2020, p. 253).

Building a network

The more time we spend in our roles as academic researchers, the more we will get to know the other researchers and staff in our institutions. Such local contacts are important, especially for providing reassurance and support through shared experiences. We will also have to look further afield to find collaborators to help us with research projects, publications, funding proposals, reference letters, and job opportunities (Defazio et al., 2009; Faria and Goel, 2010; Goel and Grimpe, 2013). To do this, we must employ one of the most divisive academic skills – networking.

An early career researcher who believes they are naturally good at networking is a rare breed (and probably someone to avoid at parties). By the time we become professional researchers, we might – if we are lucky – be decent writers, or good teachers, or even have a flair for public speaking, but most of us do not possess innate networking skills. Unfortunately, whether we like it or not, being able to reach out and connect with fellow researchers is an integral part of the job. Tracking down the right collaborators, finding suitable mentors, and successfully building a network is central to being an academic (Quinlan, 1999; Mathews, 2003).

The 'powerful magic' of academic networking can be challenging, especially to those unfamiliar with academic culture (Gillies and Alldred, 2007, p. 106). The self-serving nature of academic networking is inescapable, and can be described as 'the dynamic, socio-political practice of building, maintaining, and ending relations at work for personal and career benefits' (Van den Brink and Benschop, 2014, p. 487). As mentioned in Chapter 8, social media can be invaluable for networking when used in the correct manner (Carrigan, 2019), but are often used solely for 'self-promotion and ego-bolstering' (Meishar-Tal and Pieterse, 2017, p. 17). Regardless of how grimy the idea of improving our networking skills makes us feel, giving some thought to how we meet and connect with other professionals is an unfortunate necessity.

One of the most basic steps in establishing rapport with someone has always been the simple act of remembering their name (Carnegie, 1936). Maddeningly, this simple act still trips many of us up, especially at academic events where people are introduced in quick succession. Event organisers often try to circumvent this issue by providing lanyards or name badges, but not every professional networking situation, or even every conference, will employ such measures. Even if they do, trying to surreptitiously glance at someone's name badge, while it becomes increasingly clear that we do not remember their name, is awkward at best. Admitting we have forgotten their name is not a professional blunder; most people will not take offence, even if they feel a little undermined for not having made a big enough impression for us to commit their name to memory. If we cross paths with them again at another event, only to realise that we have once more forgotten their name ... then the professional and personal embarrassment starts to spiral.

The issue is that we do not yet have a strong enough link in our mind between the person and their name. The easiest way to create that link is to politely repeat their name back to them as soon as we are introduced, to make sure we have heard their name properly, and to confirm that we are pronouncing it correctly. By saying it aloud we have already improved our chances, but the critical part is to then connect it to something else that we will not forget. Perhaps the easiest way to remember a name is to come up with some kind of association between the person's face and their name (Lorayne and Lucas, 1974), but really any kind of meaningful association can be valuable, and will make all the difference between repeatedly forgetting their name or having it stored safely in our memory banks (Schmidt et al., 1999).

As we say their name for the first time, we should follow it up with a positive association or a connection we have with that name. Maybe it is (or sounds like) the name of a family member, a friend, or even a celebrity we admire. Personally, I go a step further; while I am repeating their name I will, in my head (and that part is crucial if I hope to ever talk to them again), put their name into a song lyric, or a pun, or a slogan. It means that a lot of people in my life have their own theme songs that play in my head whenever I meet them, which obviously makes me sound deranged, but it is an eccentricity I happily indulge to save me the embarrassment of forgetting names.

Once names are remembered, the main goal of networking is to connect with people and build rapport. Celebrity networking 'gurus' always say that the best way to connect with someone is to make them think you are interested in what they have to say. For regular people who do not earn their living being professional sociopaths, that sounds manipulative. A healthier and more honest way to achieve the same rapport with someone, is to *actually* be interested in what they have to say. No matter who we meet in the course of our academic pursuits, they are likely to have some connection to a world we can relate to. Whether they are a veteran researcher or someone at the beginning of their studies, we should be able to find enough shared experiences to be genuinely interested in their discipline, subject, or research topic. Even if we do not understand the technical details of their research, trying to understand what makes them passionate about their work can be a wonderful way of getting to know someone better. Often, they will appreciate our interest and be just as curious about our work and, before we know it, we will have a new professional contact and – if we find enough common ground and mutual interests – a potential new friend. Thankfully, this book is not about making friends; an emotionally-limited Irishman who sings people's names in his head is not your ideal guide on that particular adventure.

Conference reviews and networking

A useful way to ensure we get the most out of attending academic conferences, while turbo-charging our fledgling networking skills at the same time, is to write conference reviews for academic journals. Although not the most prestigious of academic publications (when compared with the other types of journal articles described in Chapter 4), it is one of the shortest and easiest kinds of papers to write, and still carries academic weight if published in a reputable journal.

The importance that publications have in our academic careers should be all the incentive we need to commit to writing something as relatively painless as a conference review paper, but an additional benefit is that it provides an easy way for us to kickstart our networking efforts. It may not be easy to talk to strangers about our research, especially if they happen to be senior academics whose work we admire, but if we can introduce ourselves as researchers who are writing about the conference and seeking their perspectives, then we are almost guaranteed they will be happy to talk to us. Even the keynote speakers – usually the most high-profile and in-demand conference delegates – will doubtless find a few minutes to speak to us if we let them know we wish to quote their keynote in our conference review.

Academic conferences are not widely reviewed in the literature, but most academic journals are interested in publishing a variety of article types that will be of interest to their readers, so a conference review is more attractive to journals than we might think. Before deciding to review a conference you are planning to attend, use your well-honed research skills to consult the published literature and establish if there are already any reviews of the conference in academic journals. If there are no academic publications then you may have to dig deeper to see if there is any information about the conference available elsewhere online, on previous conference websites, or anywhere there might be a mission statement, a list of objectives for the conference, or even a history of the event. Having that background knowledge of the event will help you to answer some key questions that you could consider putting into the introduction of your paper – such as when and why the conference was established, and how it has since evolved. That can help to frame your own engagement with the conference as you capture the current attendee experience.

Researcher views

Anne, on the importance of networking at conferences:

> I focused on the social aspect of conferences, more than the actual content. That is when you meet people. I mean, you have to choose who you network with and not let it go to waste. I wasn't shy at all. I spoke to professors and people who lead groups and, for me, I knew what I was looking for. The second year of my PhD, I was already looking into where I was going to do my postdoc.

If you know other people attending the conference you could consider enlisting them as co-authors by asking them to keep brief notes on their most memorable experiences at the conference. Even if you do not know anyone attending the conference, the review paper you are working on is as good an excuse as any to introduce yourself. You can even reach out to the conference organisers who may provide valuable behind the scenes perspectives and, if appropriate, could potentially be co-authors too.

Conferences are challenging to run, and rather than focusing on the problems or obstacles that arise, it is more constructive to focus on what went well and what delegates hope to see at future events. We can approach the conference review as a way of speaking about individual ideas, broader contexts, or specific perspectives. We might choose to comment on the current state of a particular field of research (Roche and Davis, 2017); provide advice to fellow professionals on whether they should consider attending a particular conference (Roche et al., 2018); or tackle a wider societal issue (Brown et al., 2020). A conference review template is available on this book's companion website.

Strength in numbers

Several of the academic skills discussed in this book can be acquired through a logical two-step process – seeking out someone to help us learn a skill, then tracking our improvement as we develop that skill. Each step in that process culminates in its own distinct area of professional development. Finding people to learn from, taken to its logical conclusion, is known as joining a 'community of practice'. Tracking how we improve in our roles is the basis of a field called 'reflective practice'. We will consider reflective practice in the next section, but first we will explore communities of practice.

Academic mentoring has long been considered vital in institutions of higher education for providing opportunities for professional growth (Baldwin and Blackburn, 1981). Although a good mentor improves academic career aspirations (Lindholm, 2004), the positive impact it has on both promotion and salary prospects are of most benefit to those who already have the highest socioeconomic status (Whitely et al., 1991). Once we have a professional network, we can reduce our dependence on mentors by starting or joining a community of practice.

A community of practice is any group of individuals who come together through a shared interest or passion and seek ways to improve themselves and to support each other. The earliest interpretations of communities of practice highlighted how any employment that involves working with others can result in a community of practice, which is a social process 'that includes, indeed it subsumes, the learning of knowledgeable skills' (Lave and Wenger, 1991, p. 29). Communities of practice were often considered a necessary means for workers to informally share knowledge and succeed in the workplace (Brown and Duguid, 1991) especially 'as members develop among themselves their own understanding of what their practice is about' (Wenger, 1998, p. 4). Over time, definitions of community of practice were expanded to describe any group of people engaging in a sustained pursuit of shared knowledge and expertise (Wenger, 2000; Wenger et al., 2002), as well as being a conceptual lens for exploring and understanding social learning (Cox, 2005), and even a managerial tool (Li et al., 2009).

Communities of practice exist for every kind of work or hobby and are not constrained by geographical location or any other demographic. Although there are countless ways a community of practice might form, with any number of topics of interest as its focus, the two obvious topics of interest for an early career researcher are academic development and research area. A community of practice focusing on academic development can coalesce in our institution with our peers. Seeking out fellow researchers who wish to improve their academic skills can provide us with professional development opportunities across all aspects of our practice. Organising a conference, for example, even a small or local meeting for a niche discipline, or solely for graduate students, can help develop skills such as teamwork, communication, and project management (Sciortino, 2018).

Although academic communities of practice can be 'turbulent', 'loosely-formed', and 'dispersed across universities nationally and internationally' (Arthur, 2016, p. 233), there is a strong tradition of forming academic communities to share teaching practices in higher education. This is often referred to as the 'scholarship of teaching and learning' (Felten, 2013, p. 121) and participating in such a community can help us investigate teaching and learning from both student and teacher perspectives (Bernstein, 2010). Wise academics share best practices, not just because of their intrinsic scholarly value, but because of the benefits that good teaching has for society (Bernstein and Bass, 2005).

The second area where a community of practice can be beneficial is in our specific research areas. Such a community will form as we grow our professional network through collaborating with other researchers and attending academic conferences. As we gain experience attending conferences, we can progress from individual conference presentations to proposing panels or round-table discussions of our research topic. This lends us the opportunity to select and convene groups of luminaries in our field, while simultaneously boosting the visibility of our work. If such sessions are well-received, our fellow panellists may consider us for employment opportunities or provide us with letters of reference.

As we submit papers to academic journals, there is sometimes an option to volunteer as a reviewer for that journal. Being called upon to review an academic paper, or to be a guest editor, is not only a valuable and necessary contribution to our field, but is an excellent way to gain first-hand insight into the peer-review process, which in turn will improve our chances of successfully navigating academic publishing. Similarly, being called upon to review research grants provides an extremely useful perspective on funding processes that may help us to aim higher in our research funding ambitions.

Sometimes such professional development opportunities arise unexpectedly, but we can be proactive in our efforts to improve our opportunities by consulting our communities of practice for their insights. As a first step, academic researchers should register a profile on the European Commission's database of external experts so that European Union Institutions can call upon us to evaluate research grant applications, monitor the progress of research projects, or provide advice on European-level programmes and policies (European Commission, 2021). Taking ownership of our skills development as we engage in professional learning communities will undoubtedly make us better academic researchers (Stoll et al., 2006).

Researcher views

Summer, on the role of mentors:

> Mentors, I think, are the pillars of a career in research. People that are encouraging of your ideas, that are genuinely interested and eager to contribute or guide you in some way to make them happen [...] I honestly believe they determine whether you make it or break it in your early career in research.

Reflecting on professional practice

Continuing professional development is not just a necessity for academic researchers, but is an implicit expectation across a growing number of professions (Friedman and Phillips, 2004). As academic researchers, thinking of our development in terms of our own professional learning is more productive than expecting an employer to manage how we grow in our professions (Webster-Wright, 2009). Being open to receiving guidance and support from others ensures professional growth. We can fortify our progress by complementing our professional learning with reflective practice.

Reflective practice can be traced back to the idea that learning through experience is enhanced when an individual deliberately reflects on that experience, rather than relying on their immediate reactions or impulses (Dewey, 1933). The process of deliberately reflecting on experience became a method of explaining the complex and often unpredictable ways that professionals acquire knowledge (Schön, 1983). Reflective practice subsequently grew to be a means of professional learning, as well as a field of theory and practice in its own right (Thompson, 2000). It became embedded in professions such as nursing (Johns and Freshwater, 1999), and social work (Knott and Scragg, 2007) but has always remained central to education professionals in schools and formal education environments (Brookfield, 1995) as well as more informal places of learning such as zoos, museums, and aquariums (Martin et al., 2019).

Early career researchers can use the act of reflecting on their work as a way of understanding their professional progress and development. Although reflective practice can be applied to all aspects of academic life, traditionally more emphasis has been placed on teaching (Campbell and Norton, 2007). While other areas of academic work receive some attention in the field of reflective practice – supervision for example (Douglas, 2003) – it is likely that research is not frequently tackled because academic researchers have different perceptions of what it means to be a researcher (Brew, 2001). When research is occasionally considered in terms of professional learning, researchers tend to reflect on their confidence, academic recognition, productivity, and sophistication as a researcher (Åkerlind, 2008). Researcher development statements and frameworks are provided by Vitae (a non-profit branch of the Careers Research and Advisory Centre funded by the UK Research Councils) and the Irish University Association to help early career researchers appraise their professional learning (IUA, 2008; Vitae, 2010).

The first stage of reflection is merely being aware of our own learning. Next, to reach beyond simple subjective and descriptive forms of reflection, critical reflection is needed. Rather than a surface-level observation of our practice, or being 'simply a matter of pausing for thought', reflection can become deeper and more meaningful when it is a systematic analysis of personal actions within wider contexts (Thompson and Pascal, 2012, p. 316). Critical reflection can be used to self-evaluate our work and determine the 'power relationships that allow, or promote, one particular set of practices over others' (Brookfield, 2009, p. 294).

For early career researchers, sustaining regular reflection can be challenging, and adopting a more methodical approach by using existing models of structured critical reflection can make personal reflections easier (Carlile and Jordan, 2007). In Chapter 6, we saw a model of reflective practice that uses four critical lenses to interpret our teaching (Brookfield, 1995). Similarly, keeping a written account of our progress as a researcher, as described in Chapter 2, provides a clear structure for reflective practice, especially as regular reflective writing is one of the most reliable ways of gaining insight into professional development (Stevens and Cooper, 2009; Bolton, 2018).

Applying a more structured and evidence-based approach to professional development can be empowering for early career researchers. Reflective practice can provide the necessary tools to gather data on our practice by observing and analysing our professional practice and subsequently making informed changes or improvements to how we work. Experience will aid our development, but deliberate and critical reflection on that experience is what will ultimately see us fulfil our potential as academic researchers.

Researcher views

Arthur, on the benefits of professional development:

> It was written into my contract that one of the stipulations was that I had to undertake leadership training. And that's something that, never in a million years, I would have done off my own bat. And at the start, I was like, ah … a tick-box exercise. But it was a really excellent course. In your day job, everything is just happening, you're firefighting and you're just getting on with work. With professional development, it just gives you that window when you actually stop and think about certain things. So in this case, it was stopping and thinking about leadership and development skills. I wouldn't have thought of myself as a leader, but I was leading modules, I was leading programmes. There were things I was doing well, probably, but definitely things that I needed to improve on.

Summary

- Manage projects efficiently. Mastering project management will make life significantly easier for you and your project teams.
- Attend academic conferences. Presenting your work at conferences will enhance your visibility as an academic researcher and provide valuable networking opportunities.
- Build a network. Connecting with other academic researchers will result in a group of professional contacts who you can call upon for advice and support throughout your career.
- Engage your professional community. Contributing to the development of your field will aid your professional learning.
- Reflect on your practice. Reviewing your progress in a structured way will highlight what you are doing well and what you may wish to improve.

Professional development is intertwined with how we feel about our work and our identity as academic researchers. No one enjoys feeling like they are no longer improving or that they have stagnated in their development. Keeping an oversight of how things are progressing, and how we are becoming more proficient, can help remind us that we are advancing in our work. Even if there are periods when we do not receive accolades, awards, or promotions, we can still find satisfaction in how we are growing as academic researchers and becoming better at what we do. Most importantly, professional development may help us to find fulfilment and contentment in our work. It will also have a role to play in our career prospects. Speaking of which, the time has come to gather up our CVs, research plans, and teaching philosophy statements – we are being summoned to our career progression review in the next chapter.

Further reading

- Badiru, A. B., Rusnock, C. F., & Valencia, V. V. (2016). *Project Management for Research: A Guide for Graduate Students*. Boca Raton, FL: CRC Press Taylor & Francis.
An easy-to-read guide for early career researchers to get to grips with the basics of project management in order to improve their research.

- Bolton, G. with Delderfield, R. (2018). *Reflective Practice: Writing and Professional Development* (5th edn). London, UK: SAGE.
This book provides an invaluable exploration of how reflective writing can be harnessed in professional development.

- Carnegie, D. (1936). *How to Win Friends & Influence People*. New York, NY: Simon and Schuster.
The original guidebook to professional networking and, though dated in parts, still eerily relevant in the modern workplace.

- Nicolson, D. J. (2017). *Academic Conferences as Neoliberal Commodities*. Cham, Switzerland: Palgrave Macmillan.
The definitive book on academic conferences, right down to the sections and chapters being styled after the different aspects of a typical conference.

- Wenger, E. (2000). *Communities of Practice: Learning, Meaning, and Identity* (2nd edn). Cambridge, UK: Cambridge University Press.
The educational theorist Etienne Wenger and cognitive anthropologist Jean Lave were the first to devise the concept of communities of practice before it was refined and expanded in this book.

Resources

Further resources for this chapter can be found at: www.JosephRoche.ie/EssentialSkills

- Gantt Chart Template
- Academic Poster Template
- Conference Review Template

References

Abbott, A. (2020). The world's biggest research programme got a lot right. *Nature, 588*(7838), 371.

Åkerlind, G. S. (2008). Growing and developing as a university researcher. *Higher Education, 55*(2), 241–254.

Arthur, L. (2016). Communities of practice in higher education: professional learning in an academic career. *International Journal for Academic Development, 21*(3), 230–241.

Badiru, A. B., Rusnock, C. F., & Valencia, V. V. (2016). *Project Management for Research: A Guide for Graduate Students.* Boca Raton, FL: CRC Press Taylor & Francis.

Baldwin, R. G. & Blackburn, R. T. (1981). The academic career as a developmental process: implications for higher education. *The Journal of Higher Education, 52*(6), 598–614.

Bernstein, D. (2010). Finding your place in the scholarship of teaching and learning. *International Journal for the Scholarship of Teaching and Learning, 4*(2), 1–6.

Bernstein, D. & Bass, R. (2005). The scholarship of teaching and learning. *Academe, 91*(4), 37–43.

Biggs, J., Hawley, P. H., & Biernat, M. (2018). The academic conference as a chilly climate for women: effects of gender representation on experiences of sexism, coping responses, and career intentions. *Sex Roles, 78*(5-6), 394–408.

Bolton, G. with Delderfield, R. (2018). *Reflective Practice: Writing and Professional Development* (5th edn). London, UK: SAGE.

Brew, A. (2001). Conceptions of research: a phenomenographic study. *Studies in Higher Education, 26*(3), 271–285.

Brookfield, S. (1995). *Becoming a Critically Reflective Teacher.* San Francisco: Jossey-Bass.

Brookfield, S. (2009). The concept of critical reflection: promises and contradictions. *European Journal of Social Work, 12*(3), 293–304.

Brown, A., Roche, J., & Hurley, M. (2020). Engaging migrant and refugee communities in non-formal science learning spaces. *JCOM: Journal of Science Communication, 19*(4), R01.

Brown, J. S. & Duguid, P. (1991). Organizational learning and communities-of-practice: toward a unified view of working, learning, and innovation. *Organization Science, 2*(1), 40–57.

Bush, G. P. & Hattery, L. H. (1956). Teamwork and creativity in research. *Administrative Science Quarterly*, *1*(3), 361–372.

Campbell, A. & Norton, L. (Eds.) (2007). *Learning, Teaching and Assessing in Higher Education: Developing Reflective Practice*. Exeter, UK: Learning Matters.

Campos, R., Leon, F., & McQuillin, B. (2018). Lost in the storm: the academic collaborations that went missing in hurricane Isaac. *The Economic Journal*, *128*(610), 995–1018.

Carlile, O. & Jordan, A. (2007). Reflective writing: principles and practice. In C. O'Farrell (Ed.), *Teaching Portfolio Practice in Ireland: A Handbook* (pp. 24–38). Dublin: AISHE.

Carnegie, D. (1936). *How to Win Friends & Influence People*. New York, NY: Simon and Schuster.

Carrigan, M. (2019). *Social Media for Academics*. London, UK: SAGE.

Cobey, K. D., Mazzarello, S., Stober, C., Hutton, B., Moher, D., & Clemons, M. (2017). Is this conference for real? Navigating presumed predatory conference invitations. *Journal of Oncology Practice*, *13*(7), 410–413.

Coser, L. A. (1997). *Men of Ideas*. New York, NY: Simon and Schuster.

Cox, A. (2005). What are communities of practice? A comparative review of four seminal works. *Journal of Information Science*, *31*(6), 527–540.

Defazio, D., Lockett, A., & Wright, M. (2009). Funding incentives, collaborative dynamics and scientific productivity: evidence from the EU framework program. *Research Policy*, *38*(2), 293–305.

Dewey, J. (1933). *How We Think. A Restatement of the Relation of Reflective Thinking to the Educative Process*. Boston, MA: DC Heath and Company.

Douglas, D. (2003). Reflections on research supervision: a grounded theory case of reflective practice. *Research in Post-Compulsory Education*, *8*(2), 213–230.

Egri, C. P. (1992). Academic conferences as ceremonials: opportunities for organizational integration and socialization. *Journal of Management Education*, *16*(1), 90–115.

European Commission (2005). The European Charter for Researchers and the Code of Conduct for the Recruitment of Researchers. Brussels, Belgium: European Commission.

European Commission (2021). *Work as an Expert*. Available at: https://ec.europa.eu/info/funding-tenders/opportunities/portal/screen/work-as-an-expert (accessed 7 October 2021).

Faria, J. R. & Goel, R. K. (2010). Returns to networking in academia. *NETNOMICS: Economic Research and Electronic Networking*, *11*(2), 103–117.

Felten, P. (2013). Principles of good practice in SoTL. *Teaching and Learning Inquiry*, *1*(1), 121–125.

Friedman, A. & Phillips, M. (2004). Continuing professional development: developing a vision. *Journal of Education and Work*, *17*(3), 361–376.

Gibert, A., Tozer, W. C., & Westoby, M. (2017). Teamwork, soft skills, and research training. *Trends in Ecology & Evolution*, *32*(2), 81–84.

Gillies, V. & Alldred, P. (2007). Making the right connections: knowledge and power in academic networking. In V. Gillies & H. Lucey (Eds.), *Power, Knowledge and the Academy* (pp. 105–121). London, UK: Palgrave Macmillan.

Goel, R. K. & Grimpe, C. (2013). Active versus passive academic networking: evidence from micro-level data. *The Journal of Technology Transfer, 38*(2), 116–134.

Gross, N. & Fleming, C. (2011). Academic conferences and the making of philosophical knowledge. In C. Camic, N. Gross, & M. Lamont (Eds.), *Social Knowledge in the Making* (pp. 151–179). Chicago, IL: University of Chicago Press.

IUA, Irish Universities Association (2008). *Irish Universities' PhD Graduates' Skills Statement*. Dublin, Ireland: IUA. Available at: www.iua.ie/publications/irish-universities-phd-graduates-skills (accessed 7 October 2021).

Johns, C. & Freshwater, D. (1999). Transforming nursing through reflective practice. *Journal of Psychiatric and Mental Health Nursing, 6*(5), 404–405.

Klöwer, M., Hopkins, D., Allen, M., & Higham, J. (2020). An analysis of ways to decarbonize conference travel after COVID-19. *Nature, 583*(7816), 356–359.

Knott, C. & Scragg, T. (Eds.) (2007). *Reflective Practice in Social Work*. Exeter: Learning Matters Ltd.

Kriwy, P., Gross, C., & Gottburgsen, A. (2013). Look who's talking: compositional effects of gender and status on verbal contributions at sociology conferences. *Gender, Work & Organization, 20*(5), 545–560.

Lave, J. & Wenger, E. (1991). *Situated Learning: Legitimate Peripheral Participation*. Cambridge, UK: Cambridge University Press.

Leahey, E. (2007). Not by productivity alone: how visibility and specialization contribute to academic earnings. *American Sociological Review, 72*(4), 533–561.

Li, L. C., Grimshaw, J. M., Nielsen, C., Judd, M., Coyte, P. C., & Graham, I. D. (2009). Evolution of Wenger's concept of community of practice. *Implementation Science, 4*(1), 1–8.

Lindholm, J. A. (2004). Pathways to the professoriate: The role of self, others, and environment in shaping academic career aspirations. *The Journal of Higher Education, 75*(6), 603–635.

Lorayne, H. & Lucas, J. (1974). *The Memory Book*. New York, NY: Ballantine Books.

Martin, L. W., Tran, L. U., & Ash, D. B. (2019). *The Reflective Museum Practitioner: Expanding Practice in Science Museums*. New York, NY: Routledge.

Mathews, P. (2003). Academic mentoring: enhancing the use of scarce resources. *Educational Management & Administration, 31*(3), 313–334.

Maylor, H. (2001). Beyond the Gantt Chart: project management moving on. *European Management Journal, 19*(1), 92–100.

Meishar-Tal, H. & Pieterse, E. (2017). Why do academics use academic social networking sites? *International Review of Research in Open and Distributed Learning, 18*(1), 1–22.

Mochal, T. & Mochal, J. (2011). Don't 'microbuild' or micromanage the workplan. In T. Mochal & J. Mochal, *Lessons in Project Management* (pp. 27–30). Berkeley, CA: Apress.

Nicolson, D. J. (2017). *Academic Conferences as Neoliberal Commodities*. Cham, Switzerland: Palgrave Macmillan.

Niner, H. J., Johri, S., Meyer, J., & Wassermann, S. N. (2020). The pandemic push: can COVID-19 reinvent conferences to models rooted in sustainability, equitability and inclusion? *Socio-Ecological Practice Research, 2*(3), 253–256.

Quinlan, K. M. (1999). Enhancing mentoring and networking of junior academic women: what, why, and how? *Journal of Higher Education Policy and Management, 21*(1), 31–42.

Roche, J. & Davis, N. (2017). Citizen science: an emerging professional field united in truth-seeking. *JCOM: Journal of Science Communication, 16*(04), R01.

Roche, J., Davis, N., Stanley, J., & Hurley, M. (2018). The Annual Ecsite Conference: an engagement and education forum for science museums. *Journal of Museum Education, 43*(1), 78–82.

Rossiter, M. W. (1993). The Matthew Matilda effect in science. *Social Studies of Science, 23*(2), 325–341.

Salas, E. (2015). *Team Training Essentials: A Research-Based Guide.* New York, NY: Routledge.

Schmidt, I. W., Dijkstra, H. T., Berg, I. J., & Deelman, B. G. (1999). Memory training for remembering names in older adults. *Clinical Gerontologist, 20*(2), 57–73.

Schön, D. A. (1983). *The Reflective Practitioner: How Professionals Think in Action.* New York, NY: Basic Books.

Sciortino, F. (2018). More than a meeting. *Nature, 559*(7714), 431.

Settles, I. H. & O'Connor, R. C. (2014). Incivility at academic conferences: gender differences and the mediating role of climate. *Sex Roles, 71*(1–2), 71–82.

Stevens, D. D. & Cooper, J. E. (2009). *Journal Keeping: How to Use Reflective Writing for Effective Learning, Teaching, Professional Insight, and Positive Change.* Sterling, VA: Stylus Publishing, LLC.

Stoll, L., Bolam, R., McMahon, A., Wallace, M., & Thomas, S. (2006). Professional learning communities: a review of the literature. *Journal of Educational Change, 7*(4), 221–258.

Thompson, N. (2000). *Theory and Practice in the Human Services.* Buckingham: Open University Press.

Thompson, N. & Pascal, J. (2012). Developing critically reflective practice. *Reflective Practice, 13*(2), 311–325.

Timperley, C., Sutherland, K. A., Wilson, M., & Hall, M. (2020). He moana pukepuke: navigating gender and ethnic inequality in early career academics' conference attendance. *Gender and Education, 32*(1), 11–26.

Van den Brink, M. & Benschop, Y. (2014). Gender in academic networking: the role of gatekeepers in professorial recruitment. *Journal of Management Studies, 51*(3), 460–492.

Vitae (2010). *Researcher Development Framework.* Cambridge, UK: Vitae.

Webster-Wright, A. (2009). Reframing professional development through understanding authentic professional learning. *Review of Educational Research, 79*(2), 702–739.

Wenger, E. (1998). Communities of practice: learning as a social system. *Systems Thinker, 9*(5), 2–3.

Wenger, E. (2000). *Communities of Practice: Learning, Meaning, and Identity* (2nd edn). Cambridge, UK: Cambridge University Press.

Wenger, E., McDermott, R. A., & Snyder, W. (2002). *Cultivating Communities of Practice: A Guide to Managing Knowledge*. Boston, MA: Harvard Business Press.

Whitely, W., Dougherty, T. W., & Dreher, G. F. (1991). Relationship of career mentoring and socioeconomic origin to managers' and professionals' early career progress. *Academy of Management Journal, 34*(2), 331–350.

Eleven

Career Progression

In this chapter, we will cover:

- seeking out employment
- job application documents
- interviews
- promotions and external opportunities
- pursuing other career paths.

The most vulnerable stage of an academic career

The typical academic career path involves doctoral study that is followed by postdoctoral experience before culminating in a faculty post that can lead to a permanent or tenured position. Describing it as a simple linear process, however, does not reflect the complexity and uncertainty that comes with finding long-term academic employment. The challenges facing early career researchers aspiring to land tenure-track jobs in academia are well-documented, with increasing competition for a dwindling number of secure positions (Whicker et al., 1993; Woolston, 2020). Being a newly qualified, accomplished, and professional researcher in academia can lead to wide-ranging employment opportunities, but many of those positions will come with temporary or short-term contracts, with little job security and uncertain future employment options (Laudel and Gläser, 2008; Gaughan and Bozeman, 2019).

As with many of the skills discussed in this book, the challenges associated with career progression are not often highlighted for academic researchers in a manner that encourages them to start preparing early in their careers. In this chapter, we will look at compiling the necessary documents for job applications, navigating the interview process, gaining professional experience, and considering employment opportunities outside of academia.

CVs, resumes, and supporting documents

Applying for academic jobs is a commitment. Those who get overwhelmed by the task are more likely to postpone seeking out and applying for positions until they urgently need a job – thus adding additional pressure to an already stressful process. We should start searching for jobs and submitting applications long before our current role or contract finishes. To ensure we have an idea of the kinds of positions open to us, we can seek advice from mentors or collaborators in our networks, and subscribe to job-posting newsletters and websites. Gaining familiarity with the type of jobs on offer will help us prepare our job application documents.

Researcher views

Tessa, on the transitional nature of postdoctoral research positions:

> I have a postdoctoral position that is a two-year position and so, as we speak, I have my eye on the job market to be applying again. So it still sort of feels like I'm in the process of it. I'm in that career progression moment, like I'm trying to find out what the next, and hopefully more permanent, step will be [...] I still feel like everything's a little precarious, what's it going to be, is this academia thing actually going to work out.

The main documents we are likely to need are a resume, or a curriculum vitae (CV), and a cover letter. Letters of recommendation may also be requested, or at least the names and contact details of individuals who can provide references. If we followed the approach to building a network outlined in Chapter 10, we should have plenty of potential referees for our applications. If the position involves teaching, we can expect a teaching philosophy statement will be needed too (covered in Chapter 6). Research posts may also require a research plan outlining our research goals and how we will achieve them. To give context to our plan, we should describe our research philosophy and the kinds of research questions we are interested in answering (as described in Chapter 2), alongside a complementary publication plan (as seen in Chapter 4), and a funding plan to make it all possible (covered in Chapter 5). A template research plan is available on this book's companion website.

Depending on the job, discipline, institution, and country, there could be other supporting documents necessary for our applications, but keeping copies of the above documents ready for use at short notice is a wise strategy, particularly when it comes to the CV: 'the production and scrutiny of CVs form an increasingly central part of routine academic life such that it is now impossible to conceive of that life without CVs' (Miller and Morgan, 1993, p. 135). The CV is so ingrained in academic career progression that some feel 'the modern academic is morbidly obsessed by them' (Metcalfe, 1992, p. 620).

The key difference between a resume and a CV is that while a CV should capture all our academic achievements and experiences, a resume is designed specifically to suit the needs of the potential employer (Basalla and Debelius, 2014). A CV can run to several pages, but a resume should be no more than two pages, and ideally just one. The words are used somewhat interchangeably, and so unless our 'Academic CV' is explicitly requested – which will become a lengthy document as our careers progress – then a bespoke one or two-page resume is the document that we should include, even if it is referred to as a 'CV' in the job listing.

The selection committee members assembled to evaluate our applications will not mistake quantity for quality – they will not enjoy combing through a long document trying to ascertain if we *might* be the right fit for the job. Instead, they are probably sifting through dozens, if not hundreds of applications, and their first pass will involve discarding those who do not immediately seem like viable candidates for the role. Our goal is to make sure our documents do not end up in the discarded pile. We can make the job of the selection committee easier by having a one or two-page resume concisely highlighting why we are exactly who they are looking for.

Job opportunities can arise unexpectedly and the easiest way to prepare an application at the last minute is to keep a 'master copy' of our full academic CV up to date (Chong and Clohisey, 2020). This document will list our publications, research grants, awards, education, previous positions, and all of our skills, along with our current contact and employment details. Of these, the most important section to develop is our list of skills. This list should include as many skills as possible, each followed by an explanation of how we developed that skill through work, education, or extracurricular activities. We can add new skills as we develop them, until we have accounted for every skill that is mentioned in the kinds of job advertisements we are considering. If the application requires a shorter CV or resume, then we can select the relevant skills from our master copy to ensure that we include everything that is needed for the job.

Having ensured the skills section of our resume matches exactly what is needed for the position, we can focus on the rest of the document. We should avoid putting a 'Curriculum Vitae' or 'Resume' title at the top of the document. Everyone knows what the document is, and the title should instead be the most important thing we want remembered by the selection committee – our name. This should be immediately followed by our contact details. If we happen to have a professional or personal website, it is acceptable to include a link in our contact details but only if it is a website that we keep updated and that we (and those in our life whose opinions we trust) are convinced presents us in the best professional light. A two-line objective, where we state why we have the skills and experience required for the position, is an easy way to demonstrate that our resume has been tailored to the job description. The education section should be clear and succinct, and should only include relevant information from third level education.

After listing any degrees or qualifications from colleges and universities, relevant previous employment, and our tailor-made skills section, we can include an oft-underappreciated 'hobbies' or 'other interests' section. This can provide an interview panel with an easy way to ask us about our interests and passions outside of work, and can demonstrate that we are well-rounded applicants. It should only be a line or two, and should be used to share an interesting aspect of our life that will stick in the memory of the selection committee. Of course, we are free to write that we 'enjoy reading and travelling', like everyone else in the history of applicants, but why not include something more unusual – competitive knitting, stone skipping, volunteering at an animal sanctuary, skydiving, coffee roasting, soap carving, writing fan fiction, beatboxing – whatever could be considered quirky or unexpected. It does not need to be an impressive pastime, and we do not even need to be good at it, but if it piques the curiosity of the selection committee, we have fulfilled our goal of being memorable and standing out among the horde of resumes. A template resume is available on this book's companion website.

Rather than having one set of documents that we submit for every job, our application and supporting documents need to be tailored to the job that is being advertised. Selection committees can easily spot a generic application that has been made for mass submission so, like the strategy for grant applications in Chapter 5, we should make sure we have as much information as possible before submitting our application. Cherry-picking the required skills from our master copy CV and tailoring the resume to be exactly what the selection committee is looking for is essential, but so too is writing a cover letter that demonstrates why we are right for the job.

The structure of the cover letter has remained the same for decades – one page with short paragraphs describing why we are interested in the position, why we believe we are suitable for the position, how we heard about the role, and a concluding paragraph describing our availability to interview (McDowell, 1987; Carr, 2019). As well as being concise, our cover letter should address a named person, use a formal tone, and be entirely free of any spelling or grammatical errors (Tomaska and Nosek, 2018). A template cover letter is available on this book's companion website.

Researcher views

Vanessa, on job applications becoming less daunting with experience:

> It's kind of like how am I gonna write a page to show how great I am when all I've done is like one research project or taught one class? As I get more experienced, the applications get easier. The first couple of years I was quite anxious about submitting applications. But I think once you get more experienced, once there's more to put in the application and you're not banking on that one paper you published, the application process gets easier. And I also know how to write them. Now I know what the search committees are looking for.

Preparing to interview

Once we have our supporting documents for job applications in good order, and we have tailored our submissions to as many suitable advertised posts as we can find, we will eventually be called to interview. This, above all others, is the part of career progression that most people would prefer not to think about until they have no choice but to face it. Rather than waiting for the elation-panic to set in when we receive an invitation to interview, we can begin our preparations much earlier, thanks to the predictability of interview questions.

As part of our preparations for the interview, we should learn everything we can about the institution, the department offering the job, and our potential new colleagues, so that we can plan how to adapt our interview answers to the appropriate context. To prepare for interviews we should practise answering different versions of standard interview questions. Despite the uncertainties inherent to the interview process (Bozionelos, 2005), we can expect several common types of questions, such as:

- Tell us about the research you have done that you are most proud of.
- How do you see your career progressing over the years ahead (five-year plan)?
- What kinds of courses would you propose to teach and what makes them innovative?
- Why did you choose this job and how do you see yourself fitting into this environment?
- Do you have any questions for us?

The most important aspect of how an early career researcher prepares for academic interviews is in successfully presenting themselves as a potential colleague rather than falling back on their identity as a graduate student (Kelsky, 2015). Our answers should help the interview panel imagine what it would be like to work with us. We want them to recognise us as someone whom they could rely on as a confident and competent colleague – someone who would inspire students, motivate staff, and enhance the reputation of the institution.

When preparing for any potential questions about research, your answers should not overly focus on your PhD. That work was carried out under the guidance of a mentor, and the interview panel needs to see you as an independent researcher. Instead, prepare to briefly describe your research area (using the *elevator pitch* from Chapter 8), before describing something you are currently working on – a paper, a book proposal, a grant application – that demonstrates how you are building on your previous research. You can outline your five-year plan by highlighting the main papers and research grants you will be targeting, using your publication plan (Chapter 4) and your funding plan (Chapter 5). Practise speaking confidently about your ambition to supervise researchers and build a research group, as well as how your publication and funding plans are designed to deal with any setbacks along the way. It is important to get comfortable hearing yourself saying those words out loud, so that by the time you are saying it to an interview panel your answers will be full of belief and will demonstrate your understanding of the role.

When preparing for questions on your teaching, bear in mind that the panel will want to be convinced that you are ready to seamlessly fit into their department. They will want to know if you can teach one of their existing courses at short notice, and bring fresh perspectives and innovative new modules that could strengthen their current course offerings. Preparing your answers to such questions provides an opportunity to demonstrate your knowledge of the institution – mention the current modules and courses that are offered, and describe how your teaching would fit into those programmes, or expand them, as needed. It is also an opportunity to show how your research, teaching, and public engagement experience aligns with, and consolidates, the work that is already happening in the institution and its wider community.

An additional type of question that warrants a prepared answer is the kind a panel uses to test how serious you are about taking the job. They may even ask you directly if you would accept the job if it were offered to you (Herreid and Full, 2010). That directness can trip up interviewees, as their answers might indicate that they have not seriously considered the logistics of accepting the position. It can also be a difficult question for candidates who have several job applications being processed at the same time. If you cannot honestly say that you would accept the job, then a polite way to answer the question is to express how honoured you would be to be offered a position, how you would give any offer due consideration, but that you would also need to discuss it with your family and loved ones before making any decision that would affect them. If pressed about applying for other positions, you are not obliged to give specific details – you can simply confirm that you are investigating all the options open to you, and that you are committed to finding employment at a prestigious institution.

After seeing a candidate perform flawlessly over the course of an interview it is always disheartening to watch them bungle the final question, especially as there is no excuse for not expecting it. Prepare for the inevitable 'Have you any questions for us?' part of the interview by having one or two well-rehearsed questions that will conclude the interview on a positive note and demonstrate how much research and consideration you have given the role (Onwuegbuzie and Hwang, 2014). Avoid general questions about the department or institution that you could easily have found the answer to by searching online, and resist the urge to ask questions about things like salary and annual leave – those questions can be dealt with if you are made an offer and move to the contract negotiation stage. Instead, ask an open-ended question about something unique to that department that you would genuinely like to hear more about; for example, 'All of my main questions have already been addressed, but I would love to hear about how your graduate-run seminar series came about, and was wondering if that is something that academic staff can get involved in supporting?'. Someone on the panel is bound to be delighted to talk about any initiative that casts the institution in a good light, and it means the lasting image the panel members will have of you is that of a confident and enthusiastic potential colleague who would be an asset to the department.

Presenting the best version of yourself

Practising mock interviews with friends, peers, and mentors is a great way to improve your interview performance, especially if you can talk to people who have experience as either an academic interviewer or interviewee. The interview format itself is often the main distraction to candidates. The more you practise, the more comfortable you will become with the format, enabling you to focus instead on your responses to questions, and your overall performance.

During the interview, the panel will be imagining their students being taught by you. They will expect to see someone who is professorial in their conduct – calm and deliberate, comfortable pausing to consider questions, projecting a balance of self-belief and humility. Of course, most of us do not feel like that all the time. Chapter 12 explores how we can often be battling our own neuroses, but a job interview is not the ideal place to be exploring those anxieties. Having rehearsed answers to the common kinds of interview questions will allow you to take a moment to compose your thoughts, before confidently giving your answers, safe in the knowledge that you have repeatedly practised such conversations.

Online interviews are becoming increasingly common and require some adjusting to the lack of real-time nonverbal communication (Peper et al., 2021). Dress as professionally as you would for an in-person meeting and make sure to test that your video, audio, and choice of venue are all appropriate for the interview. As academic career coach Karen Kelsky notes, the key thing to remember for the online interview is to keep your answers short. Rather than trailing off at the end of a sentence – decisively conclude your answer. Be content to leave a few seconds of silence to allow for any lag or delay on the call and to give the panel a chance to respond or to decide who is asking the next question. It is more stilted than a natural conversation would be, but if you present your answers succinctly and confidently, you can expect it to proceed like a regular interview (Kelsky, 2015).

As well as the interview itself, you may be asked to make a short presentation to the interview panel, or even to the whole department. If you are requested to present an overview of your work, use your *back pocket* lecture (Chapter 6) to provide a high-level but accessible account of your research and teaching, and how they would complement the existing work in the department. You may instead be asked to present on a more specific topic or concept chosen by the panel. Either way, you should practise your presentation as many times as needed until you feel confident in your delivery.

Record your practice presentations and critique them afterwards, to see if you are convincingly projecting yourself as a potential future colleague. Solicit feedback on whether your presentation is clear, engaging, and shows you and your work in the best light. If you are given 20 minutes in the interview schedule for a presentation and questions, then your talk should take 10–15 minutes at most. It is entirely acceptable to have a presentation that takes up less than the allotted time, but going over your time could potentially ruin the interview schedule, and your chances with it.

You can improve your interview skills faster with first-hand experience – apply for positions regularly, even if you are not certain you would take the job if it were offered to you. As you gain more interview experience, you can begin trusting in your abilities, and by the time you interview for your dream job, you can ignore the distractions of the interview format itself and concentrate on giving a stellar performance. If you are offered a position, take your time with what will be a significant decision to make. It is not a decision you should make alone, and seeking advice from peers and mentors will help you decide if it is the right job for you. Relocating is common for early career researchers, and there are countless implications to consider before moving, especially for families (Nerad and Cerny, 1999; Richardson and Zikic, 2007). Ultimately, if you accept a job offer, you can take pride in having successfully navigated the interview process, and can be confident of doing so again if you decide to pursue other employment opportunities in the future.

Researcher views

Summer, on observing women struggle in research when adequate support was not available:

> They took on much more responsibility of care work and domestic labour than their partners or than most male co-workers, which meant they had way less time to work on their own research projects [...] New mothers, from different cities or countries, often dropped out of their degrees and careers as they had no access to a support system to care for their children and be able to continue working at the same time.

Promotions and moonlighting

After the success of landing an academic post, it can be tempting to get swept up in the responsibilities that come with the role, and to focus on teaching, supervision, public engagement, or the myriad administrative duties that will materialise on our desks, to the detriment of our research, writing, publishing, and funding applications. As we have seen in previous chapters, all of those duties provide valuable experience, but when it comes to career progression in an academic research-performing environment, more value is placed on our research than any other aspect of our work (Dobele and Rundle-Theile, 2015; Glausiusz, 2019). Achieving excellence in the non-research aspects of our work is commendable, but if we apply for academic promotion having accomplished little with our research, we will be overlooked in favour of colleagues making steady progress with their research, even if they are underperforming in many of the non-research aspects of the job. To prevent such a situation, we need to have a strategy that prepares us for the promotion process.

As long as your institution has an application process for promotions, you should be able to acquire an application form, and even if the decision-making around promotions remains opaque, the criteria that are used to make those decisions should be transparent in the application form (Kiely et al., 2019). Use the promotion criteria as your way of judging how you will prioritise your time, and if you need to re-allocate any effort away from tasks that will not be recognised by a promotion committee.

Having a steady output of research publications, and a steady income of research grants, will put you in a strong position, but there may be other criteria you are expected to address. These could include memberships of discipline-specific associations, awards, and honours you have won or been nominated for, and any other ways you have contributed to your field and to the wider academic community (Macfarlane, 2007). You may also be expected to demonstrate evidence of your leadership skills, and how you have assumed positions of responsibility (Lonsdale, 1998; Buller, 2013). These are not the type of achievements that can be quickly addressed when you start your promotion application. Instead, they should form part of your long-term planning, ideally as soon as you start in your role. That way, you can address all your professional obligations in good time, and give the promotion committee no reason to delay your advancement.

Researcher views

Séamus, on being strategic about research grants to secure employment:

> Your greatest asset to the people that sign your cheques is that you can bring in funding. They are indifferent to your brilliance and your beautifully crafted theories. If you can bring in money by winning grants for the most derivative, uninspired research, it is a far safer path to a secure position.

Job security and recognition are vital for providing academic researchers with the freedom and motivation to keep pursuing new ideas and endeavours (Nir and Zilberstein-Levy, 2006). This can make the promotion process particularly discouraging. Despite efforts to recognise more academic duties – such as teaching (Subbaye and Vithal, 2017) – as being important criteria for promotion assessments, there remains enduring issues of inequity throughout the academic promotion process (Moses, 1986; Baker, 2010; Barrow and Grant, 2019). While oblique promotion processes and low starting salaries can be frustrating for junior academics, it is more often difficulties with colleagues, and a perceived lack of opportunities that lead to outright job dissatisfaction (Manger and Eikeland, 1990; Dorenkamp and Weiß, 2018). Having a contract – temporary or permanent – grants us the credibility and freedom to at least consider external opportunities, whether we wish to gain additional experience or supplement our income.

Although traditional university posts sometimes limit academics to a single employer, forward-thinking universities are now recognising the benefits of allowing their staff to explore other opportunities (Hayter et al., 2017). Staff morale is likely to be higher when academics are entitled to more control over their income and job satisfaction through external endeavours which, for better or worse, can offset the frustration caused by a lack of promotion opportunities. Once obligations to primary contracts are fulfilled, having staff moonlighting in other roles can strengthen the research and teaching expertise of the institution. Depending on your area of research, you may be able to explore freelance work, side-projects, part-time industrial or clinical positions, or set up your own professional practice (Clarysse et al., 2011).

Consulting work is always an option for academic researchers, and some universities now offer formal routes to secure such opportunities through the institution itself (Perkmann and Walsh, 2008). In return for the university taking a small cut of any such income, the institution handles all the additional financial and legal paperwork that goes with increasing your income through consulting. This can be very useful if you are unsure about how much you should charge for your time – even if universities may not always be able to recognise the value of their staff through promotions, they certainly know how much to charge when it is an external organisation that is paying.

As well as supporting freelance and consulting opportunities, modern universities recognise that academic researchers are innovative, creative, and can make excellent entrepreneurs, especially when given access to business incubators or technology transfer offices to explore their options in establishing start-up or spin-out companies (Perkmann et al., 2013; Garcia-Martinez, 2014). Setting up a business and building a company can be rewarding on many levels, but can also be incredibly demanding. While involving your university – usually granting it a share of profits or ownership – in such a process might not seem immediately appealing, having the support of expert financial and legal teams can allow you to focus on the parts of the process that you find most interesting.

If you are worried that the organisation you are joining is not progressive enough to support or even allow moonlighting, you can address it at the contract negotiation stage. Rather than accepting the opening offer from the university, you should enquire if your additional skills (which could be grant-writing, public engagement, or any other skill that you could foresee resulting in occasional external work opportunities) can be recognised with a higher starting salary. In the rare situation where the university agrees, then you should be content in having successfully negotiated a better position for yourself. In the more likely scenario, where you receive some variation of 'while we appreciate your experience, we unfortunately do not recognise those skills as warranting an increase in salary', then you can ask for that sentiment to be made explicit in the conditions of your employment. If an employer does not recognise those skills as warranting a higher income, it can have few grievances if those skills generate an external income for you.

If your external commitments are confined to evenings or weekends there should be no issues, especially if you continue to do an excellent job for your main employer.

You may have to seek permission, however, if an external opportunity will affect your regular working hours. In such situations, taking annual leave or vacation days might be your only option. Finding time for other opportunities is no easy feat – most academics work far more than their contracted hours, just to feel like they are staying on top of their primary responsibilities (Gillespie et al., 2001). If you find you are struggling in your role, however, moonlighting might be a way to maintain motivation. If part-time or freelance work starts to become more interesting or rewarding, you may consider reducing your contracted hours in your academic role. Having knowledge and experience of external work opportunities can also help if you decide at some point that your future lies outside academic research.

Researcher views

Lilly, on seeing how her part-time doctoral research helps her in her employment:

> What was really fascinating was when I realised how much my research actually helps me in my day job. I work for two start-ups and at some point I was going back to my PhD work and I realised *Oh my God, here's my answer*. What I was struggling with at work, the answer to some of those things was not in some books, but it was actually in my own research and I was answering my own questions right there. And so at that moment I felt like what I'm doing is actually significant, it actually makes sense, it's actually applicable. That really woke me up and gave me a lot of motivation to keep working on it.

Brave new career paths

The percentage of doctoral students who progress to tenured academic posts is not as high as might be expected – it varies by country and discipline, but it is generally less than 10% (Caterine, 2020). When it comes to career progression, missing out on a job or a promotion can feel like a rejection or even a failure if we let it (Carson et al., 2013). The sheer number of applications, and the competition in academia, mean that there are bound to be setbacks along the way. If we can see these events less as failures and more as necessary stepping stones, or even as opportunities for learning and growth, we are more likely to succeed. That is easier said than done, however, if our self-confidence is unsteady and if we are prone to occasional bouts of imposter syndrome (Chapter 12).

Even after securing employment, academics worry about their chosen career path, especially if there are parts of their job they dislike (Lacy and Sheehan, 1997). Although promotions are one of the most obvious ways to gauge if we are excelling in our job, it is more important to determine if our jobs are providing us with the kind of challenges, opportunities, rewards, and fulfilment that motivates us to keep working. Within any academic job there should be freedom to adapt and evolve in our roles to ensure we are playing to our strengths. Focusing on the tasks we enjoy, the ones we are good at, and finding a way to make them central to our work, will make us happier in our jobs.

More research is needed to better understand the trends in typical academic career paths (Zacher et al., 2019), but there is broad agreement that it helps no one if we pour every waking moment into our job to the detriment of our life outside work; Leaving an academic job to explore other career paths can be difficult, but there are always ways to explore our options outside of academic careers with mentors, career advisors, or coaches (Savage, 2015). As well as moonlighting in other roles, a sabbatical can provide a route to exploring aspects of our work in new ways (Davidson et al., 2010). It is not unusual for people to return to academia having explored other roles (Lieberman, 2019), and a career break can provide just such an opportunity to try a new profession.

The more time we spend working as academic researchers, the more difficult it can become to imagine alternative careers, but the skills we develop are compatible with countless professions (Baruch and Hall, 2004). Researchers are highly skilled individuals and finding employment opportunities outside of the academy is not just realistic, but for a host of reasons to do with our own situations, might even be more appealing. Regardless of where we find ourselves on the academic career path, it is always worth keeping our options open. 'The best professors rarely make the mistake of feeling they are serving their students or disciplines by spending every available moment' working, and instead 'become well rounded as faculty members because they've already discovered the secret of how to remain well rounded as people' (Buller, 2010, p. 405).

Summary

- Look for opportunities. Rather than waiting for someone to offer you your dream job, seek it out.
- Keep a master copy of your CV updated. Refine your job application documents regularly so that they are ready at short notice.
- Practise interviewing. Interview skills are too valuable to develop only when you urgently need a job.
- Consider your opportunities. If you are unsatisfied within your role, expand your horizons with side projects or freelance work.
- Be open to working outside of the academy. The academic career path is winding and uncertain, and any external opportunities that appear stimulating and rewarding are worthy of consideration.

The life of an academic researcher can be immensely gratifying, but it is not without occasional (sometimes recurring) setbacks. No academic researcher should ever feel that their career path is predetermined; facing the challenges and opportunities that will arise along the way is the only part of the journey that can be guaranteed.

Although inescapable, career prospects should not be our primary consideration as academic researchers. Thriving in our work is even more important, and our jobs are bearable only if they provide some kind of professional satisfaction. We will conclude our quest through academic skills by focusing on what is at once intrinsic to our success, as well as being more important than anything else we have discussed – the final chapter reminds us to prioritise our health and wellbeing.

Further reading

- Basalla, S. & Debelius, M. (2014). *'So What Are You Going To Do With That?': Finding Careers Outside Academia* (3rd edn). Chicago, IL: University of Chicago Press.
Full of real-world anecdotes, this book is an engaging guide to translating academic experience into diverse career options.

- Buller, J. L. (2010). *The Essential College Professor: A Practical Guide to an Academic Career.* San Francisco, CA: John Wiley & Sons.
A well-considered guide to dealing with the career challenges and opportunities that arise for college professors.

- Caterine, C. L. (2020). *Leaving Academia: A Practical Guide.* Princeton, NJ: Princeton University Press.
A recent account of the state of academic opportunities in the US and what is needed to make the transition from higher education to pastures new.

- Kelsky, K. (2015). *The Professor Is In: The Essential Guide to Turning your PhD into a Job.* New York, NY: Three Rivers Press.
Karen Kelsky draws on her expertise as an academic career consultant to provide a brutally honest depiction of navigating the academic job market.

- Whicker, M. L., Kronenfeld, J. J., & Strickland, R. A. (1993). *Getting Tenure.* Newbury Park, CA: SAGE.
This book demystifies the tenure process and provides practical advice on what needs to be prioritised in order to boost the likelihood of being offered a permanent position.

Resources

Further resources for this chapter can be found at: www.JosephRoche.ie/EssentialSkills

- Research Plan Template
- Resume Template
- Job Application Cover Letter Template

References

Baker, M. (2010). Career confidence and gendered expectations of academic promotion. *Journal of Sociology, 46*(3), 317–334.

Barrow, M. & Grant, B. (2019). The uneasy place of equity in higher education: tracing its (in)significance in academic promotions. *Higher Education, 78*(1), 133–147.

Baruch, Y. & Hall, D. T. (2004). The academic career: a model for future careers in other sectors? *Journal of Vocational Behavior, 64*(2), 241–262.

Basalla, S. & Debelius, M. (2014). *'So What Are You Going To Do With That?': Finding Careers Outside Academia* (3rd edn). Chicago, IL: University of Chicago Press.

Bozionelos, N. (2005). When the inferior candidate is offered the job: the selection interview as a political and power game. *Human Relations, 58*(12), 1605–1631.

Buller, J. L. (2010). *The Essential College Professor: A Practical Guide to an Academic Career.* San Francisco, CA: John Wiley & Sons.

Buller, J. L. (2013). *Positive Academic Leadership: How to Stop Putting out Fires and Start Making a Difference.* San Francisco, CA: John Wiley & Sons.

Carr, L. (2019). *How to Write a Cover Letter for Academic Jobs: An Ebook with Tips and Examples to Create the Perfect Cover Letter.* London, UK: Jobs.ac.uk eBooks.

Carson, L., Bartneck, C., & Voges, K. (2013). Over-competitiveness in academia: a literature review. *Disruptive Science and Technology, 1*(4), 183–190.

Caterine, C. L. (2020). *Leaving Academia: A Practical Guide.* Princeton, NJ: Princeton University Press.

Chong, Z. S. & Clohisey, S. (2020). How to build a well-rounded CV and get hired after your PhD. *The Journal of the Federation of European Biochemical Societies.* doi:10.1111/febs.15635

Clarysse, B., Tartari, V., & Salter, A. (2011). The impact of entrepreneurial capacity, experience and organizational support on academic entrepreneurship. *Research Policy, 40*(8), 1084–1093.

Davidson, O. B., Eden, D., Westman, M., Cohen-Charash, Y., Hammer, L. B., Kluger, A. N., ... & Spector, P. E. (2010). Sabbatical leave: who gains and how much? *Journal of Applied Psychology, 95*(5), 953–964.

Dobele, A. R. & Rundle-Theile, S. (2015). Progression through academic ranks: a longitudinal examination of internal promotion drivers. *Higher Education Quarterly, 69*(4), 410–429.

Dorenkamp, I. & Weiß, E. E. (2018). What makes them leave? A path model of postdocs' intentions to leave academia. *Higher Education, 75*(5), 747–767.

Garcia-Martinez, J. (2014). The third way: becoming an academic entrepreneur. *Science,* 20 March. Available at: www.sciencemag.org/careers/2014/03/third-way-becoming-academic-entrepreneur (accessed 4 April 2021).

Gaughan, M. & Bozeman, B. (2019). Institutionalized inequity in the USA: the case of postdoctoral researchers. *Science and Public Policy, 46*(3), 358–368.

Gillespie, N. A., Walsh, M. H. W. A., Winefield, A. H., Dua, J., & Stough, C. (2001). Occupational stress in universities: staff perceptions of the causes, consequences and moderators of stress. *Work & Stress, 15*(1), 53–72.

Glausiusz, J. (2019). Tenure denial, and how early-career researchers can survive it. *Nature*, *565*(7737), 525–528.

Hayter, C. S., Lubynsky, R., & Maroulis, S. (2017). Who is the academic entrepreneur? The role of graduate students in the development of university spinoffs. *The Journal of Technology Transfer*, *42*(6), 1237–1254.

Herreid, C. F. & Full, R. J. (2010). How to survive an academic job interview. *Journal of College Science Teaching*, *39*(3), 10–15.

Kelsky, K. (2015). *The Professor Is In: The Essential Guide to Turning your PhD into a Job*. New York, NY: Three Rivers Press.

Kiely, K., Brennan, N., & Hayes, A. (2019). Measuring research in the University via senior academic promotions and faculty research metrics. *Procedia Computer Science*, *146*(1), 173–181.

Lacy, F. J. & Sheehan, B. A. (1997). Job satisfaction among academic staff: an international perspective. *Higher Education*, *34*(3), 305–322.

Laudel, G. & Gläser, J. (2008). From apprentice to colleague: the metamorphosis of early career researchers. *Higher Education*, *55*(3), 387–406.

Lieberman, L. (2019). Leaving and returning to academia: can you ever go home again? In J. B. Urban & M. R. Linver (Eds.), *Building a Career Outside Academia: A Guide for Doctoral Students in the Behavioral and Social Sciences* (pp. 21–29). Washington, DC: American Psychological Association. doi: 10.1037/0000110-003

Lonsdale, A. (1998). Performance appraisal, performance management and quality in higher education: contradictions, issues and guiding principles for the future. *Australian Journal of Education*, *42*(3), 303–320.

Macfarlane, B. (2007). Defining and rewarding academic citizenship: the implications for university promotions policy. *Journal of Higher Education Policy and Management*, *29*(3), 261–273.

Manger, T. & Eikeland, O. J. (1990). Factors predicting staff's intentions to leave the university. *Higher Education*, *19*(3), 281–291.

McDowell, E. E. (1987). Perceptions of the ideal cover letter and ideal resume. *Journal of Technical Writing and Communication*, *17*(2), 179–191.

Metcalfe, A. W. (1992). The curriculum vitae: confessions of a wage-labourer. *Work, Employment and Society*, *6*(4), 619–641.

Miller, N. & Morgan, D. (1993). Called to account: the CV as an autobiographical practice. *Sociology*, *27*(1), 133–143.

Moses, I. (1986). Promotion of academic staff. *Higher Education*, *15*(1), 135–149.

Nerad, M. & Cerny, J. (1999). Postdoctoral patterns, career advancement, and problems. *Science*, *285*(5433), 1533–1535.

Nir, A. E. & Zilberstein-Levy, R. (2006). Planning for academic excellence: tenure and professional considerations. *Studies in Higher Education*, *31*(5), 537–554.

Onwuegbuzie, A. J. & Hwang, E. (2014). Interviewing successfully for academic positions: a framework for candidates for asking questions during the interview process. *International Journal of Education*, *6*(2), 98–113.

Peper, E., Wilson, V., Martin, M., Rosegard, E., & Harvey, R. (2021). Avoid Zoom fatigue, be present and learn. *NeuroRegulation, 8*(1), 47–56.

Perkmann, M. & Walsh, K. (2008). Engaging the scholar: three types of academic consulting and their impact on universities and industry. *Research Policy, 37*(10), 1884–1891.

Perkmann, M., Tartari, V., McKelvey, M., Autio, E., Broström, A., D'este, P., … & Sobrero, M. (2013). Academic engagement and commercialisation: a review of the literature on university–industry relations. *Research Policy, 42*(2), 423–442.

Richardson, J. & Zikic, J. (2007). The darker side of an international academic career. *Career Development International, 12*(2), 164–186.

Savage, N. (2015). Career counselling: pick a path. *Nature, 517*(7536), 645–647.

Subbaye, R. & Vithal, R. (2017). Teaching criteria that matter in university academic promotions. *Assessment & Evaluation in Higher Education, 42*(1), 37–60.

Tomaska, L. & Nosek, J. (2018). Ten simple rules for writing a cover letter to accompany a job application for an academic position. *PLoS Comput Biol, 14*(5), 1–4.

Whicker, M. L., Kronenfeld, J. J., & Strickland, R. A. (1993). *Getting Tenure.* Newbury Park, CA: SAGE.

Woolston, C. (2020). Uncertain prospects for postdoctoral researchers. *Nature, 588*(7836), 181–184.

Zacher, H., Rudolph, C. W., Todorovic, T., & Ammann, D. (2019). Academic career development: a review and research agenda. *Journal of Vocational Behavior, 110,* 357–373.

Twelve
Health and Wellbeing

In this chapter, we will cover:

- the state of health and wellbeing in early career researchers
- preparing to cope with the challenges of academia
- maintaining a work–life balance
- asking for help
- supporting others.

Taking good care

We conclude our journey through academic skills by reminding ourselves that prioritising our health and wellbeing is non-negotiable. The skills needed to bolster physical and mental health in academia are vitally important, yet they are oftentimes neglected. One of the most worrying findings from studies of early career researchers is the growing rate of mental health related issues. Symptoms of psychiatric distress – ranging from nervousness, irritability, and stress, to anxiety, depression, and suicidal thoughts – present in early career researchers at an ever-increasing rate (Garcia-Williams et al., 2014; Levecque et al., 2017; Evans et al., 2018).

In this chapter, we will explore the extent of this worrying trend in academia, while also preparing for some of the inevitable challenges of the academic environment. We will also discuss the importance of keeping some semblance of a work-life balance and practising self-care. Finally, we will see how becoming more aware of the challenges facing those around us can allow us to support our colleagues in their times of need, building a stronger and more supportive academic research environment.

The gravest cause for concern

The precarious working conditions of early career researchers have been a cause for concern for decades (Kubie, 1954; Herschberg et al., 2018). One of the more obvious problems with doctoral and early career research programmes across the world is that, despite the number of people obtaining doctorates dramatically increasing, a coherent strategy for supporting this rising number of highly qualified people has not been responsibly considered (Cyranoski et al., 2011). On top of this, and probably worsened by it, there is growing evidence that the state of mental health of people studying and working in university environments is deteriorating (Kadison and DiGeronimo, 2005).

While students at all academic levels experience distress, for researchers at an early stage of their careers, the demands of academia can be compounded by factors such as high expectations, isolating environments, and sleeplessness, all of which can lead to 'debilitating depression, agonizing bouts of anxiety or even suicide attempts' (Gewin, 2012, p. 299). In 2014, a research development officer wrote an anonymous post on *The Guardian*'s higher education blog that warned of a culture of acceptance around mental health issues in academia, and called attention to instances of depression, sleep and eating disorders, alcohol abuse, self-harm, and suicide among doctoral students. The post was shared hundreds of thousands of times and sparked an unprecedented debate over unacceptable levels of distress among early career researchers (Shaw and Ward, 2014).

In 2018, a survey of 2,279 researchers from different disciplines across 26 countries suggested that early career researchers were six times more likely to experience depression and anxiety, resulting in urgent calls to tackle the 'mental health crisis' and the 'strikingly high rates of anxiety and depression' among early career researchers (Evans et al., 2018, pp. 283–284). Another survey of more than 7,600 postdoctoral researchers across 93 countries found that this mental and emotional strain can cause early career researchers to question whether they should stay in academic research (Woolston, 2020). The high-pressure nature of the work, long hours, comparatively low wages, and inherent job insecurity each contributed to this uncertainty. A separate survey of 13,000 researchers from more than 160 countries found that even though 65% of respondents felt 'under tremendous pressure to publish papers, secure grants, and complete projects', 49% said they would 'not discuss work-based feelings of severe stress or anxiety with relevant people/authorities in their workplace' often because these feeling were considered 'normal in academic life' (Cerejo et al., 2020, p. 6).

Researcher views

Sarah, on how her research affects her wellbeing:

> You have to have some sort of wellness self-discipline. You end up sometimes pulling all-nighters and chasing deadlines and other times you really have so much free time that you just take too much of it. What I found to be most hurtful for my wellbeing is the nonlinearity of success [...] You cannot really say at some point *Okay I'm really done with this*. And the fact that there's always this thing that you know is not finished ... it's kind of like nibbling on your wellbeing in the background. It's always in the back of my mind. Every time I go on holiday, every time I have a weekend away, every time I try to relax in the evenings ... sometimes I dream about it.

This normalisation of stress is endemic in academia, where 'high levels of job satisfaction can co-exist with elevated levels of stress' (Kinman, 2014, p. 224). Academic environments are becoming ever more punishing places to work (Taberner, 2018). Even after securing an academic post, there is evidence that the demands placed on junior professors can have a detrimental effect on their research (Powell, 2016), and to survive, some even succumb to unethical practice (Martinson et al., 2005). In addition to the challenges raised by workload, poor management, job insecurity, and insufficient recognition (Gillespie et al., 2001), women and ethnic minorities additionally endure marginalisation, patronisation, and discrimination within academic environments (Martinez et al., 2007; Housee and Richards, 2011; Ysseldyk et al., 2019). Academia can be a 'cold, lonely, comparative and competitive place' for people who experience 'the intersections of marginalized identities' (Edwards, 2019, p. 32).

Researcher views

Vanessa, on her experience of being a woman in academia:

> It was very amplified at [that university] that I was a woman. I was young. I was a little girl. I didn't know what I was doing. I didn't know what I was saying. If I was assertive, I was defensive or I had attitude. If I knew what I was talking about, and I was confident in what I was talking about, I had attitude about it. My actions were always being twisted and manipulated to benefit what other people needed me to do [...] And how they do that is probably by controlling you a bit and manipulating you a bit. I think that's quite common in academia for women [...] If you feel like you're being made to self-reflect on your own actions, it's probably not you, it's probably the older white academic men who are projecting shit on to you so that you can do their work. And they can get the praise.

Occupational stressors such as time pressure, work overload, and complex interpersonal relationships have long existed in universities (Brown et al., 1986), but little progress has been made in dealing with them, with 'acceptance of the problem' sometimes reported as the main coping strategy (Abouserie, 1996, p. 54). This can result in burnout – 'chronic workplace stress that has not been successfully managed' (Obradovitz, 2020, p. 10). Burnout can stem from the social, economic, and cultural pressures related to career development (Schaufeli et al., 2009), and affects university staff at a level comparable to schoolteachers and healthcare professionals (Watts and Robertson, 2011).

There are, however, suggested interventions that could help address the health and wellbeing crisis in academic research. These include establishing or expanding support services and resources, training to better recognise mental health issues, clear referral paths to appropriate resources and services, and cultural changes in academic environments to reduce psychological stressors (Garcia-Williams et al., 2014; Evans et al., 2018). Given the looming challenges awaiting early career researchers, our goal should be to expect these challenges and to ensure we are well prepared to meet them.

Facing the challenges of academic life

One of the first and most enduring challenges of embarking on a career in academia is in seeing ourselves as academic researchers and accepting that as our identity. At some point we *will* question our place in the research environment, and that doubt can quickly affect our sense of self-worth. This erosion of self-belief is known as 'imposter syndrome' – a phenomenon in which an individual perceives themselves undeserving of the position they are in. Successes are attributed to luck, and such individuals often have an unfounded fear of being discovered as a fraud, despite the lack of any external evidence to support this feeling (Clance and Imes, 1978; Clance, 1986; Bravata et al., 2019). This kind of self-doubt has long been associated with academic researchers (Topping and Kimmel, 1985) and, unchecked, can pose serious problems for our wellbeing (Morris, 2013; Mount and Tardanico, 2014). It can endure throughout an academic career (Edwards, 2019; Wilkinson, 2020) and can be especially pronounced for those entering academia later in life, or returning after time away (Chapman, 2017).

Recognising feelings of self-doubt and insecurity is the first step in being able to deal with them. A good way to combat feelings of inadequacy is to develop a more realistic view of our abilities and values, and to refrain from comparing ourselves to the select few academics – usually those more advanced in their careers – who are treated like celebrities (Woolston, 2016). Acknowledging that we are not the only ones experiencing self-doubt opens up the opportunity to seek social support from mentors or peers, which is one of the best ways to address the stress that results from questioning our academic legitimacy and expertise (Hutchins and Rainbolt, 2017).

Overcoming imposter syndrome requires not only seeking regular feedback, but subsequently internalising the evidence that we are performing well in our roles (Nedegaard, 2016). That evidence can come from external evaluations (such as feedback from supervisors, peers, and students), or through having a tool for introspection and accurate self-evaluation. Engaging in reflective practice (as described in Chapter 10), such as keeping a reflective diary, can be a constructive means of working through and coping with stress in a university environment (Travers, 2011). Reflective writing is also a valuable way to tackle imposter syndrome directly, and can be even more constructive in a peer-group setting (Coryell et al., 2013; Wynne et al., 2014).

The challenge of coming to terms with an academic identity, along with the development of new skills, and maintaining motivation, are a few of the common personal or internal issues that an early career researcher can face (Barry et al., 2018). There are also external demands such as maintaining supervisory relationships, navigating career progression, and keeping a work–life balance (Levecque et al., 2017; Sverdlik et al., 2018; Barry et al., 2019). Finding a healthy balance is a challenge that almost every academic researcher faces. The independence that comes with academic life is one of the most attractive parts of the job. This academic freedom, as explained in Chapter 9, grants a level of autonomy that can be difficult to find in many other careers. With this independence, however, can come a sense of isolation.

Prolonged periods of feeling isolated can lead to loneliness (Janta et al., 2014) and is one of the reasons why depression is 'rife among graduate students and postdocs' (Gewin, 2012, p. 299). Research establishments have a duty of care to their employees to actively foster communities of support and to help researchers recognise that they are valued members of the institution. When these communities are not in place or are not maintained, then our best option is to follow the advice in Chapter 10 and find or establish our own community. Engaging empathetically with our peers and colleagues can reduce feelings of isolation while providing a support system for ourselves and others.

Another indispensable academic experience is in learning how to cope with rejection. Rejection is an intrinsic part of academic life that can be difficult for high-achieving early career researchers to accept if they have grown used to effortless success. The ever-lurking imposter syndrome skulks in the shadows, waiting to strike at the first sign of an academic setback. A deep-rooted driver of imposter syndrome is an innate fear of failure (Sakulku, 2011), yet failure awaits us at every turn in our efforts to carry out meaningful research. Most of our experiments will not succeed on our first try, and the constant learning, iterating, adapting, and retesting is why progress can be made at all (Parkes, 2019; Young, 2019). As soon as we have risen to the challenge of carrying out meaningful research, we are faced with running the gauntlet of academic writing (Chapter 3), publishing (Chapter 4), seeking research funding (Chapter 5), and applying for jobs or promotions (Chapter 11) – all competitive processes where our submissions are more likely to be rejected than accepted.

Seeing setbacks less as failures and more as learning opportunities is the approach of the academic survivor (Timmermans and Sutherland, 2020). It takes time to embrace failure, to depersonalise it, to learn that it is not an endpoint but rather a fundamental part of the process (Holdsworth, 2020). One response to a perceived failure or rejection could be to work harder – surmising that longer hours are needed to achieve a higher level of success. This can lead to an even more unhealthy work–life balance, and result in workaholism (Leung et al., 2000; Hogan et al., 2016). Instead, a common recommendation for higher education institutions to improve wellbeing among staff is to offer more robust forms of support in coping with rejection, such as training in resilience and managing stress (Blix et al., 1994; Hegney et al., 2021). Becoming more resilient and prepared for academic rejection certainly makes things more bearable, but that is only the start of what we need to do to look after our mental, emotional, and physical health.

Practising self-care

Self-care starts with finding ways to be happy. Although it can be as easy as 'doing something nice for yourself or doing something which you enjoy', many of us do not take the time to reflect on our happiness (Vye et al., 2007, p. 60). In academic research, we are often guilty of valuing the wrong part of the job when it comes to our happiness. We strive to contribute new knowledge that we hope may benefit society, and sometimes that is enough to keep us happy. Too often, however, we value the outputs, and what they might mean for us, more than we value carrying out the work itself. Rather than enjoying the work, we endure it, in the hope that it will bring us published papers, successful research grants, professional recognition, jobs, promotions, money, a house, a car, a pony, a holiday, or whatever we are pursuing that we think will bring us happiness. Despite ostensibly being places where intelligent people gather, universities are not renowned for their students and staff knowing what makes them happy.

Researcher views

Lilly, on finding motivation and support in whatever form that works:

> When you constantly have this feeling that you should be doing something and it's not being done, it impedes you. And if you carry that for many years, it really messes you up [...] I had to reach out for support, for help. At some point, I put pictures of Henry Cavill in a motivational folder on my computer, so that I can look at them before I start my PhD work each day. Whatever it takes. If Henry can help, Henry can help.

As we have seen, the levels of distress on campus are startling. It is not surprising that when Yale psychology professor Laurie Santos offered a module on happiness, it quickly became her university's most popular class (Shimer, 2018). A free online version of the course saw more than three million people enrol in just three years, showing just how much interest people have in learning how to be happy (Oswaks, 2021). As academic researchers, we should prioritise our happiness. If we are happy in and with our lives then we can give our job, along with everything else in our lives – like our relationships and family responsibilities – the attention and the best versions of ourselves that they deserve. Instead of sacrificing our happiness in pursuit of a career we can only hope will bring us contentment, we should strive to enjoy the journey itself. If we have a quality of life that keeps us happy, we are more likely to thrive in our work, and when the world sees us at our happiest and healthiest, we are more likely to succeed in everything else.

If we are not looking after ourselves, we are not going to fulfil our academic potential. We may survive for a while, or even convince ourselves that everything is fine, but eventually we will have to deal with the physical, mental, and emotional toll that our work is taking on us. Sleep deprivation is a common cause for concern for early career researchers (Allen et al., 2021). Stress caused by work, along with working irregular hours, can have a detrimental effect on our sleeping patterns. The COVID-19 global pandemic caused much of the academic workforce to work remotely, and brought both challenges and opportunities in terms of wellbeing (Issa and Jaleel, 2021). Flexible working hours have long been touted as a way to alleviate stress – although who gains access to such arrangements has raised concerns about historical inequity in higher education (Smyth et al., 2020). Some have found that the rise of 'working from home' has had the opposite effect in that the boundaries between the personal and professional have become blurred (Burgio et al., 2020). To reduce the impact on our work–life balance, and on our sleep, we should set firm limits on our working hours and have 'non-negotiable periods for time off […] especially at the weekend' (Gewin, 2020, p. 717).

To give ourselves the best chance of quality sleep, we should keep our bedroom cool and comfortable (Wiseman, 2014) and, if possible, free of any work activities such as checking emails before bed (Chapter 9 has advice on email efficiency). Avoiding alcohol, caffeine, and nicotine (Caviness et al., 2019) will help, but the single most important decision is resolving to get eight hours of sleep every night (Walker, 2017). Complementary sleep habits include eating well and staying active. Researchers often spend long periods indoors, seated, looking at screens, so all of us need to ensure we are eating healthily and getting enough exercise, especially if we are spending most of our time working or studying on a university campus (Haberman and Luffey, 1998; Irwin, 2004). Taking breaks to walk in the countryside, parks, or any greenspaces available to us, can be hugely beneficial (Barton et al., 2009; Roe and Aspinall, 2011; O'Mara, 2019).

Once we are getting enough sleep, exercising regularly, and eating healthily, we can explore other ways of improving our wellbeing. Some people find self-help books useful as a form of active coping or bibliotherapy – reading books for the specific purpose of healing (Norcross, 2000; Bergsma, 2008). With a deluge of self-help books to choose from, early career researchers often gravitate towards books that help them to strive for success (Robertson, 2012), change their mindset (Dweck, 2006), become more vulnerable (Brown, 2012), become more resilient (Duckworth, 2016), or explore the benefits of therapy (Gillihan, 2016). The therapeutic benefits of practising mindfulness – exercises designed to focus our attention on the here and now without trying to interpret or judge the experience – are frequently recommended for academics (Lemon and McDonough, 2018; Nicklin et al., 2019; Barry et al., 2019).

Researcher views

Genevieve, reflecting on her PhD experience:

> There were things I could have done differently, that would have made me happier, I guess, and just more able to deal with the stresses of doing a PhD [...] I realised quite a while after my PhD, maybe a year or two after I finished, I remember having this kind of realisation that I have done all this work and I had so much to be proud of, and at no point had I felt proud of myself for what I had achieved. I always just felt like it wasn't enough and I had to do more. I didn't realise until later that I was doing this massive piece of work and it was bringing lots of experiences that I would never have again and I forgot to actually pause and enjoy any of it. I was just so stressed, I was just trying to get through it, and I wasn't in the present at all. Now I have the kind of tools to recognise that. I really wish I had known more about mindfulness when I was a PhD student.

Along with our self-care efforts, it is vital to remember that it is normal to ask for help, particularly when it comes to our mental health. Removing any stigma around speaking about mental health is something all of us can support. Similarly, we can all be more proactive in checking in on our own mental health. We should ask ourselves if we feel able to do our work, if we think we are being productive, and if we are deriving satisfaction from it. If we cannot answer those questions positively, it could be a sign that we need to talk to someone. Other symptoms to look out for include difficulties in staying motivated and maintaining focus, while seeing changes in appetite, sleep pattern, energy levels, sociability, and mood – any of which can be signs of anxiety or depression, the mental-health disorders most commonly experienced by early career researchers (Gewin, 2012). The first step we need to take in asking for help is to recognise that any mental health problems we are facing are not personal weaknesses or failings, and could well be conditions that require treatment (Gewin, 2012; Eva, 2019). A list of health and wellbeing resources is available on this book's companion website.

Helping those in need

If we are lucky enough to find ourselves in a position of relative comfort – where we are healthy, happy, and enjoying our work – we probably reached such a position through a combination of hard work and receiving the right support at critical moments. That might serve as a reminder for us to check in on those around us, either our fellow academic researchers, or any students we are working with. Most people will face challenges in academia, and perhaps even moments of crisis. Who they turn to – assuming they have someone to turn to – in those moments, could be the difference between them overcoming the problems they are facing, or being consumed by them.

The importance of advice and support from mentors has cropped up repeatedly in this book, and while it may seem more natural to wait until people come to us seeking advice, early career researchers do not always realise they need help, or even that they are struggling, until they talk to someone. Checking in on others might lead to us offering help, but supportive listening can be just as important (Bodie et al., 2013). As we saw in Chapter 7, fostering a positive supervisory relationship can have a significant impact on wellbeing (Al Makhamreh and Stockley, 2020), and providing feedback – the kind of regular informal and low-stakes formative assessment described in Chapter 6 – can be particularly useful for students and researchers wrestling with their academic identities (Chapman, 2017). Helping our students to discover their academic identities is far more valuable than helping them to discover new knowledge (Green, 2005). Some of our students and colleagues may have to manage ongoing and permanent issues of health, and we should encourage them to utilise every support available to them to ensure their work is not compromised unnecessarily by issues of health. In particular, we should advocate for the mental health of those around us, and if appropriate, encourage them to seek professional counselling (Hyun et al., 2006).

As our careers progress, we might realise that we do not have mentors anymore, and that we are the ones doing the mentoring. That does not mean we will no longer face challenging moments or times when we need help, as mid-career researchers are often a neglected group in academia who could benefit from more support (Kandiko Howson et al., 2018). Peer-mentoring is essential at such times; if researchers have no one else they can turn to for support, then they must look out for each other. In Chapter 11, we saw just how frustrating academic career progression can be; sometimes people feel trapped in a role where they do not see a satisfying future for themselves. In such scenarios, reminding people how skilled and employable they are, and how many options are open to them, can be a panacea for the pressures of their job (Kruger, 2018). We all have times when we can benefit from collegial support, and any help we provide to those who are most in need is time well spent.

As we have seen, imposter syndrome is endemic to academic environments, and it is likely a symptom of a much larger problem in academic research – inequity (Mullangi and Jagsi, 2019). Academic research, by its nature, should be open and accessible to all (Nosek et al., 2015). Institutions of higher education are environments where diversity of race, ethnicity, age, language, sexual orientation, ability, socioeconomic status, gender, and belief need to be welcomed and encouraged to lead to a more equitable society. Despite their diversity, university campuses remain places where people encounter both conscious and unconscious biases (Stellar et al., 2020). Improving diversity throughout academic environments, especially in leadership and senior academic positions, is vital to help early career researchers identify with leaders and mentors in their fields. A final moral consideration, if we find ourselves in a privileged position of power, is that we may have the ability to affect change. In this, and the preceding chapters, we have seen the kinds of problems that can arise across all aspects of academic research. If we can do anything to help academic systems become more accessible, supportive, and inclusive, then we will have taken responsibility for bringing about positive change. Having a stable, secure, and rewarding job in academia is a position of privilege. If we are fortunate enough to find ourselves in such a position, we must consider those who are trying to follow in our footsteps. We do not have a professional responsibility to help others, but having firsthand experience of the countless obstacles facing those pursuing an academic career path should be all the motivation we need to offer our support.

Summary

- Keep sight of the big picture. As absorbing as it is to be an academic researcher, it is unequivocally just a job, and your happiness and quality of life are far more important.
- Practise self-care. Maintain a healthy work–life balance and prioritise your diet, your fitness, and especially your sleep.
- Seek support. Whether you are looking for advice, guidance, or just someone to talk to, asking for help when you need it is central to taking care of yourself.
- Offer your colleagues help. Remember that you have the benefit of skills, knowledge, and experience that could be incredibly supportive to others.
- Affect change. If you stay in the field of academic research, keep in mind that the system needs to be improved for those to come.

Throughout this book, we have seen how developing a range of academic skills can open up new opportunities and bring personal and professional success. Getting to grips with basic research skills can build our confidence; taking ownership of our academic writing, publishing, and funding can lead to more autonomy; gaining experience teaching, supervising, and engaging public audiences can provide a sense of accomplishment; while administration and professional development will ensure we are tasked with the responsibilities that can raise our career to new heights. More important than being happy with work, however, is being happy with life. Our skills as academic researchers are vital to new knowledge and societal progress, but above all else, we must prioritise our health and wellbeing.

Thank you for taking the time to consider your academic skills by reading this book. I hope you enjoyed the journey as much as I did, and I wish you well on your coming academic adventures.

Further reading

- Duckworth, A. (2016). *Grit: The Power of Passion and Perseverance*. New York, NY: Scribner.

The self-help book market is oversaturated, but Angela Duckworth's recounting of how perseverance and resilience can help us succeed is a favourite of early career researchers.

- Kadison, R. & DiGeronimo, T. F. (2005). *College of the Overwhelmed: The Campus Mental Health Crisis and What to Do About It*. San Francisco, CA: Jossey-Bass.

A well-considered guide to tackling stress and mental health disorders in university environments.

- Pretorius, L., Macaulay, L., & de Caux, B. C. (Eds.) (2019). *Wellbeing in Doctoral Education: Insights and Guidance from the Student Experience*. Cham, Switzerland: Springer Nature.

This book provides first-person accounts of doctoral student experiences to highlight the importance of supporting the wellbeing of early career researchers.

- Stellar, J., Martinez, C., Eggan, B., Poy, B., Weisser C. S., Eager, R., Cohen, M., & Buras, A. (2020). *Diversity at College: Real Stories of Students Conquering Bias and Making Higher Education More Inclusive*. Washington, DC: Ideapress Publishing.

An insight into the biases present in higher education institutions, co-written by people who have experienced them firsthand.

- Walker, M. (2017). *Why We Sleep: Unlocking the Power of Sleep and Dreams*. New York, NY: Simon and Schuster.

If ever you needed a book to scare you into getting your eight hours of sleep each night.

Resources

Further resources for this chapter can be found at: www.JosephRoche.ie/EssentialSkills

- List of Health and Wellbeing Online Resources

References

Abouserie, R. (1996). Stress, coping strategies and job satisfaction in university academic staff. *Educational Psychology*, *16*(1), 49–56.

Al Makhamreh, M. & Stockley, D. (2020). Mentorship and well-being: examining doctoral students' lived experiences in doctoral supervision context. *International Journal of Mentoring and Coaching in Education*, *9*(1), 1–20.

Allen, H. K., Barrall, A. L., Vincent, K. B., & Arria, A. M. (2021). Stress and burnout among graduate students: moderation by sleep duration and quality. *International Journal of Behavioral Medicine*, *28*(1), 21–28.

Barry, K. M., Woods, M., Warnecke, E., Stirling, C., & Martin, A. (2018). Psychological health of doctoral candidates, study-related challenges and perceived performance. *Higher Education Research & Development*, *37*(3), 468–483.

Barry, K. M., Woods, M., Martin, A., Stirling, C., & Warnecke, E. (2019). A randomized controlled trial of the effects of mindfulness practice on doctoral candidate psychological status. *Journal of American College Health*, *67*(4), 299–307.

Barton, J., Hine, R., & Pretty, J. (2009). The health benefits of walking in greenspaces of high natural and heritage value. *Journal of Integrative Environmental Sciences*, *6*(4), 261–278.

Bergsma, A. (2008). Do self-help books help? *Journal of Happiness Studies*, *9*(3), 341–360.

Blix, A. G., Cruise, R. J., Mitchell, B. M., & Blix, G. G. (1994). Occupational stress among university teachers. *Educational Research*, *36*(2), 157–169.

Bodie, G. D., Vickery, A. J., & Gearhart, C. C. (2013). The nature of supportive listening, I: exploring the relation between supportive listeners and supportive people. *International Journal of Listening*, *27*(1), 39–49.

Bravata, D. M., Watts, S. A., Keefer, A. L., Madhusudhan, D. K., Taylor, K. T., Clark, D. M., ... & Hagg, H. K. (2019). Prevalence, predictors, and treatment of impostor syndrome: a systematic review. *Journal of General Internal Medicine*, *35*(4), 1252–1275.

Brown, B. (2012). *Daring Greatly: How the Courage to be Vulnerable Transforms the Way We Live, Love, Parent, and Lead*. London, UK: Penguin Publishing.

Brown, R. D., Bond, S., Gerndt, J., Krager, L., Krantz, B., Lukin, M., & Prentice, D. (1986). Stress on campus: an interactional perspective. *Research in Higher Education*, *24*(1), 97–112.

Burgio, K. R., MacKenzie, C. M., Borrelle, S. B., Ernest, S. M., Gill, J. L., Ingeman, K. E., Teffer, A., & White, E. P. (2020). Ten simple rules for a successful remote postdoc. *PLoS Computational Biology*, *16*(5), 1–7.

Caviness, C. M., Anderson, B. J., & Stein, M. D. (2019). Impact of nicotine and other stimulants on sleep in young adults. *Journal of Addiction Medicine*, *13*(3), 209–214.

Cerejo, C., Awati, M., & Hayward, A. (2020). *Joy and Stress Triggers: A Global Survey on Mental Health Among Researchers — CACTUS Mental Health Survey Report*. Cactus Foundation. Available at: www.cactusglobal.com/mental-health-survey (accessed 4 April 2021).

Chapman, A. (2017). Using the assessment process to overcome Imposter Syndrome in mature students. *Journal of Further and Higher Education*, *41*(2), 112–119.

Clance, P. R. (1986). *The Impostor Phenomenon: When Success Makes You Feel Like a Fake*. New York, NY: Bantam Books.

Clance, P. R. & Imes, S. A. (1978). The imposter phenomenon in high achieving women: dynamics and therapeutic intervention. *Psychotherapy: Theory, Research & Practice*, *15*(3), 241–247.

Coryell, J. E., Wagner, S., Clark, M. C., & Stuessy, C. (2013). Becoming real: adult student impressions of developing an educational researcher identity. *Journal of Further and Higher Education*, *37*(3), 367–383.

Cyranoski, D., Gilbert, N., Ledford, H., Nayar, A., & Yahia, M. (2011). Education: the PhD factory. *Nature*, *472*(7343), 276–279.

Duckworth, A. (2016). *Grit: The Power of Passion and Perseverance*. New York, NY: Scribner.

Dweck, C. (2006). *Mindset: The New Psychology of Success*. New York, NY: Random House.

Edwards, C. W. (2019). Overcoming imposter syndrome and stereotype threat: reconceptualizing the definition of a scholar. *Taboo: The Journal of Culture and Education*, 18(1), 18–34.

Eva, A. L. (2019). *How Colleges Today Are Supporting Student Mental Health*. The Greater Good Science Center. Available at: https://greatergood.berkeley.edu/article/item/how_colleges_today_are_supporting_student_mental_health (accessed 4 April 2021).

Evans, T. M., Bira, L., Gastelum, J. B., Weiss, L. T., & Vanderford, N. L. (2018). Evidence for a mental health crisis in graduate education. *Nature Biotechnology*, 36(3), 282–284.

Garcia-Williams, A. G., Moffitt, L., & Kaslow, N. J. (2014). Mental health and suicidal behavior among graduate students. *Academic Psychiatry*, 38(5), 554–560.

Gewin, V. (2012). Mental health: under a cloud. *Nature*, 490(7419), 299–301.

Gewin, V. (2020). Ways to look after yourself and others in 2021. *Nature*, 588(7839), 717–718.

Gillespie, N. A., Walsh, M. H. W. A., Winefield, A. H., Dua, J., & Stough, C. (2001). Occupational stress in universities: staff perceptions of the causes, consequences and moderators of stress. *Work & Stress*, 15(1), 53–72.

Gillihan, S. J. (2016). *Cognitive Behavioral Therapy in 7 Weeks: A Workbook for Managing Depression and Anxiety*. Berkeley, CA: Althea Press.

Green, B. (2005). Unfinished business: subjectivity and supervision. *Higher Education Research & Development*, 24(2), 151–163.

Haberman, S. & Luffey, D. (1998). Weighing in college students' diet and exercise behaviors. *Journal of American College Health*, 46(4), 189–191.

Hegney, D., Tsai, L., Craigie, M., Crawford, C., Jay, S., & Rees, C. (2021). Experiences of university employees of the impact of a mindful self-care and resiliency program on their well-being. *Higher Education Research & Development*, 40(3), 524–537.

Herschberg, C., Benschop, Y., & Van den Brink, M. (2018). Precarious postdocs: a comparative study on recruitment and selection of early career researchers. *Scandinavian Journal of Management*, 34(4), 303–310.

Hogan, V., Hogan, M., & Hodgins, M. (2016). A study of workaholism in Irish academics. *Occupational Medicine*, 66(6), 460–465.

Holdsworth, C. (2020). A manifesto for failure: depersonalising, collectivising and embracing failure in research funding. *Emotion, Space and Society*, 37(100744), 1–4.

Housee, S. & Richards, E. (2011). And still we rise: stories of resilience and transgression. *Enhancing Learning in the Social Sciences*, 3(3), 1–22.

Hutchins, H. M. & Rainbolt, H. (2017). What triggers imposter phenomenon among academic faculty? A critical incident study exploring antecedents, coping, and development opportunities. *Human Resource Development International*, 20(3), 194–214.

Hyun, J. K., Quinn, B. C., Madon, T., & Lustig, S. (2006). Graduate student mental health: needs assessment and utilization of counseling services. *Journal of College Student Development*, 47(3), 247–266.

Irwin, J. D. (2004). Prevalence of university students' sufficient physical activity: a systematic review. *Perceptual and Motor Skills, 98*(3), 927–943.

Issa, H. & Jaleel, E. (2021). Social isolation and psychological wellbeing: lessons from Covid-19. *Management Science Letters, 11*(2), 609–618.

Janta, H., Lugosi, P., & Brown, L. (2014). Coping with loneliness: a netnographic study of doctoral students. *Journal of Further and Higher Education, 38*(4), 553–571.

Kadison, R. & DiGeronimo, T. F. (2005). *College of the Overwhelmed: The Campus Mental Health Crisis and What to Do About It.* San Francisco, CA: Jossey-Bass.

Kandiko Howson, C. B., Coate, K., & de St Croix, T. (2018). Mid-career academic women and the prestige economy. *Higher Education Research & Development, 37*(3), 533–548.

Kinman, G. (2014). Doing more with less? Work and wellbeing in academics. *Somatechnics, 4*(2), 219–235.

Kruger, P. (2018). Why it is not a 'failure' to leave academia. *Nature, 560*(7716), 133–135.

Kubie, L. S. (1954). Some unsolved problems of the scientific career. *American Scientist, 42*(1), 104–112.

Lemon, N. & McDonough, S. (Eds.) (2018). *Mindfulness in the Academy: Practices and Perspectives from Scholars.* Singapore: Springer.

Leung, T. W., Siu, O. L., & Spector, P. E. (2000). Faculty stressors, job satisfaction, and psychological distress among university teachers in Hong Kong: the role of locus of control. *International Journal of Stress Management, 7*(2), 121–138.

Levecque, K., Anseel, F., De Beuckelaer, A., Van der Heyden, J., & Gisle, L. (2017). Work organization and mental health problems in PhD students. *Research Policy, 46*(4), 868–879.

Martinez, E. D., Botos, J., Dohoney, K. M., Geiman, T. M., Kolla, S. S., Olivera, A., ... & Cohen-Fix, O. (2007). Falling off the academic bandwagon: women are more likely to quit at the postdoc to principal investigator transition. *EMBO Reports, 8*(11), 977–981.

Martinson, B. C., Anderson, M. S., & De Vries, R. (2005). Scientists behaving badly. *Nature, 435*(7043), 737–738.

Morris, C. (2013). What is researcher wellbeing and how can we manage and nurture it? *The Guardian,* 20 May. Available at: www.theguardian.com/higher-education-network/blog/2013/may/20/researcher-wellbeing-staying-productive (accessed 4 April 2021).

Mount, P. & Tardanico, S. (2014). *Beating the Impostor Syndrome.* Greensboro, NC: Center for Creative Leadership.

Mullangi, S. & Jagsi, R. (2019). Imposter syndrome: treat the cause, not the symptom. *JAMA, 322*(5), 403–404.

Nedegaard, R. (2016). Overcoming imposter syndrome: how my students trained me to teach them. *Reflections: Narratives of Professional Helping, 22*(4), 52–59.

Nicklin, J. M., Meachon, E. J., & McNall, L. A. (2019). Balancing work, school, and personal life among graduate students: a positive psychology approach. *Applied Research in Quality of Life, 14*(5), 1265–1286.

Norcross, J. C. (2000). Here comes the self-help revolution in mental health. *Psychotherapy: Theory, Research, Practice, Training, 37*(4), 370–377.

Nosek, B. A., Alter, G., Banks, G. C., Borsboom, D., Bowman, S. D., Breckler, S. J., ... & Yarkoni, T. (2015). Promoting an open research culture. *Science, 348*(6242), 1422–1425.

Obradovitz, C. (2020). Managing stress and employee burnout. *Risk Management, 67*(10), 10–11.

O'Mara, S. (2019). *In Praise of Walking: The New Science of How We Walk and Why It's Good for Us.* London, UK: Random House.

Oswaks, M. (2021). Over 3 million people took this course on happiness. Here's what some learned. *New York Times,* 13 March. Available at: www.nytimes.com/2021/03/13/style/happiness-course.html (accessed 4 April 2021).

Parkes, E. (2019). Scientific progress is built on failure. *Nature.* Available at: https://doi.org/10.1038/d41586-019-00107-y (accessed 4 April 2021).

Powell, K. (2016). Young, talented and fed-up: scientists tell their stories. *Nature News, 538*(7626), 446.

Robertson, I. (2012). *The Winner Effect: The Science of Success and How to Use It.* London, UK: Bloomsbury.

Roe, J. & Aspinall, P. (2011). The restorative benefits of walking in urban and rural settings in adults with good and poor mental health. *Health & Place, 17*(1), 103–113.

Sakulku, J. (2011). The impostor phenomenon. *The Journal of Behavioral Science, 6*(1), 75–97.

Schaufeli, W. B., Leiter, M. P., & Maslach, C. (2009). Burnout: 35 years of research and practice. *Career Development International, 14*(3), 204–220.

Shaw, C. & Ward, L. (2014). Dark thoughts: why mental illness is on the rise in academia. *The Guardian,* 6 March. Available at: www.theguardian.com/higher-education-network/2014/mar/06/mental-health-academics-growing-problem-pressure-university (accessed 4 April 2021).

Shimer, D. (2018). Yale's most popular class ever: happiness. *New York Times,* 26 January. Available at: www.nytimes.com/2018/01/26/nyregion/at-yale-class-on-happiness-draws-huge-crowd-laurie-santos.html (accessed 4 April 2021).

Smyth, C., Cortis, N., & Powell, A. (2020). University staff and flexible work: inequalities, tensions and challenges. *Journal of Higher Education Policy and Management.* doi: 10.1080/1360080X.2020.1857504

Stellar, J., Martinez, C., Eggan, B., Poy, B., Weisser C. S., Eager, R., ... & Buras, A. (2020). *Diversity at College: Real Stories of Students Conquering Bias and Making Higher Education More Inclusive.* Washington, DC: Ideapress Publishing.

Sverdlik, A., Hall, N. C., McAlpine, L., & Hubbard, K. (2018). The PhD experience: a review of the factors influencing doctoral students' completion, achievement, and well-being. *International Journal of Doctoral Studies, 13*(1), 361–388.

Taberner, A. M. (2018). The marketisation of the English higher education sector and its impact on academic staff and the nature of their work. *International Journal of Organizational Analysis, 26*(1), 129–152.

Timmermans, J. A. & Sutherland, K. A. (2020). Wise academic development: learning from the 'failure' experiences of retired academic developers. *International Journal for Academic Development*, *25*(1), 43–57.

Topping, M. E. & Kimmel, E. B. (1985). The imposter phenomenon: feeling phony. *Academic Psychology Bulletin*, *7*(1), 213–226.

Travers, C. (2011). Unveiling a reflective diary methodology for exploring the lived experiences of stress and coping. *Journal of Vocational Behavior*, *79*(1), 204–216.

Vye, C., Scholljegerdes, K., & Welch, I. D. (2007). *Under Pressure and Overwhelmed: Coping with Anxiety in College*. Westport, CT: Praeger – Greenwood Publishing Group.

Walker, M. (2017). *Why We Sleep: Unlocking the Power of Sleep and Dreams*. New York, NY: Simon and Schuster.

Watts, J. & Robertson, N. (2011). Burnout in university teaching staff: a systematic literature review. *Educational Research*, *53*(1), 33–50.

Wilkinson, C. (2020). Imposter syndrome and the accidental academic: an autoethnographic account. *International Journal for Academic Development*, *25*(4), 363–374.

Wiseman, R. (2014). *Night School: Wake Up to the Power of Sleep*. London, UK: Pan Macmillan.

Woolston, C. (2016). Faking it. *Nature*, *529*(7587), 555–557.

Woolston, C. (2020). Postdocs under pressure: 'Can I even do this anymore?'. *Nature*, *587*(7835), 689–692.

Wynne, C., Guo, Y. J., & Wang, S. C. (2014). Writing anxiety groups: a creative approach for graduate students. *Journal of Creativity in Mental Health*, *9*(3), 366–379.

Young, M. (2019). The utility of failure: a taxonomy for research and scholarship. *Perspectives on Medical Education*, *8*(6), 365–371.

Ysseldyk, R., Greenaway, K. H., Hassinger, E., Zutrauen, S., Lintz, J., Bhatia, M. P., … & Tai, V. (2019). A leak in the academic pipeline: identity and health among postdoctoral women. *Frontiers in Psychology*, *10*(1297), 1–17.

Index